James Madison and Constitutional Imperfection

This book presents a provocative account of James Madison's political thought by focusing on Madison's lifelong encounter with the enduring problem of constitutional imperfection. In particular, it emphasizes Madison's alliance with Thomas Jefferson, liberating it from those long-standing accounts of Madisonian constitutionalism that emphasize deliberation by elites and constitutional veneration. Contrary to much of the scholarship, this book shows that Madison was aware of the limits of the inventions of political science and held a far more subtle understanding of the possibility of constitutional government than has been recognized. By repositioning Madison as closer to Jefferson and the Revolution of 1800, this book offers a reinterpretation of one of the central figures of the early republic.

Jeremy D. Bailey is the Ross M. Lence Distinguished Teaching Chair at the University of Houston, where he holds a dual appointment in the Department of Political Science and the Honors College. He is the author of *Thomas Jefferson and Executive Power* and coauthor of *The Contested Removal Power, 1789–2010.*

James Madison and Constitutional Imperfection

JEREMY D. BAILEY

University of Houston

CAMBRIDGE
UNIVERSITY PRESS

CAMBRIDGE
UNIVERSITY PRESS

32 Avenue of the Americas, New York NY 10013-2473, USA

Cambridge University Press is part of the University of Cambridge.

It furthers the University's mission by disseminating knowledge in the pursuit of education, learning and research at the highest international levels of excellence.

www.cambridge.org
Information on this title: www.cambridge.org/9781107121607

First published 2015

A catalogue record for this publication is available from the British Library

Library of Congress Cataloguing in Publication data
Bailey, Jeremy D., 1974–
James Madison and constitutional imperfection / Jeremy D. Bailey.
    pages   cm
Includes bibliographical references and index.
ISBN 978-1-107-12160-7 (hardback) – ISBN 978-1-107-54742-1 (paperback)
1. Madison, James, 1751–1836 – Political and social views.   2. United States –
Politics and government – Philosophy.   3. Republicanism – United States –
History – 18th century.   4. Constitutional history – United States.   I. Title.
E342.B235   2015
973.5′1092–dc23   2015012683

ISBN 978-1-107-12160-7 Hardback
ISBN 978-1-107-54742-1 Paperback

For Wilson Alexander Bailey

Contents

Preface

This book's cover includes a photograph of James Madison's letter to John G. Jackson, written in 1821. In that letter, clearly revised with care, Madison made an extraordinary confession to Jackson. He confessed that some of the delegates to the Federal Convention of 1787 had been overly influenced by Shays' Rebellion in Massachusetts. By overestimating the importance of that rebellion, these delegates imparted a "higher toned system than was perhaps warranted."

This confession should surprise readers who are familiar with Madison's political thought and with the history of the early republic. It is not surprising because an important American Founder said it. After all, Madison's friend and lifelong accomplice made that point over and over again as soon as the text of the new Constitution reached him in France. To Madison, Thomas Jefferson wrote, "The late rebellion in Massachusetts has given more alarm than I think it should have done."[1] Jefferson was more descriptive to William S. Smith: "Our Convention has been too much impressed by the insurrection of Massachusetts: and in the spur of the moment they are setting up a kite to keep the hen-yard in order."[2] It is surprising because, according to our accepted understandings of Madison, Shays' Rebellion represents the critical difference between him and Jefferson.

In what follows, I argue for a new reading of Madison, and this new reading emphasizes the alliance between Madison and Jefferson. In this, I have followed the path blazed by Lance Banning. I do not, however, agree with all of Banning's conclusions. Most importantly, I do not share Banning's central assumption that, for Madison, republicanism presupposed a particular variety

---

[1] Thomas Jefferson to Madison, 20 December 1787, in Merril D. Peterson, ed., *Thomas Jefferson: Writings* (New York: Library of America, 1984), 917.
[2] Thomas Jefferson to William S. Smith, 13 November 1787, in *Thomas Jefferson: Writings*, 911.

of federalism. I think Banning's otherwise definitive account is distorted on that point, and readers will see that I am not all that interested in determining the extent to which Madison was a nationalist.

This requires another clarification. At an earlier stage of this project, I aspired to write what I believed would be the first comprehensive account of Madison's political thought and practice over the course of his entire career. After some time, it occurred to me that this was not what I actually have done, for I leave many features of Madison's political thought unexamined (I do not discuss religious liberty, for example). While I do cover most of Madison's career (from ratification to retirement), I focus on one important feature of Madison's political thought: the problem of constitutional imperfection. Moreover, rather than offering new interpretations of familiar events in Madison's career, I instead spend more time on those that have received little and sometimes no attention. With both of these choices, my intention is to create space in the scholarship on the early republic by reconceiving how we understand Madison's constitutionalism by detaching it from what I call Madisonian constitutionalism. My intention is not to settle or end debate, but rather to push that debate forward and open it to more participants. It remains for another day, and hopefully for another scholar, to write that comprehensive and definitive treatment of Madison's political thought.

Acknowledgments

I must begin by saying that I am humbled by the fact that the United States has carved a place for university professors to do this kind of work. The State of Texas and the University of Houston afforded me two sabbaticals, one in Spring 2010 and the other in Fall 2014, without which this book would have been delayed for several more years. I should also thank the State of Texas and the University of Houston for preserving the institution of tenure. Tenure has given me the freedom and the will to undertake the necessary research, work that takes a long time and is often not recognized in annual merit reviews. I must acknowledge, however, that academic freedom at my university and in my state has declined since I arrived in 2007, and the changing incentive structure makes work of this kind less rewarding and more vulnerable to the meddling of the powerful and the rich. I fear that my son's generation will find university life less appealing and scholarly research less possible.

On a happier note, my graduate students at the University of Houston have been a source of energy and several deserve special mention. Between 2008 and 2014, Robert Ross and Shellee O'Brien came to UH and wrote doctoral dissertations related to Madison; they provided the intellectual community that is possible only in a doctoral program and cannot be taken for granted. Likewise, Sarah Mallams followed one rabbit trail after another, and was especially helpful in helping me understand the background of the famous Jefferson letter to Henry Lee. One undergraduate, Madison West, helped with the project in Spring 2013 and assisted with sorting out what was missing from Madison's correspondence and what was not.

This book is a continuation of a project that I began in the Fall of 1999. It thus has benefited from fifteen years of conversations ranging from academic chitchat to formal conference presentations, from anonymous reader reports of articles to intense debates into the night. There are more participants in these conversations, and more friends, than I can call to memory and as a result more people deserving of thanks than are listed here. Early drafts of individual chapters of this book have benefited from the reading of friends and colleagues who share my interest in American political thought. Among those are David Alvis, Wyndham Bailey, James Ceaser, Daniel Cullen, Todd Estes, Dustin Gish, Ben Kleinerman, Daniel Klinghard, Marc Landy, Bill McClay, Jim Stoner, Flagg Taylor, George Thomas, Jeffrey Tulis, Steve Wirls, Scott Yenor, and Michael Zuckert. Deserving special mention are Rafe Major and Alan Gibson. Rafe read conference paper after conference paper and helped me find my argument; Alan shared his vast knowledge of Madison and the Madison literature and took the time to help me catch up and to correct many of my errors. I must also thank the reviewers for Cambridge University Press. Simply put, their hard work made this better. I remain indebted to Lew Bateman, whose support has been important for me, and who has been an aegis for many of us working in the field of the early republic. Thanks also to Mike Andrews and Pamela Edwards and the Jack Miller Center for providing an opportunity for me to discuss the early republic with many historians and political theorists. Of particular value to this project was their 2009 conference at Georgetown, where I was given the chance to introduce my Madison to many of the aforementioned friends.

It is customary to say that the persons thanked should not be held responsible for any errors of the author. That custom is especially warranted in this case, because the argument in what follows runs counter to much of what is normally taught and written about Madison. The argument is my own, and it will stand or fall as it is tested against the evidence. A version of Chapter 2 was published in 2012 as "Should We Venerate That Which We Cannot Love?: James Madison on Constitutional Imperfection" in *Political Research Quarterly*, 732–44. Portions of Chapter 4 were previously published in 2008 as "The New Unitary Executive and Democratic Theory: The Problem of Alexander Hamilton" in *American Political Science Review*, 453–65, and in 2012 as "Was James Madison Ever for the Bill of Rights?" in *Perspectives on Political Science*, 59–66. This material is used with permission of the publishers.

Finally, my deepest debts are to my wife Wyndham and my son Wilson, who have to put up with my excursions to the past. Wyndham is a far better teacher than I am, and her sense of the present continues to light my way. Namaste. This book is dedicated to Wilson, whose birth coincided with Game 4 of the 2004 American League Championship Series and whose mental toughness continues to be a source of fatherly pride and wonder. The earth indeed belongs to the living, but its peaks and mysteries belong to the courageous and to the true.

Abbreviations

Hunt	*The Writings of James Madison*, ed. Gaillard Hunt, vol. 9 (New York: G. P. Putnam's, 1910).
Koch	James Madison, *Notes of Debates in the Federal Convention of 1787 as Reported by James Madison*, ed. Adrienne Koch (Athens: Ohio University Press, 1966).
Madison Papers Presidency	*The Papers of James Madison, Presidential Series*, 8 vols., ed. J. C. A. Stagg, Jeanne Kerr Cross, and Susan Holbrook Perdue (Charlottesville: University of Virginia Press, 1984–2015).
Madison Papers Retirement	*The Papers of James Madison, Retirement Series*, 2 vols., ed. David B. Mattern, J. C. A. Stagg, Mary Parke Johnson, and Anne Mandeville Colony (Charlottesville: University of Virginia Press, 2009–2013).
Madison Writings	*James Madison: Writings*, ed. Jack N. Rakove (New York: Library of America, 1999).
PJM	*The Papers of James Madison, Congressional Series*, 17 vols., ed. William T. Hutchinson, William M. E. Rachal, Robert E. Rutland, and John C. A. Stagg (Chicago: University of Chicago Press; Charlottesville: University of Virginia Press, 1962–1991).

Republic of Letters   *The Republic of Letters: The Correspondence*
                                between Thomas Jefferson and James Madison,
                                1776–1826. 3 vols., ed. James Morton Smith
                                (New York: Norton, 1995).
Scigliano   *The Federalist,* ed. Robert Scigliano
                                (New York: Modern Library, 2000).

I

The Madison Problem

"We must refer to the monitory reflection that no government of human device and human administration can be perfect; that that which is least imperfect is the best government."

James Madison, 1833[1]

This book attempts to answer a question that arose during my examination of Thomas Jefferson's transformation of executive power. That question is this: Given James Madison's critique of Jefferson's proposals for frequent appeals to the people, why did Madison collaborate with Jefferson to bring about and institutionalize a version of those frequent appeals? Put another way, if we assume that Jefferson's Revolution of 1800 was actually a revolution, why did Madison go along with it?[2]

In answering this question, this book introduces and attempts to answer a second question. Specifically, what was Madison's solution to the problem of constitutional imperfection? By constitutional imperfection I mean the gaps that necessarily arise because no constitution can anticipate every contingency and opportunity, and I mean the flaws that derive from the errors of the founders. Constitutions are doomed to have both, so, as a result, those who live under one must determine whether their own constitution has a doctrine with respect to the problem of constitutional imperfection. That doctrine will have to first determine the extent of the imperfection as well as provide a remedy. The remedy might be formal amendment, judicial interpretation, legislative deliberation, executive discretion, appeals to the people, or some combination of any of these. I believe studying Madison with an eye to the problem of

---

[1] Madison to unknown, 1833, Hunt 9: 528.
[2] Jeremy D. Bailey, *Thomas Jefferson and Executive Power* (New York: Cambridge University Press, 2007).

I

constitutional imperfection will liberate his thought from what can be called
Madisonian constitutionalism. By examining Madison's political thought and
practice unburdened by the assumptions of Madisonian constitutionalism, this
book seeks to offer a fresher and more accurate account of Madison himself.

Madisonian Constitutionalism

Studies of American constitutionalism often rely on one of two well-known
dichotomies. The first is the famous contest between Jefferson and Alexander
Hamilton, between a strict construction of the Constitution with an emphasis
on consent and a broad construction of the Constitution with an emphasis
on sovereignty. The second dichotomy pits Jefferson against Madison. Under
Jeffersonian constitutionalism, institutions should represent and embody the
will of the people, and constitutional change should be frequent because each
generation has the right to give its consent to its fundamental laws. Under
Madisonian constitutionalism, institutions should mediate the will of the people, and constitutional change should be relatively infrequent because people
need a constitution they can "venerate" and tinkering with it every generation
would undermine this requirement of government.[3]

There is much to be said for these dichotomies. The first one helps us classify
and understand the way ideas and partisan politics have interacted throughout American politics.[4] The second one is perhaps less well worn, but equally
important. In particular, it is useful in distinguishing a republic from a democracy, and perhaps in separating presidential from parliamentary regimes, as well
as those in which there is a tradition of strong judicial review from those where
there is not.[5] Unsurprisingly, this literature overlaps with the increasing calls
for a new Constitution. For example, in a recent book recommending a new
constitutional convention, Sanford Levinson urges readers to reject Madison
and embrace Jefferson.[6] In his view, the problem is that where there had once
been a healthy debate between Jeffersonians and Madisonians, victories over
totalitarianism abroad and Jim Crow at home have allowed twentieth-century
Jeffersonians to join the Madisonians "in support of the Constitution in all
respects." This is a mistake, in Levinson's view, because Madison's victory
over Jefferson stands in the way of fixing important structural defects in the

[3] See also Michael P. Zuckert, *The Natural Rights Republic: Studies in the Foundation of the American Political Tradition* (South Bend, IN: University of Notre Dame Press, 1996), 232–43.
[4] A good example is Franklin D. Roosevelt's recommendation to employ Hamiltonian means to achieve Jeffersonian ends.
[5] Robert A. Dahl, *How Democratic Is the American Constitution?* Second Edition (New Haven, CT: Yale University Press, 2003).
[6] Sanford Levinson, *Our Undemocratic Constitution: Where the Constitution Goes Wrong (And How We the People Can Correct It)* (Oxford: Oxford University Press, 2006). See also Barber's discussion of the corrosive effects of Madisonian constitutionalism in Sotirios A. Barber, *Constitutional Failure* (Lawrence: University Press of Kansas, 2014).

Constitution. Levinson goes on to compare the newly converted Madisonian to the "battered wife who continues to profess the 'essential goodness' of her abusive husband."[7]

In addition to providing a convenient historical framework for would-be constitutional reformers, the distinction between Jefferson and Madison has served as a useful measure of constitutional change across governments. In his study of what he calls the state constitutional tradition, John Dinan concludes that even though Madison might have won the contest with respect to the U.S. Constitution, Jefferson clearly scored many victories at the level of the state constitutions.[8] Likewise, in their *The Endurance of National Constitutions*, Elkins, Ginsburg, and Melton collected data on every national constitution since 1787 to determine what it is that makes a constitution last over time. Their argument is framed in terms of Jefferson versus Madison, and they find that both visions of constitutional life win: the average length of endurance for a constitution just happens to be Jefferson's nineteen years, yet constitutions seem to "improve" with age.[9]

In addition to offering a handy formula for social scientists who aim to classify democratic regimes, the difference between Jefferson and Madison is especially important for ongoing scholarship in political theory, as political theorists and intellectual historians have returned to considering what it is that constitutes any particular people. This literature is rapidly expanding, but what animates it is the difficulty in determining the moment at which, to borrow the formulation of the Declaration, "one people" becomes dissolvable from "another." Or as Brian Steele put it in his groundbreaking study of Jefferson and American nationhood, the problem is that "two peoples cannot become two overnight."[10]

The importance of the idea of Madisonian constitutionalism can also be seen in the renewed scholarly attention to "constitutional identity" and "constitutional maintenance." For example, Walter F. Murphy quotes from Madison's *Federalist* No. 49 to reveal a distinction between "constitutionalists" and "democrats": constitutionalists are "more pessimistic about human nature than are democrats" and, unlike democrats, "they are concerned, sometimes obsessed with humanity's propensity to act selfishly and abuse power."[11] Further, Murphy appeals to Madison several times to distinguish constitutional

---

[7] Ibid., 20.

[8] John J. Dinan, *The American State Constitutional Tradition* (Lawrence: University Press of Kansas, 2009).

[9] Zachary Elkins, Tom Ginsburg, and James Melton, *The Endurance of National Constitutions* (Cambridge: Cambridge University Press, 2009).

[10] Brian Steele, *Thomas Jefferson and American Nationhood* (New York: Cambridge University Press, 2012), 12. See also Jason Frank, *Constituent Moments: Enacting the People in Postrevolutionary America* (Durham, NC: Duke University Press, 2010).

[11] Walter F. Murphy, *Constitutional Democracy: Creating and Maintaining a Just Political Order* (Baltimore: Johns Hopkins University Press, 2009), 8.

maintenance from mere constitutional change, especially constitutional change "run amok."[12] Similarly, Gary Jeffrey Jacobsohn points to Madison, who, "like Burke, calculated the benefits of consistency in terms of winning over the 'prejudices of the community'."

> Implicit in Madison's calculation is the idea that a constitution, however clear and reasonable in its articulation of rules and principles, can only succeed in translating word into deed (and thereby establish a discernible identity) if fundamental continuity in basic law and actual constitutional practice are seen as two sides of the same coin.[13]

Jacobsohn's invocation of Madison, however, is not a complete endorsement. Madisonian and Burkean consistency is important as it serves as a kind of a capital to help constitutional theorists navigate the inevitable challenges of what Jacobsohn calls constitutional disharmony, but for Jacobsohn, this consistency is insufficient as a solution because sometimes "it is innovation that is in fact required." Like Murphy, Jacobsohn sees this innovation as required by the universal claims made by natural law, which inevitably force serious constitutional theorists to look abroad to solve constitutional difficulties at home. "Constitutional imperfection is, then, the setting within which constitutional interpretation, especially as it looks outward, takes places."[14]

From these accounts, we can see that the dichotomy between Madison and Jefferson still plays a role in the way political scientists and constitutional theorists think about constitutional design. This book, however, argues that this dichotomy is flawed or at least under-examined. Specifically, it argues that our notion of Madisonian constitutionalism has stood in the way of examining Madison's political thought and practice on its own terms.[15] In particular, it ignores the inconvenient fact that Madison spent the vast majority of his life helping Jefferson bring about changes that inevitably made the United States and its Constitution more Jeffersonian. If Madisonian constitutionalism is what scholars say it is, did Madison believe it?

Recent Work on Madison

Given the stakes, it is perhaps no surprise that there has been a resurgence of interest in Madison's political thought. While the discussion so far suggests that there is basic unity among political scientists and constitutional theorists about Madisonian constitutionalism, there is in fact less unity among Madison

---

[12] Ibid., 498–99, 512.

[13] Gary Jeffrey Jacobsohn, *Constitutional Identity* (Cambridge, MA: Harvard University Press, 2010), 97.

[14] Ibid., 203.

[15] I should acknowledge that there has been very good work revising Madisonian constitutionalism with respect to Madison and judicial review. See, for example, George Thomas, *The Madisonian Constitution* (Baltimore: The Johns Hopkins University Press, 2008), 1–38.

scholars about the important contours of Madison's thought. In short, Madison scholars are still divided concerning Madison's commitment to democracy and concerning the consistency of his political thought.

Years ago, Charles Beard and Robert Dahl found in Madison's *Federalist* essays an antidemocratic effort to divide and check the landless majority, but these accounts were challenged by Martin Diamond, who emphasized the freedom assumed by *The Federalist*'s vision of a "commercial republic" and concluded that Madison was a "friend" to democratic government.[16] Later, in the seminal study of Madison in the 1780s, Lance Banning argued that Madison's efforts to strengthen the national government were consistent with Madison's previous commitment to popular government.[17] For the past two decades, the question of Madison's democratic commitments has remained unsettled. Eminent scholars such as Gary Wills, Isaac Kramnick, and Drew McCoy still find Madison to be suspicious of democracy, and a few, such as Sheldon Wolin and Richard Matthews, even go as far as to conclude that Madison was hostile to it.[18] On the other side, Alan Gibson, Larry Kramer, Robert Martin, and Colleen Sheehan have built on Banning's argument by emphasizing Madison's democratic credentials.[19]

The question regarding Madison's commitment to democratic principles has also become entangled with another, namely whether there is "a Madison problem" with respect to Madison's consistency over time.[20] Broadly, the problem is that Madison's efforts in the 1790s to form and organize the Republican party seem inconsistent with Madison's efforts in the 1780s to form and ratify the Constitution of 1787.[21] This problem can be formulated in numerous

---

[16] Charles A Beard. *An Economic Interpretation of the Constitution* (New York: The Free Press, 1913); Robert Dahl, *Preface to Democratic Theory* (Chicago: University of Chicago Press, 1956); Martin Diamond, "Democracy and the Federalist: A Reconsideration of the Framers' Intent," *American Political Science Review* 53 (1959): 52–68.

[17] Lance Banning, *The Sacred Fire of Liberty: James Madison and the Founding of the Federal Republic* (Ithaca, NY: Cornell University Press, 1995), 250–52.

[18] Garry Wills, *Explaining America: The Federalist* (Garden City, NY: Doubleday, 1991); Drew R. McCoy, *The Last of the Fathers: James Madison and the Republican Legacy* (New York: Cambridge University Press, 1991); Richard K. Matthews, "James Madison's Political Theory: Hostage to Democratic Fortune," *Review of Politics* 67 (2005): 49–67; Sheldon Wolin, "Fugitive Democracy," *Constellations* 1 (1994): 11–25.

[19] As discussed later, scholars within these groupings disagree among themselves about the contours of Madison's democratic theory as well as about the degree to which its form in the 1790s was a departure from that in the 1780s. See Colleen A. Sheehan, *James Madison and the Spirit of Republican Self-Government* (New York: Cambridge University Press, 2009); Alan Gibson, "Veneration and Vigilance: James Madison and Public Opinion, 1785–1800," *Review of Politics* 67 (2005): 5–35; Robert W. Martin, "James Madison and Popular Government: The Neglected Case of the Memorial," *Polity* 42 (2010): 185–209.

[20] The phrase comes from Wood's chapter, "Is There a 'James Madison Problem'," in Gordon S. Wood, *Revolutionary Characters: What Made the Founders Different* (New York: Penguin, 2006), 141–72.

[21] Alan Gibson, "The Madisonian Madison and the Question of Consistency: The Significance and Challenge of Recent Research," *Review of Politics* 64 (2002): 331–38.

ways: the Madison of the 1780s was concerned with empowering the national government, yet the Madison of the 1790s defended the prerogatives of the states; the Madison of the 1780s warned of the dangers of faction, yet the Madison of the 1790s cofounded and organized the nation's first opposition party; and the Madison of the 1780s worried about the dangers of a tyrannical majority, yet the Madison of the 1790s worried about the threat to the disorganized majority constituted by an organized minority. According to Robert Dahl, whereas the Madison of 1787 was motivated by his fear of the majority, "the mature and experienced Madison of 1821 might have done less to check majority rule and more to facilitate it."[22]

There are, to be sure, potential solutions to this problem. One possible solution is that one period should be considered an outlier and therefore not part of the real Madison. So it could be, as Gordon Wood argued, that the Madison of the 1780s is the problem, because Madison's actions as secretary of state and president are consistent with the Madison of the 1790s. Or it could be, as Drew McCoy has argued, that the Madison of the 1820s is more like the Madison of the 1780s. A second solution, as Jack Rakove argues, is that the essential point is not that Madison's solution changed, but rather that Madison's perception of the threat to liberty changed. Under this view, and as Rakove puts it, Madison in the 1780s was most concerned about a powerful legislature and thus designed a constitution to check legislative power. But in the 1790s, Madison perceived that the greater threat to liberty came from the executive branch, so he shifted his focus to designing a constitution that checked the president. A third solution is that Madison was more or less consistent over time. So, for example, Banning argues that Madison was never a "nationalist," so the tension between the 1780s and 1790s has been overstated.[23] Colleen Sheehan reads Madison's writings in the 1780s to confirm her argument that Madison believed public opinion was "sovereign" but also something that needed to be shaped by the laws, an argument drawn from her study of Madison's party press essays in the 1790s.[24] Alan Gibson disagrees with this solution, but he too finds consistency in Madison's efforts to create what Gibson calls an "impartial" republic.[25]

These potential solutions are important early steps in understanding Madison, but in my view they all share a common problem. That problem with the existing scholarship on the Madison "problem" is that the period under consideration is frequently too narrow to provide a representative sample of Madison's career. So, for example, Banning and Rakove emphasize the constitution-building period of the 1780s, Sheehan the opposition period of

[22] Dahl, *How Democratic?*, 33.
[23] Banning, *Sacred Fire*, 158, 172.
[24] Sheehan, *James Madison and the Spirit of Republican Self-Government*.
[25] Alan Gibson, "Madison's 'Great Desideratum': Impartial Administration and the Extended Republic," *American Political Thought* 1 (2012): 181–207.

the 1790s, and McCoy the retirement period of the 1820s and 1830s. With the exception of one or two biographies, the scholarly literature just has not yet connected the dots over the whole course of Madison's career, and it has left some important periods almost completely unexplored.[26] As a result, we have very good accounts of Madison in one period or another, but we lack the perspective to place these accounts in the larger context of Madison's political thought and practice throughout his career. The real Madison problem might just be that our scholarship is still in the early stages.

The Problem of Constitutional Imperfection

Madison's records of the Federal Convention of 1787 inform most of our understanding of the Constitution, yet, throughout his life, Madison carefully recorded his doubts about the process and result of that Convention. In his first letter to Jefferson after the Convention, Madison described the Convention as a "miracle" and emphasized difficulties that were "peculiarly embarrassing" and "created more embarrassment." He called the absence of the congressional negative "materially defective."[27] Madison repeated some of this language in his important yet understudied *Federalist* No. 37, which was written in January 1788. In 1819, Madison quoted with approval Benjamin Franklin's joke at the expense of the "poor sample" of "human reason" displayed at the Convention of 1787.[28] In 1821, he wrote that the deliberations at the Convention operated in too temporary a horizon, and were constrained by extreme negotiating tactics; he also admitted that he would have held different opinions at the Convention had he known then either how the Convention would proceed or how the government would eventually operate under the Constitution.[29] In 1823, and to explain the ongoing problems with presidential selection, Madison wrote that the Convention made mistakes at the end because the delegates were tired and hurried.[30] In 1831, he recalled that Gouverneur Morris distinguished himself at the Convention for his "rare willingness" to change his mind after discussion.[31]

---

[26] The leading biography is Ralph Ketcham, *James Madison: A Biography* (Charlottesville: University Press of Virginia, 1990). See also Jeff Broadwater, *James Madison: A Son of Virginia & a Founder of a Nation* (Chapel Hill: University of North Carolina Press, 2012); Kevin R. C. Gutzman, *James Madison and the Making of America* (New York: St. Martins, 2012); Lynn Cheney, *James Madison: A Life Reconsidered* (New York: Viking, 2014).

[27] Madison to Jefferson, 24 October 1787, *Madison Writings*, 144, 152, and 149.

[28] In his 1819 Detached Memoranda, Madison recalled a story that Benjamin Franklin told a story of a man with no sense of smell who, upon observing sailors on a ship debating whether a piece of meat stunk or smelled sweet, concluded that "what you call smelling" is "nothing but fancy & mere prejudice." Madison, "Detached Memoranda," *Madison Writings*, 746.

[29] Madison to John Jackson, 28 December 1821, *Madison Papers Retirement*, 2: 441–44.

[30] Madison to Hay, 23 August 1823, Hunt 9: 155.

[31] Madison to Jared Sparks, 8 April 1831, Hunt 9: 447–51.

These were no doubt the reflections of someone well versed in the complex politics of constitutional controversy. After the Convention and before the rise of parties, Madison served as one of two principal exponents of the document (the *Federalist*), shepherded the first major revision through debate in Congress (the Bill of Rights), and assumed the leading role in the first debate regarding separation of powers (the removal debate of 1789). As Jefferson's sidekick and partisan politician in his own right, Madison tried to resolve imprecision with regard to the bank, the treaty power, presidential selection, the power to incorporate territory, and internal improvements. In Madison's retirement, would-be reformers turned to Madison to learn how to answer constitutional debates brought up by the Missouri Compromise, the Election of 1824, John Quincy Adams's national program, and the nullification crisis. As tirelessly as Madison worked to maintain the Constitution of 1787, he was inconsistent on whether that Constitution was better illuminated by debate in the Federal Convention or debate in the state ratifying conventions. Madison's treatment of constitutional imperfection could be the line connecting his efforts as the "Father of the Constitution" to those as the "last of the Fathers."

To be sure, scholars have long noted that Madison was dissatisfied with particular provisions of the Constitution, and much of the scholarship on the Madison problem has been focused on Madison's theories of constitutional interpretation and change. The difficulty has been that, at first glance, there is no clear unity in Madison's treatment of the problem of constitutional imperfection. There were times when he thought a policy was great policy but absolutely required a constitutional amendment (internal improvements, the national university, and recolonization of slaves). There were times, however, when he thought an amendment might be desirable in the abstract but unnecessary in practice (his first position on the Bill of Rights, and his later opinion on the bank). Similarly, even though he often advised that an amendment to the Constitution should not be proposed during a national controversy, he made calls for the states to begin the amendment process (the Alien and Sedition Acts), drafted amendments (the Louisiana Purchase), and distributed proposed amendments widely (the election controversy of 1824) precisely during moments of national controversy. And yet there were times when he thought a call for an amendment or appeal to the people would undermine the judiciary (Jefferson's 1823 protest message for the Virginia legislature), which he sometimes thought should be the necessary "final arbiter" in constitutional disputes. On another occasion, Madison worried that an error within the Constitution would become permanently attached to the public mind, as the Constitution would shape "opinions and commitments" into "settled obstacles" to much needed reform.[32] Finally, there were times when Madison argued eloquently against extra-constitutional appeals to the people, yet there was at least one occasion (the election controversy of 1800) when he advocated just that.

[32] Madison to George Hay, 23 August 1823, Hunt, 9: 155.

One potential solution to this problem could be that Madison's solutions were aimed not only at particular constitutional difficulties but also at what he saw as excesses in the methods advocated to solve them. To the strict constructionist who worried that the Constitution would be made blank by construction, Madison argued that imperfections sometimes have to be settled by deliberation over time and ultimately by judges. To the broad constructionist who grounded his argument on what all sovereign governments must do, Madison argued that the Constitution was a specific compact among the sovereign people and rested on their consent. To the advocate of frequent appeals to the people, Madison argued that constitutions need to be venerated if they are going to endure. Each was a solution that Madison himself embraced at one time or another, yet each, as Madison knew better than any of his contemporaries, carried its own dangers. There is no better example than that of Jefferson.

The Problem of Jefferson as Possible Solution

If there were one object of study that could provide the most clarity to the political thought and practice of Madison over his entire career, it would be his political alliance with Thomas Jefferson. The two worked together for the first time in 1776 in Williamsburg, where each was a member of the Virginia House of Delegates, and then again in 1779, when Jefferson was governor of Virginia and Madison member of the executive council. Jefferson and Madison turned this relationship into an alliance at least as early as the 1780s, when they collaborated in an ambitious and failed attempt to transform Virginia's legal order by liberalizing punishment, ending slavery, and creating a new system of education. With Jefferson in France, Madison focused on reforming the Articles of Confederation, and that collaboration continued in the form of an extraordinary series of letters that would span six years of their geographical separation and would include their famous exchange about constitutional change. From 1789, the date of Jefferson's return to the United States, to 1826, the year of Jefferson's death, the two collaborated to organize the nation's first political party, get each other elected as president, found the University of Virginia, and, finally, protect each other's legacies. In the final months of his life, Jefferson wrote Madison to ask that Madison "take care of me when dead."

This important collaboration has of course received previous scholarly attention. Adrienne Koch's *Jefferson and Madison: The Great Collaboration* was the first book-length attempt to understand the relationship between the two Virginians, particularly by examination of the intellectual exchange between the two.[33] But it was published in 1950. The more recent *Madison and Jefferson* by Andrew Burstein and Nancy Isenberg is the essential history

---

[33] Adrienne Koch, *Jefferson and Madison: The Great Collaboration* (Oxford: Oxford University Press, 1950).

of the relationship. The difference between the two works is evident from the titles. Burstein and Isenberg place Madison first in order to make Madison more equal to Jefferson, elevating Madison from the standard description of a "faithful lieutenant." Accordingly, Burstein and Isenberg point out the times when Madison disagreed with Jefferson and when Madison was indispensable in guiding Jefferson's career.[34] But, like Koch, much of the disagreement they find is isolated around the ratification of the Constitution, and, unlike Koch, they are less interested in understanding the political thought of each. This book, then, is more like Koch's in its attentiveness to political ideas, both as a cause and as an effect, but it will focus more closely on the way the relationship helps us understand Madison.

More than a touching and historically significant example of friendship in politics, the problem of Jefferson is essential to understanding Madison's dealing with the imperfections of the Constitution.[35] In prior work, I have argued that Jefferson saw his election in 1800 as an opportunity to transform executive power by democratizing it. That is, as Hamilton noted, Jefferson did not fear an energetic executive per se. Rather, Jefferson feared the energetic executive that he perceived Hamilton was creating, one that relied on expansive interpretations of constitutional authority. Jefferson sought to change this version of executive power to one that would be in his view more accountable and therefore more clearly tied to the majority will by electoral politics and by way of declarations of principle offered by the president. Accordingly, the Twelfth Amendment and the two-term tradition were designed by Jefferson to institutionalize what he called "his" principle, a single term of seven to eight years with the opportunity to remove midway in the term. Likewise, Jefferson changed the Inaugural Address to de-emphasize the formal transfer of power by way of the oath of office, and to reorient it around a declaration of principles, a declaration that would create a "union of sentiment" where it had not previously existed. The presidency, then, was remade to become the institutional path for appeals to the people to happen on a regular basis. Indeed, for Jefferson, the presidency made public opinion possible. If this is a correct rendering of Jefferson, then it is clear that we need to determine Madison's view of the Revolution of 1800. Did he understand it differently, or did he seek to moderate it? More directly, did Madison believe that the Revolution of 1800 was a revolution?

If this rendering is too focused on Jefferson, the question can be rephrased in a way that arises more directly out of Madison's political thought. In *Federalist* No. 37, Madison wrote that one of the difficulties faced by the delegates to

---

[34] Andrew Burstein and Nancy Isenberg, *Madison and Jefferson* (New York: Random House, 2010).

[35] For a useful comparison of Jefferson's "political friendship" with Madison to that of his "philosophic friendship" with John Adams, see Jean M. Yarbrough, *American Virtues: Thomas Jefferson in the Character of a Free People* (Lawrence: University Press of Kansas, 1988), 165–82.

the Convention of 1787 was how to combine energy and stability with "the genius of republican liberty." In his view, the problem is that every government requires both energy and stability, but the Americans also desired republican liberty. Further, the problem is that the necessary ingredients do not mix easily with the desired one. This is because energy requires the rule of the one, stability requires the rule of the few, and republican liberty requires the rule of the many. Likewise, energy requires an adequate length of term and stability requires a long length of term, but republican liberty demands a short length of term. The difficulty, then, is that the Constitution tries to mix principles that are in some fundamental way unmixable. As a result, the Constitution forces constitutional actors to privilege the alliance of two of the principles against a third.

This book argues that Madison veered toward republican liberty and away from stability. To be sure, Madison did not go as far as Jefferson would have, but the fact of Madison's lifetime alliance with Jefferson suggests that Madison was more than comfortable in choosing republican liberty over stability. But it also argues that this captures Madison's thinking even when we separate out the influence of Jefferson and the emergence of partisan politics. This is to say that we have long overestimated the importance of stability for Madison.

The Plan of the Book

Chapter 2 begins the analysis by revisiting Madison's argument for constitutional veneration. After summarizing Madison's response to Jefferson in *Federalist* No. 49, it returns to the context and timing of that essay to show that Madison also offered reasons to be wary of veneration. This chapter reveals that Madison had previously endorsed Jefferson's argument, at least in the context of the Kentucky constitution, only a few years earlier in his underappreciated letter to Caleb Wallace.[36]

The chapter next turns to Madison's personal correspondence to show that the recommendation in No. 49 had a specific audience and particular purpose, namely convincing moderates like Edmund Randolph that a second convention would be dangerous. Because Madison believed that deliberation would be impossible at such a convention, he had to make the difficult case that more constitutional deliberation was a bad thing, so he resurrected Jefferson's argument for frequent appeals to the people to take it off the table. Finally, the chapter provides a textual interpretation of *Federalist* No. 49 that links that essay to Madison's discussion of constitutional imperfection in *Federalist* No. 37.

Chapter 3 continues the analysis of the early Madison by revisiting his treatment of deliberation and its relationship to public opinion. In *Federalist*

[36] Jeremy D. Bailey, "Should We Venerate That Which We Cannot Love?: James Madison on Constitutional Imperfection," *Political Research Quarterly* 65 (2012): 732–44.

No. 38 Madison introduces deliberation as a feature of republican government, but deliberation seems to disappear from Madison's later essays, most
importantly in his discussions of ratification and Congress. This suggests that
Madison did not believe deliberation to be essential to republican government,
in part because Madison did not expect deliberation to happen among representatives either during times of ratification or during debate in Congress.

Chapter 4 considers two constitutional debates from the early 1790s: the
debate over the removal power and the debate over the Bill of Rights. Both
debates are especially important for this study because both happened before
the emergence of political parties, and in each, Madison took the lead and won.
From the episode of the Bill of Rights, we learn that Madison offered, but did
not wholeheartedly embrace, the claim that declarations could educate and
unite the whole people. Others made that argument, and Jefferson would make
it central to the Revolution of 1800. With Jefferson, Madison had already used
such declarations to reform Virginia politics, and, with Jefferson, he would do
it again in 1798 to protest the Alien and Sedition Acts. But, when he fathered
the Bill of Rights, Madison believed that liberty would be better secured by
institutional arrangements, not the attentiveness of the people. This reading
offers an important qualification of the Madison presented by political theorists, especially Colleen Sheehan and Robert Goldwin.

If the discussion of the Bill of Rights offers a chance to examine Madison's
thinking about the effect constitutions have on citizens, the removal debate sheds
important light on the way the institutional arrangements of the Constitution
would work. In particular, Madison's argument that the Constitution gives the
president alone the power to remove executive branch officials offers a chance
to assess the way Madison went about resolving constitutional difficulties. In
particular, Madison associated the president with the principle of responsibility
and the Senate with the principle of stability, and argued that the Senate's participation in the removal would give "too much stability" to the government.
At a minimum, this reveals that Madison thought that too much stability could
be a bad thing.

Chapter 5 considers Madison's decision in the 1790s to organize an opposition party to the Washington administration. Like Sheehan's account, it emphasizes Madison's turn to public opinion as a legitimate source of authority,
especially in his essays for the *National Gazette*. It also shows that his argument
against the national bank relied on a method of constitutional interpretation that
links his arguments for ratification to his efforts in retirement to preserve the
correct history of the Constitution. For Madison, the history of the particulars
of ratification, and not the requirements of good government, was most essential to understanding the meaning of the Constitution. But this forced him to
articulate his understanding of the role of public opinion under the Constitution.
Importantly, all of this was done in the context of Jefferson's return to the United
States, and Madison eventually came to endorse at least one application of
Jefferson's famous argument that the earth belongs to the living.

Chapter 6 examines what might be called the "middle Madison," or the period from the election of 1800 to the election of 1824. This period has received very little attention from Madison scholars, yet this is the period where we can get the best handle on Madison's view of the Revolution of 1800. Accordingly, this chapter focuses on Madison's understanding of the presidency in the constitutional order as a point of comparison with Jefferson. In particular, it considers the middle Madison on removals as well as Madison's acquisition of West Florida while president. Moreover, because this period had two election crises, this chapter considers Madison's response to constitutional reforms surrounding debates about the connection between the presidency and public opinion. During the election crisis of 1800, Madison favored a direct appeal to the people rather than a constitutional path. As Ackerman has argued, it was Federalists who proposed a remedy that could be grounded in constitutional text, and Republicans who used the threat of a second convention as leverage against moderate Federalists.[37] In this context, Madison endorsed what Ackerman calls an "irregular" appeal to the people, without worrying in the slightest that such an appeal would undermine the people's respect for the Constitution. Again, in 1823, during the buildup to the election crisis of 1824, Madison believed that an appeal to the people in the form of a constitutional amendment was the better path. This time, Madison attempted to correct what he had long regarded as a constitutional error – the equality of states in the contingency election in the House for presidential selection. In fact, he went so far as to support his proposal with the historical claim that the delegates at the Convention in 1787 grew tired and hurried at the end and thus made mistakes. Rather than being concerned about the consequences of the amendment process during a heated national controversy intertwined with the crisis of sectionalism, he instead returned to the argument he had made in 1785, namely that constitutions need to be corrected before they become fixed in the public mind. Importantly, Andrew Jackson's opponents, like the Federalist opponents of the Twelfth Amendment, had by then embraced the argument from veneration to counter these reforms to presidential selection, reforms that they correctly perceived were aimed at making the president more directly connected to the national electorate.

Chapter 7 examines the last period of Madison's life, the period studied by Drew McCoy in his masterful *Last of the Fathers*. Instead of replicating McCoy's work, this chapter considers Madison's last endeavor to understand the Constitution, namely his organization of his *Notes on the Federal Convention* for posthumous publication. Madison's decision to preserve the *Notes* is itself worthy of study, as it established Madison as the primary authority of the Constitution while at the same time revealing the messiness of the convention debates. Accordingly, this chapter situates Madison's work in the competing

---

[37] Bruce Ackerman, *Failure of the Founding Fathers: Jefferson, Marshall, and the Rise of Presidential Democracy* (Cambridge, MA: Harvard University Press, Belknap Press, 2005).

claims about who deserved the credit for the arguments in the Declaration of Independence and who had the best records of the Constitutional Convention. In fact, Madison collaborated with Jefferson in composing Jefferson's famous letter to Henry Lee about the "object" of the Declaration, and, although scholars have not noticed it, Madison's suggested version of the letter has important differences from the version Jefferson eventually sent. Moreover, this chapter challenges Jack Rakove's claim that Madison believed that the state ratifying conventions offered the best guide to original meaning.

Toward a New Madison

Madison went out of his way in the *Federalist* to dismantle Jefferson's proposal for frequent appeals to the people, and he returned to that argument several times in their correspondence. Because of the power of that critique, it is tempting to conclude that the dialogue between Madison and Jefferson was a contest between two visions of constitutionalism, between Madisonian veneration and Jeffersonian revolution.[38] It is probably for this reason that, among political scientists at least, Madison's reputation has long outshone his normally more sparkling companion, Thomas Jefferson, in part because Madison's *Federalist* essays resist Jefferson's tendency to hyperbole and display a kind of sober rigor that is attractive to practitioners of social science.

The problem with this characterization of Madison is that it does not line up with the facts. In particular, it enables us to too easily forget that Madison's concern with a second convention was that the first convention had demonstrated how dangerous, and how flawed, all such conventions must be. So, like the argument that Madison came to believe a bill of rights would serve as a valuable maxim of republican government, and the argument that Madison believed in the sovereignty of public opinion, the emphasis on Madison's recommendation of veneration focuses too closely on only one aspect of Madison's lifelong involvement with the politics of constitutional imperfection.

---

[38] For example, Greg Weiner writes that Madison's views "were far more Burkean than Jeffersonian," and that Madison's emphasis on "constitutional veneration evoked the linchpin of so much of Madison's democratic theory." Likewise, Gary Rosen argues that Madison "had no desire to encourage informal amendment through what Bruce Ackerman has called 'constitutional politics' – that is, through 'mobilized deliberation' of the people outside the provisions of Article V." See Gary Rosen, *American Compact*, 173, and Greg Weiner, *Madison's Metronome: The Constitution, Majority Rule, and the Tempo of American Politics* (Lawrence: University Press of Kansas, 2012), 59.

2

Appeals to Tradition

The Case for and against Veneration

According to scholars, the most important difference between James Madison and Thomas Jefferson has long been Madison's argument that constitutional government requires "veneration" of the constitution. Madison's *Federalist* No. 49 is the most well known of his recommendations of constitutional veneration, but as will be discussed in later chapters, Madison made this argument several times over the course of his life, often when responding to Jefferson's enthusiastic recommendations for appeals to the people.[1] This chapter focuses on *Federalist* No. 49, where Madison's argument first occurs and where it was given in its most public form, and it argues that the scholarly account is not quite accurate. Indeed, the evidence shows that Madison did not fully endorse constitutional veneration and even that Madison offered reasons to be wary of it.

In *Federalist* No. 49, Madison criticized a provision of Thomas Jefferson's 1783 proposed constitution for Virginia, which would have provided for a new constitutional convention whenever two-thirds of any two of the three departments called for it. Madison noted that Jefferson's proposal had "great force" because it seemed "strictly consonant with republican theory" in that it would refer constitutional disputes back to the people, who "are the only legitimate fountain of power." But Madison also listed "insuperable objections against the proposed recurrence to the people." In particular, Madison argued that appeals to the people would undermine "veneration" toward the law and would at the

---

[1] See Chapter 5's discussion of Madison's response to Jefferson's "earth belongs to the living" letter. Madison to Jefferson, 4 February 1790, *Madison Writings*, 474. See also Madison to Jefferson, 27 June 1823, *Madison Writings*, 800; Madison to Edward Everett, 28 August 1830, *Madison Writings*, 845, and Madison, "Charters," in *Madison Writings*, 503.

A version of this chapter was published in 2012 as "Should We Venerate That Which We Cannot Love?: James Madison on Constitutional Imperfection" in *Political Research Quarterly*, 732–44. Copyright © 2012, University of Utah.

same time raise regime-level questions that would appeal to the passions rather than to the reason of the public.[2]

Because Madison so clearly says that prejudice is a necessary substitute for reason, there has been little interpretative uncertainty about No. 49. Scholars have typically found in this essay support for the larger argument that Madison was a "conservative" in the likes of David Hume and perhaps even Edmund Burke.[3] To be sure, as was discussed in the introduction, scholars are still divided concerning Madison's commitment to democracy and the consistency of his political thought over time.[4] But even those scholars who emphasize a more democratic Madison acknowledge the difficulty the essay makes for their case.[5] More generally, *Federalist* No. 49 is the clearest indication for scholars that Madison did not share Jefferson's belief in constitutional change by appeal to the people. Jack Rakove, for example, appeals to *Federalist* No. 49 as a counterweight to Bruce Ackerman's reading of No. 40, which Ackerman reads as supporting Ackerman's theory of recurring constitutional moments.[6] Likewise, Dustin Gish and Daniel Klinghard argue that Madison wrote No. 49 to counter what they see as Jefferson's attempt to use his *Notes on the State of Virginia* to influence the writing and ratification of the Constitution. In their words, Madison believed that reason was an insufficient foundation for republican politics, so he argued that the Constitution, like the Almighty, had to be *"venerated* and *revered."*[7]

This chapter challenges this consensus. After presenting the main argument and difficulties of No 49, the chapter offers two reasons to qualify Madison's

---

[2] Madison, *Federalist* No. 49, in Scigliano, 322–5.

[3] See Douglass Adair, "'That Politics May Be Reduced to a Science': David Hume, James Madison, and the Tenth Federalist," in *Fame and the Founding Fathers: Essays by Douglass Adair,* ed. Trevor Colbourn (New York: Norton, 1974), 93–106; Marvin Meyers, "Founding and Revolution: A Commentary on Publius-Madison" in *The Hofstadter Aegis: A Memorial,* ed. Stanley Elkins and Eric McKitrick (New York: Knopf, 1974), 3–35; Garry Wills, *Explaining America: The Federalist* (Garden City, NY: Doubleday, 1981); Drew R. McCoy, *The Last of the Fathers: James Madison and the Republican Legacy* (New York: Cambridge University Press, 1991), 41–61; Andrew Burstein and Nancy Isenberg, *Madison and Jefferson* (New York: Random House, 2010), 178.

[4] I should also add that some scholars see Madison's veneration as compatible with philosophic reason and therefore more than prejudice. See Rosen, *American Compact,* 137–39 and 178–84. See also James Ceaser, *Nature and History in American Political Development* (Cambridge, MA: Harvard University Press, 2008), 65.

[5] Alan Gibson, "Veneration and Vigilance: James Madison and Public Opinion, 1785–1800," *Review of Politics* 67 (2005): 5–35; Colleen A. Sheehan, "Public Opinion and the Formation of Civic Character in James Madison's Republican Theory," *Review of Politics* 67 (2005): 37–48.

[6] Jack Rakove, "The Super-Legality of the Constitution, or, a Federalist Critique of Bruce Ackerman's New-Federalism," *Yale Law Journal* 55 (1999): 473–505; Bruce Ackerman, "The Storrs Lectures: Discovering the Constitution," *Yale Law Journal* 93 (1984): 1013–72; Bruce Ackerman, *We the People: Foundations* (Cambridge, MA: Harvard University Press, Belknap Press, 1991).

[7] Dustin A. Gish and Daniel P. Klinghard, "Republican constitutionalism in Thomas Jefferson's *Notes on the State of Virginia,*" *Journal of Politics* 71 (2012): 35–51.

defense of constitutional veneration. First, it argues that the historical context suggests that the argument for veneration fits Madison's strategic objective in preventing a second convention. Second, it offers a new reading of the *Federalist* to show that Madison's recommendation of veneration offers its own reasons to be wary of constitutional veneration.

The historical context offers reason enough to be cautious about hanging too much on the argument from veneration. As we will see, Madison did not always think that Jefferson's proposal was a bad idea. In fact, he endorsed it in 1785 when making recommendations for a new constitution in Kentucky. Madison's concern then was that constitutional mistakes become more settled over time and thus more difficult to correct – a concern he repeated throughout his life. With regard to his critique of Jefferson and praise of veneration, it is obvious that Madison wrote and published his *Federalist* essays for a particular objective, convincing Americans to ratify the Constitution.[8] But what is often underappreciated in studies of the *Federalist* is that Madison wrote his essays on the republican credentials of the Constitution just at the time when the prospects for ratification had taken a turn for the worse. Specifically, at this time, Madison's goal was convincing moderates, particularly in Virginia, that a second convention would not get them what they wanted. It is likely that Madison wrote the essays on the republicanism of the Constitution with these moderates in mind. Because these moderates could have been attracted to a second convention as a compromise, Madison focused these essays on the problems of deliberation. Because Jefferson's proposal could potentially give rhetorical and democratic heft to this compromise, Madison brought up Jefferson's proposal in order to remove deliberation in the form of a second convention as a possible alternative.

In addition to the historical context, the *Federalist* suggests reasons to be wary of constitutional veneration. Instead of reading the essay as a discreet treatment of Jeffersonian appeals to the people (Nos. 49–50), or as a step in the argument concerning separation of powers (Nos. 47–51) simply, this chapter examines the essay as closing Madison's larger discussion of the requirements of republican government (beginning in No. 37). Read this way, we are reminded that Madison goes out of his way, and further than any other supporter of the Constitution, to clearly elucidate the ways in which the Constitution, and any conceivable constitution, is flawed. Moreover, Madison does not attempt to understate these flaws by calling them unimportant or solvable in the future. Rather, he attributes them to the problems of deliberation, not only by the people but also by elites, and in an important part of this argument, Madison makes the troubling confession that the republican remedy

---

[8] Pauline Maier and other historians have concluded that it is unlikely the *Federalist* influenced ratification decisions outside of New York. This does not present a problem for my argument, as my argument is concerned primarily with Madison's objectives. See Pauline Maier, *Ratification: The People Debate the Constitution, 1787–1788* (New York: Simon & Schuster, 2010).

for the republican disease, the extended republic, makes deliberation worse during times of founding.

The Case for Veneration in *Federalist* No. 49

In *Federalist* No. 49, Madison offered four reasons to reject Jefferson's proposal. The first objection was that it would not accomplish its goal, that is, it would not prevent the legislative branch from benefiting from the arrangement by allying itself with one of the other two departments. The second brings us to the subject of this chapter: such appeals would deprive the government of "that veneration which time bestows on everything." This veneration is necessary, because "government rests on opinion." The problem, however, is that "the reason of man, like man himself, is timid and cautious when left alone, and acquires firmness and confidence in proportion to the number with which it is associated." Here, Madison perhaps looked to Hume's examination of constitutional imperfection in his "Idea of a Perfect Commonwealth." In particular, Hume contrasted philosophers with the wiser magistrate "who will bear a reverence for what carries the mark of age."[9] It is also worth noticing that Madison's reference to the "reason" of men, combined with his discussion of the "veneration" men have toward their governments, calls attention to the tension between unattached pursuit of truth and love of country. But even while seeming to remind readers of this perhaps irreconcilable tension between philosophy and citizenship, Madison made a different point about reason. Rather than emphasizing the danger reason presents to the political order, Madison instead depicted reason among individuals as needing "firmness and confidence." Reason needs to be "fortified," and time and agreement with other citizens "are known to have a double effect" in such fortification. Veneration seems to support reason rather than work against it.[10]

Madison's discussion of public reason makes sense when we see that Madison's understanding of reason rests on the compatibility between reason and respect for the laws. Madison wrote that considerations on how to fortify reason should be disregarded "in a nation of philosophers," because "a reverence for the laws would be sufficiently inculcated by the voice of an enlightened reason."[11] Further, such a "nation of philosophers is as little to be expected as the philosophical race of kings wished for by Plato," but he did not explain what characterizes the difference between the reason of the philosophic and that of the ordinary.[12] One possible explanation is that philosophic reason is

---

[9] David Hume, "Idea of a Perfect Commonwealth," in *Essays: Moral, Political, and Literary*, Revised Edition, ed. Eugene Miller (Indianapolis, IN: Liberty Fund, 1985), 512.

[10] Madison, *Federalist* No. 49, Scigliano, 322–25.

[11] Ibid., 323.

[12] It is worth noting here that Madison referred to Jefferson as a "philosopher" many times after Jefferson died. See Chapters 7 and 8.

not at odds with republican politics. Support for this explanation can be found in the logic that animates *Federalist* No. 10. In that essay, Madison acknowledged that there is such a thing as a "permanent and aggregate interest of the community," but it seems that the "reciprocal influence" between passions (especially self-love) and opinions alters what might otherwise be a rational estimation of the community's permanent and aggregate interest.[13] But this is to say that a proper regulation of the passions could allow for a better calculation of interest, even those interests that are permanent and aggregate. Instead of being fundamentally opposed to the law, philosophic reason elevates timid and cautious reason, which, if left alone, would disrespect the law because it wrongly regards the law as standing in the way of interest. If philosophic reason were widespread, republican politics would spring naturally and rationally from interest.

Madison turned more explicitly to the passions in the third, and what he calls a "more serious," objection to Jefferson's proposal. Such appeals to the people, he writes, would disturb the "public tranquility by interesting too strongly the public passions." Because constitutional conventions are "experiments" that "are of too ticklish a nature," it is best not to attempt them when unnecessary. But having just undergone a revolution, Madison had to explain how the recent revolution can be distinguished from others:

> We are to recollect that all the existing constitutions were formed in the midst of a danger which repressed the passions most unfriendly to order and concord; of an enthusiastic confidence of the people in their patriotic leaders, which stifled the ordinary diversity of opinions on great national questions; of a universal ardor for new and opposite forms, produced by a universal resentment and indignation against the ancient government; and whilst no spirit of party connected with the changes to be made, or the abuses to be reformed, could mingle its leaven in the operation.

In this striking passage, Madison cataloged the ways in which the passions were aligned for a change in government that could be compatible with respect for the laws. The thrust of this argument is that passions arising from local and particularistic concerns were pushed aside by passions against the common enemy and passions for common leaders against that enemy. In other words, because philosophic reason is not to be expected, constitutional founding rests on the dubious hope that benign passions will rule the more ordinary, more dangerous passions that typically arise to answer ticklish questions. By this logic, a founding should not be repeated.[14]

The fourth objection to Jefferson's proposal was that the appeal to the people would not solve the problem requiring the appeal in the first place, because, as the department closest to the people, the legislative branch would most likely benefit from such an appeal. Even when the executive and judicial departments call for an appeal to the people to correct an overbearing legislature, it would

[13] Madison, *Federalist* No. 49, Scigliano, 54–55.
[14] Ibid., 323–24.

be likely that the people would side with the legislative branch and further constitutionalize legislative tyranny. This practical point helps clarify why the ordinary passions would be dangerous. Because the executive and judicial departments are "too few in number" and, in the case of the latter, too separated by their tenure from the people, it is likely that the people will favor the legislative department. After all, the members of the legislative branch are "distributed and dwell among the people at large." Further, they have "connections of blood, of friendship, and of acquaintance" with the most "influential part of society," and the "nature of their public trust implies a personal influence among the people." To be sure, there would be times when the "usurpations of the legislature might be so flagrant and so sudden, as to admit of no specious coloring," so that the executive and judicial departments would enjoy an advantage. But even in these moments, Madison predicted, the "public decision" "could never be expected to turn on the true merits of the question." Rather,

> [i]t would inevitably be connected with the spirit of preexisting parties, or of parties springing out of the question itself. It would be connected with persons of distinguished character and extensive influence in the community. It would be pronounced by the very men who had been agents in, or opponents of, the measures to which the decision would relate.

From this catalog of the advantages of the legislative branch, and from Madison's prediction of the outcome of an appeal to the public, perhaps even in periods of ordinary politics, we catch a glimpse of what Madison saw as the character of public opinion during periods of founding or re-founding. The people seem to be unable to serve as judges in the contest between the departments either because they lack the ability to see beyond their own immediate connection to a member of Congress, or because they fall under the influence of legislative coalition leaders who have a stake in the outcome of the appeal to the public. The problem with appeals to the people then is that during such occasions, "the passions, therefore, not the reason, of the public would sit in judgment."

This argument is striking for the clarity in which Madison recorded his doubts about the ability of the public to sort through appeals, but Madison did not stop there. Instead he argued that "it is the reason, alone, of the public, that ought to control and regulate the government." Given the scholarship that points to Madison's borrowing from Hume, it should be mentioned that this points to a difference with Hume, who wrote in "Idea of a Perfect Commonwealth" that the "bulk of mankind" was governed "by authority, not reason."[15] More important for the present purposes, Madison's statement

---

[15] Hume, "Idea of Perfect Commonwealth," 512. On the influence of Hume, and in addition to Adair, see, for example, Robert A. Manzer, "A Science of Politics: Hume, *The Federalist*, and the Politics of Constitutional Attachment," *American Journal of Political Science* 45 (2001): 508–18. For a summary of the literature, see Alan Gibson, *Interpreting the Founding: Guide to the Enduring Debates Over the Origins and Foundations of the American Republic* (Lawrence: University Press of Kansas, 2006), 41–43.

is also notable for its apparent tension with his previous comment concerning reason. In the previous passage about this not being a nation of philosophers, Madison went out of his way to write that philosophers can see that reason and reverence for the laws are compatible, but ordinary citizens cannot, because their reason is timid and cautious. Here, however, Madison offered *public* reason as an alternative to passion, which is to say, at least, that public reason is possible.

There are two possible ways to resolve this tension. The first, or strong, explanation is that public reason is possible only when the passions of the people are "controlled and regulated by the government."[16] This in turn suggests that veneration stands in as a milder form of governmental control and regulation of the passions. That is, it seems for Madison that the discoveries of the modern science of politics – the extended republic and legislative checks and balances – are insufficient in that they require a prior grounding on allegiance to a particular constitution. This allegiance must be almost spiritual in its devotion, which is to say that the constitution must be beyond contestation and deliberation. For those scholars such as Colleen Sheehan who emphasize ancient and/or conservative strands in Madison, this passage is important in its suggestion that government shapes its citizens.[17] The second, or soft, explanation is that public reason emerges from constitutional deliberation. Under this explanation, separation of powers and other institutional arrangements elevate the public passions and interests into something close to public reason. That is, the constitutional process itself stands in as a substitute to the appeal to the people and renders unnecessary the question whether the people are able to sort through an appeal to the public.

Even if either or both explanations were persuasive, they leave other puzzles about the argument for veneration. First, consider Madison's rhetorical strategy. Why would Madison take the time to consider and dismantle a friend's proposal about the Virginia constitution when nobody else had proposed applying that solution to the national Constitution?[18] Second, given the lack of discussion regarding Jefferson's proposal, it is somewhat strange that Madison went out of his way to recommend veneration on the grounds that veneration is necessary for any constitution when the actual task at hand was to replace one constitution (the Articles) with another (the Constitution of 1787). That is, why would Madison argue so vigorously for veneration when moderates or fence-sitters might want the assurance that they would be able to tinker in the future? Third, and more broadly, if we must venerate the constitution only because the alternative is worse, we then venerate even though the object of

[16] Madison, *Federalist* No. 49, Scigliano, 325.
[17] For the classical influences on Madison, see Colleen A. Sheehan, *The Mind of James Madison: The Legacy of Classical Republicanism* (New York: Cambridge University Press, 2015).
[18] I have yet to find a mention of Jefferson's proposal by an anti-Federalist before or after publication of Madison's No. 49.

our veneration is perhaps unworthy of our longtime attachment. This could be
a matter of choosing the less bad option, but what does veneration recommend
when the opportunity arises for the people or their representatives to form a
better constitution? Madison, after all, had praised Americans in *Federalist* No.
14 for "having not suffered a blind veneration for antiquity." These questions
are amplified by Madison's prior treatment of Jefferson's proposal.

The Kentucky Constitution in 1785

There is no lack of scholarship on Madison's thinking before the Convention of
1787. What has not been noticed, however, is that Madison's first written analysis of Jefferson's 1783 proposal was not *Federalist* No. 49, but rather his underappreciated 1785 letter to Caleb Wallace.[19] Wallace was a friend from Princeton
who had moved to the Kentucky territory and solicited Madison's advice on
writing a constitution for a state "in embryo."[20] Although scholars have treated
the letter in solving other problems within Madison's constitutional thought,
none has commented on the tension between this letter and No. 49.[21]

    In contrast to *Federalist* No. 49, Madison used the 1785 letter to endorse
the idea of a planned review of the constitution. Wallace had asked whether
there should be a "periodical review of the Constitution." Madison answered,
"Nothing appears more eligible in theory nor has sufficient trial perhaps been
yet made to condemn it in practice." Without naming Jefferson, Madison
brought up the proposal from Jefferson's 1783 constitution: "That a Majority
of any two of the three departments should have authority to call a pleni-
potentiary convention whenever they may think their constitutional powers
have been Violated by the other Department or that any material part of the
Constitution needs amendment." In contrast to No. 49, Madison offered at
least a limited endorsement: "I should think it both imprudent & indecent
not to leave a door open for at least one revision of your first Establishment."
The reason why it would be imprudent is because constitution makers would
have more "resources" for support of a constitution as well as more "lights" in

[19] Madison, *PJM* 8: 350–59.
[20] Rakove calls Wallace a college friend. *Madison Writings*, 926.
[21] See Jack N. Rakove, "The Great Compromise: Ideas, Interests, and the Politics of Constitution
    Making," *William and Mary Quarterly*, Third Series 44 (1987): 429; Rakove, *Original
    Meanings: Politics and Ideas in the Making of the Constitution* (New York: Knopf, 1996);
    Rakove, "Origins of Judicial Review: A Plea for New Contexts." *Stanford Law Review* 47
    (1997): 1056; Rakove "The Super-Legality of the Constitution, or, a Federalist Critique of
    Bruce Ackerman's New-Federalism" 1946; Rakove, "Thinking like a Constitution," *Journal
    of the Early Republic* 24 (2004): 8. See also Larry D. Kramer, *The People Themselves: Popular
    Constitutionalism and Judicial Review* (New York: Oxford University Press, 1999), 626;
    Kramer, "'The Interest of the Man': James Madison, Popular Sovereignty, and the Theory of
    Deliberative Democracy," *Valparaiso University Law Review* 41 (2006): 738; Gary Rosen,
    James Madison and the Problem of Founding (Lawrence: University Press of Kansas, 1999).

framing one in "15 to 20 years hence." The reason why it would be indecent is because a "handful of settlers" ought not frame a perpetual constitution for what will be a "populous country." Accordingly, Madison recommended that the framers of the Kentucky constitution make "necessary and certain" a future revision of the constitution, which, in this context, meant including a provision like Jefferson's proposal.

Before we consider the significance of this letter, we should consider three alternative explanations. The first is that there is a difference between a single appeal in the shape of a convention and a *process* for repeated appeals to the people. So, under this explanation, Madison's reference to "revision" is closer to the amendment process than to a new convention. And this would not be all that surprising, because Madison in No. 49 does allow the amendment process as a "constitutional road" to constitutional correction.[22] But this explanation is unsatisfactory. In the letter to Wallace, Madison clearly specified "at least one revision" of the Kentucky constitution, not amendment, and the necessary implication from the exchange is that he endorsed Jefferson's proposal, at least for Kentucky. In fact, Madison changed Jefferson's proposal to make such constitutional conventions *more frequent* by requiring only a "majority" instead of two-thirds of two of the three departments. It must be pointed out, too, that even Jefferson later wrote that he was "not an advocate for frequent and untried changes in laws and constitutions," because "moderate imperfections had better be borne with."[23] The second alternative explanation is that there is a difference between writing a constitution for a new territory or state and writing a new Constitution for the United States. The premise for this objection is clear: Madison might have believed that the stakes were lower and therefore the states could experiment with and even rewrite their constitutions. But this is not a distinction Madison employed in No. 49. Rather he considered and rejected Jefferson's proposal for appeals to the people as a proposal for *any* constitution. A third and related explanation is that Madison changed his mind. Perhaps the deepening crisis under the Articles, or Shay's Rebellion, prompted a new appreciation for the law. Or, to apply Banning's thesis that Madison learned from the Convention, perhaps Madison learned from his participation in the Convention that writing a constitution was more difficult and dangerous than he and Jefferson had supposed.

Even if the second and third explanations were true, they would still leave some questions unanswered. If it is true that Madison believed that a state rather than the Union should use Jefferson's proposal, we would then have to conclude that Madison believed constitutional veneration is not always a good. Similarly, if it is true that Madison changed his mind because he came to see how fragile Union really was, then we must again understand how the special importance of this particular Union factors in Madison's understanding

[22] Madison, *Federalist* No. 49, Scigliano, 322.
[23] Jefferson to Samuel Kercheval, 12 July 1816, *Jefferson Writings*, 1401.

of veneration. Both points suggest that we need to consider in greater detail the context of Madison's endorsement of veneration. As Chapter 5 discusses, this point is illustrated by yet another of Madison's analyses of Jefferson's 1783 proposed constitution. Only several months after writing No. 49, Madison sent another friend in Kentucky his criticisms of Jefferson's constitution. In this otherwise extensive analysis, Madison this time omitted any discussion of the proposal for institutionalized appeals to the people or of veneration.[24] Perhaps Madison had changed his mind again, or, this time, did not think Jefferson's proposal merited notice.

It is possible, then, that the 1785 endorsement of Jefferson's proposal reveals an important aspect of Madison's constitutional thought. In an argument that Jefferson himself might have made, Madison claimed that time brings about certain resources, and that these resources suggest a kind of progress. The people would become more ready for constitutional government, perhaps because they would improve their skills in constitutional design by additional discoveries in the science of politics. Further, Madison's distinction between a handful of settlers and a populous country underscores the differences between the few who make the law and the many who are governed by them. Under this explanation, then, Madison did support constitutional veneration in certain instances, but he also believed that progress and basic considerations of justice could outweigh unwavering attachment to a flawed constitution.

This is precisely what Madison said about the Articles of Confederation. As he put it in the letter to Wallace, the Articles of Confederation was "faulty" in two ways: the authority by which it was formed and its actual form. Nevertheless, "the Issue of an experiment has taught the difficulty of amending it." More important, the prospects for reforming the Articles were getting worse with time. With each passing year, the "depths to which it will have stricken its roots" will "counterbalance any more auspicious circumstances for overturning it." Because progress and justice require a way to transform the constitution, the framers of the Articles were imprudent and indecent for making their constitution perpetual. Experience under the Articles shows that veneration of the constitution is not always a virtue.

Madison's Political Objective in 1788

When Madison published No. 49 in February 1788, the advocates for the Constitution had lost momentum and were facing an increasingly difficult problem in the ratification process. In the weeks following the Convention, Madison had anticipated the problem in a letter to George Washington: on the one hand, there was a "very strong probability" that at least nine states will "pretty speedily" ratify, yet, on the other, nobody knew what would happen

[24] Madison, "Observations on Jefferson's Draft Constitution for Virginia," *Papers* 11: 281–295.

to the states that refused.[25] By December, this possibility was becoming more likely, and the practical problem had the potential to have enormous political consequences, as at this point Madison knew that ratification was uncertain in two of the most important states – New York and Virginia. Madison hoped that the ratification problem would solve itself: difficult states such as New York and Virginia would have no choice but to ratify because nine states already had.

But the practical political problem was given a theoretical twist when opponents to the Constitution in those two states proposed amendments to the Constitution in the form of a bill of rights. The problem was that these proposals took on the language of "conditional" ratification, ratification only on the condition that the Constitution was amended to include a bill of rights. From Madison's perspective, then, these amendments were disconcerting not only because they had the potential to undo the structural arrangements of the Constitution but also because even an innocuous declaration of rights threatened to create varying levels of ratification and thus make a legitimate basis for Union impossible.

By January, Madison and his allies had lost ground. Massachusetts was no longer a sure bet: Madison had asked Washington in late December to use his influence in Massachusetts and, on 20 January, he wrote letters to Washington and Randolph calling the situation there "very ominous to the Constitution."[26] At the same time, Madison learned that, instead of ratifying, North Carolina had surprised everyone by deciding to postpone its decision until Virginia had decided. Now, because the anti-Federalists in Virginia were gaining momentum, and because he thought South Carolina and Georgia might follow North Carolina in waiting on Virginia, Madison had reason to fear that no more than eight states would ever ratify.[27] On 10 January, he wrote to Randolph: "I consider everything therefore as problematical from Maryland Southward."[28] Madison's strategy, that nine states would easily ratify and force the more reluctant states into the fold, was in shambles. When No. 49 was published on 2 February, Madison had reason to believe that the prospects for ratification had improved in Georgia and South Carolina, but there was a new cause for Madison's concern.[29] A new version of Jefferson's *Notes on the State of Virginia* had been published in Philadelphia on 23 January 1788.[30] According to Burstein and Isenberg,

[25] Madison to Washington, 28 October 1787, *PJM* 10: 225.
[26] Madison to Washington, 20 December 1787, and Madison to Randolph, 20 January 1788, *PJM* 10: 334 and 398–99.
[27] Madison did not yet know that Georgia had ratified a few days earlier.
[28] Madison to Randolph, 10 January 1788, *PJM* 10: 356.
[29] Madison to Washington, 1 February 1788, *PJM* 10: 455.
[30] Scigliano, *The Federalist*, xxviii. I am indebted to Gish and Klinghard for alerting me to this date. These scholars argue that Jefferson intended for his *Notes* to influence the forming of the Constitution.

Jefferson had long "sought to undermine the ratification process" and "hoped to prompt a supplementary second convention."[31] And, according to Gish and Klinghard, Jefferson had arranged for his *Notes* to be published in order to influence the ratification and even the Constitution itself. Even if we do not accept these arguments about Jefferson's intentions (and I do not), it is possible that Madison believed that Jefferson's proposal for an appeal to the people in a different context would help the anti-Federalist cause by providing a second convention as a compromise with the authority of Jefferson's name and the normative argument from democracy. Madison, after all, knew that Jefferson's proposal had so much force that Madison himself had praised it in 1785.

Madison's concern about a second convention is revealing in that it rested on his assumption that the supporters of the amendments would find it impossible to agree on *any* list of amendments.[32] The problem, then, was not only that the opponents to the Constitution would change the Constitution, but rather that they would disagree so much about how to change the Constitution that they would agree only to call a convention to discuss future changes to the Constitution. This is to say that, from Madison's calculations, the seemingly safe fallback position to a set of amendments was actually the more likely and the more dangerous scenario. Madison's task in the winter of 1788, then, was to show well-intended critics of the Constitution that a conditional ratification would, first, result not in a bill of rights but rather a convention, and, second, that this convention would be dangerous. This second point would be especially difficult, because, as Madison's 1785 letter so nicely shows, both justice and progress seemed to be on the side of planning for "at least one revision" of the Constitution.

There is no better indication of Madison's anxiety than his 10 January 1788 letter to the governor of Virginia, Edmund Randolph. Randolph was crucial to ratification in Virginia, and Madison could not be sure about his intentions. As a member of the Virginia delegation to the Convention of 1787, Randolph had set the convention in the direction toward a strong national government by introducing Madison's Virginia Plan, yet Randolph refused to sign the final document on the grounds that he would first need to assess opinion in Virginia. Randolph was different than George Mason, who Madison thought was growing more opposed to the Constitution because of self-love, and different from Patrick Henry, who Madison thought was attempting to create a Southern confederacy. Although Randolph did hold several objections to the Constitution, he stated he was most concerned that the requirement of accepting or rejecting to the Constitution "in toto" would lead to "anarchy and civil convulsions," particularly if nine states did not ratify it.[33]

---

[31] Burstein and Isenberg, *Madison and Jefferson*, xix, 180.
[32] Madison to Archibald Stuart, 14 December 1787, *PJM* 10: 325–26.
[33] Madison, Koch, 656–57.

Madison wrote his letter in response to Randolph's letter of 27 December, in which Randolph had enclosed his own letter to the Virginia Assembly recommending a second convention. This letter had been published in pamphlet form and reprinted in newspapers "from Virginia to Massachusetts."[34] Madison's response contained three parts. First, Randolph was making a mistake in letting his name be connected with men like Patrick Henry and the disaffected elements in Massachusetts, whose opposition was ultimately aimed at destroying the Union. Second, even if a second convention did not include those who wanted to dissolve the union, it would be counterproductive because the "ground" taken by even the honest critics of the Constitution in the "different quarters" "forbids any hope of concord among them." Third, and most important, because the "bulk of mankind" is not up to forming a constitution and instead "must follow the judgment of others not their own," a second convention would undermine the respect for the leading characters of *both* the first and the second conventions, thus rendering a constitution by convention impossible.

Madison's distinction between the bulk of mankind and men like Randolph calls to mind his argument in No. 49 that Jefferson's proposal might work for philosophers but not for ordinary citizens. What has not been appreciated seriously enough, however, is how clearly Madison recorded his skepticism of deliberation among leading politicians during moments of founding. Madison warned Randolph that a second convention would "give a loose to human opinions," which "must be as various and irreconcilable concerning theories of Government, as doctrines of religion." This point reveals that the source of concern for Madison was not the men who would be doing the discussing, but rather the subject matter itself. That is, the problem is that opinions on constitution making are various and irreconcilable, not that the men considering the constitution were too unwise or virtuous to do the work. A second convention of leading politicians could not work, and it would undermine the first. Like an appeal to the wider public, it would reveal the shaky ground on which the first Convention rested.

Madison did not keep this unsettling view private, for he made this very point in No. 37, which was published one day after he had composed his letter to Randolph. The connection between Nos. 37 and 49 and the letter to Randolph is not a new discovery, but the chronological proximity of Madison's surprisingly dark assessment of constitutionalism in the letter and in *Federalist* No. 37 is reason enough to return to the context in which the praise of veneration emerges.[35] Read in light of Madison's larger discussion of republicanism

---

[34] According to Maier, Madison read Randolph's letter "with relief" because it supported a strong national government and because it stated that Randolph would support the Constitution if it came to an up or down vote. My interpretation emphasizes Randolph's efforts to prevent this up-or-down vote. Maier, *Ratification*, 89.

[35] For a discussion of the connection, see Rakove, "Super-Legality of the Constitution," 1955.

within the *Federalist*, Madison's recommendation of veneration is considerably more circumscribed than scholars have noted.

The Case against Veneration in the *Federalist*

Madison's *Federalist* No. 37 expanded on the comment to Randolph and provides more reason to be wary of constitutional veneration. Broadly, the object of the essay was to make the transition in the *Federalist* to discussion of the republican credentials of the Constitution. It includes the claim that the Federal Convention enjoyed an unusual "exemption" from the usual "party animosities" in most "deliberative bodies," going so far as to conclude that the Federal Convention was evidence of divine intervention.

But what is important about No. 37 is the degree to which Madison went out of his way to catalog the ways in which the Constitution was less than perfect.[36] This point stands out in comparison to Hamilton's No. 1. In each case, the rhetorical strategy for Publius was to position himself as a moderate speaking to other fair-minded moderates and to characterize the arguments of his critics as originating in interests or passions. Unlike Madison, however, Hamilton wrote that the arguments against the Constitution suffered from defects in the characters of the men who made them. Madison's frank discussion of the difficulties of the Constitution thus stands in clear contrast to that of Hamilton as a rhetorical strategy.

Indeed, this strategy and this language of difficulty had already been pursued by James Wilson. In a speech to the Pennsylvania ratifying convention on 6 November 1787, Wilson began his defense of the Constitution by "unfolding the difficulties which the late convention were obliged to encounter."[37] Wilson named five, listed below:

1. The extent of the country; republics are usually small.
2. The spiritedness of the people; love of freedom might interfere with efficient government.
3. The absence of a clear model or guide; history of confederacies is inadequate.
4. The science of government is still new.
5. Drawing the line between the general and state governments.

Wilson explained that his purpose in calling attention to these five difficulties was not to praise the delegates for their heroic efforts, but rather to remind listeners that perfection should not be expected and that the goal was not to find a constitution that "every citizen" would accept "in every part." Rather,

---

[36] Alexander Hamilton, *Federalist* No. 1, Scigliano, 3–4.
[37] James Wilson, "Remarks of James Wilson in the Pennsylvania Ratifying Convention," in *Collected Works of James Wilson*, Volume 1, ed. Kermit L. Hall and Mark David Hall (Indianapolis, IN: Liberty Fund, 2007), 178.

"all which can be expected is, to form such a constitution as, upon the whole, is the best that can possibly be obtained."[38] Like Wilson, Madison noted five difficulties faced by the Convention:

1. The novelty of the undertaking; prior confederacies were marked by failure, not success.
2. Combining energy and stability with republican principles.
3. Marking the partition between the general and state governments.
4. The pretensions of the large and small states.
5. The pretensions arising from other combinations and rivalries.

In comparing the two lists of difficulties, two points immediately stand out. The first is their similarity. Two of the five – the novelty of the project and the difficulty of drawing lines – are precisely the same. A third is similar: Wilson talks about the difficulty of balancing the free disposition of the American people with the necessities of efficient government, while Madison talks about the more abstract problem of balancing republican principles with stability and energy. In addition, both Wilson and Madison compare the difficulty of line drawing in political science with the more precise rigor of the hard sciences.[39] Both use a form of the word "embarrassing" to describe the difficulties faced by the Convention.[40] More simply, both use the language of difficulty, language they perhaps derived from Edmund Randolph's speech on 10 September in the Convention listing his objections to the Constitution.[41]

The second point is that Madison's version emphasized the difficulties that emerged within the deliberation itself. That is, Madison's fourth and fifth difficulties are unlike Wilson's in that these two could have been willed away by delegates who chose to do so. That is, Madison's difficulties seem to deliberately call attention to the failures in deliberation at the Convention, whereas Wilson's instead emphasize the more general problems of the extent of the country and the youth of the new science of politics. As will be shown in a latter discussion, this move by Madison reveals how far he went in explicating just how deep the problem of constitutional imperfection is.

Before we turn to Madison's presentation, more must be said on the similarity between Wilson's speech and Madison's *Federalist* No. 37. Did Madison

---

[38] Ibid., 185.

[39] "It is only in mathematical science, that a line can be described with mathematical precision." Ibid., 184.

[40] Wilson uses it in the context of marking the line between state and national governments. Madison uses it in the context of creating the executive. Madison to Jefferson, 24 October 1787, in *Madison Writings* 144; Wilson, "Remarks of James Wilson in the Pennsylvania Ratifying Convention," 424. Wilson also used the word on 30 June in the Convention to describe the conundrum regarding his preference for proportional representation and his preference for a small Senate. Madison, Koch, 226.

[41] Madison, Koch, 614–15. Madison treats two of the difficulties mentioned by Randolph: the "want of a more definite boundary between the General & State governments" and Congress's power to tax exports.

simply steal the idea from Wilson?[42] It would appear not, because Madison
employed a similar list in his letter to Jefferson on 24 October 1787.[43] That
list spoke in terms of the "objects which presented themselves" and listed four
instead of five. The omitted difficulty was the difficulty deriving from the novelty of the undertaking. Given that Madison sent this letter to Jefferson in
late October, it is impossible that Madison had heard about or read Wilson's
speech in early November. Likewise, given that Jefferson was in France, it is
unlikely that Wilson read the letter to Jefferson and impossible that he had
read *Federalist* No. 37, which was not published until early January. However,
it is possible that Wilson and Madison compared notes, that at some point
during the Convention or immediately afterward Madison showed Wilson a
version of his letter to Jefferson.[44] Moreover, on Madison's end, given the sim-
ilarities, it is likely that Madison read Wilson's speech and sharpened his own
presentation when he returned to it in *Federalist* No. 37.

The clearest indication for this is Madison's first difficulty, the novelty of the
undertaking. Madison did not mention this in his letter to Jefferson; indeed,
that letter was organized around the objects of the Convention, not its problems. As indicated earlier, Wilson's version emphasized the problems in the
histories of republics. "The facts recorded concerning their constitutions are
so few and general, and their histories so unmarked and defective, that no satisfactory information can be collected from them concerning many particular
circumstances."[45] As Chapter 7 discusses, Madison makes a similar point late
in life when he returns to the preparing of his records of the Convention for
publication. In the *Federalist*, however, he makes a different point. The problem is not that the delegates lacked records of other confederacies. Rather,
the problem is that those confederacies were "vitiated by the same erroneous
principles" on which the Articles of Confederation was founded. Thus, these
ancient governments were only negative examples, "warning of the course to
be shunned, without pointing out that which ought to be pursued."[46] Madison
appears to have added this point after he was exposed to Wilson's speech, and

---

[42] More precisely, it might be more accurate to ask who was the first to apply a problem of
Enlightenment philosophy to the situation. See especially Locke's discussion of the imperfec-
tion of words in Book III, chapter 9 of *Essay Concerning Human Understanding*, ed., Peter H.
Nidditch (Oxford: Oxford University Press, 1979), 475–90.

[43] Madison to Jefferson, 24 October 1787, in *Madison Writings*, 144–53.

[44] Madison's 20 September report to Edmund Pendleton, written in Philadelphia, contained the
central part of the letter to Jefferson: "The double object of blending a proper stability & energy
in the Government with the essential characters of the republican Form, and of tracing a proper
line of demarcation between the national and State authorities, was necessarily found to be as
difficult as it was desirable, and to admit of an infinite diversity concerning the means among
those who were unanimously agreed concerning the end." Madison to Pendleton, 20 September
1787, *PJM*, 10: 171.

[45] Wilson, *Works*, 181.

[46] Madison, *Federalist* No. 37, Scigliano, 223.

he seems to have thought that the friends of the Constitution needed to give the point a different emphasis than Wilson had given it.

The rest of Madison's list of difficulties tracks the list in the letter to Jefferson. The next was combining the "inviolable attention to the Republican form" with the "requisite stability and energy in government."[47] Wilson had cast this problem as one of American exceptionalism: the American people were especially free in spirit.[48] Wilson was not alone; a key debate in the Convention was the extent to which European examples could apply to the United States because of the extent to which Americans were distinguished by equality.[49] Madison, however, cast this as a problem with republican government more generally. "The genius of republican liberty" requires power in the hands of the many for a short duration, yet stability requires power in the hands of the few for a long period of time, and energy requires power in the hands of the one for an adequate tenure. In this key discussion, Madison thus transformed a conversation about class and the mixed constitution to one about separation of powers among the opposing principles of government. This abstraction allowed him to avoid the historically prickly question as to the extent to which the poor or the rich would be represented, and, just as important, it provided a principle by which controversies in separation of powers might be judged. As discussed in the examination of the removal power debate in Chapter 4, this treatment of separation of powers was more than a convenient rhetorical device, for it appears to be central in Madison's understanding of separation of powers. But the point here is that Madison thus modified what might have been merely a debate about the match between the Constitution and the spirit of the people into a reflection about the necessary and enduring difficulty of separation of powers. In a few short lines, Madison revealed that the most basic republican dogma, that there must be separation of powers, required the complex and perhaps impossible task of a separation of principles. It was "peculiarly embarrassing," he told Jefferson.[50]

This seemingly unsolvable problem was not as bad as Madison's third and central difficulty, "marking the proper line of partition" between the national and state governments. In his letter to Jefferson, Madison described this object as "perhaps of all, the most nice and difficult."[51] Wilson described this problem as one of "peculiar delicacy and importance."[52] As we have seen,

---

[47] Ibid., 223–24. In the letter to Jefferson, Madison wrote that the object was "to unite a proper energy in the Executive and a proper stability in the Legislative departments, with the essential characteristics of Republican Government." Madison to Jefferson, 24 October 1787, *Madison Writings*, 144.

[48] Wilson, *Works*, 179–80.

[49] See, for example, Charles Pinckney's speech on 25 June arguing, "The people of the U. States are perhaps the most singular of any we are acquainted with." Madison, *Notes*, 181–88.

[50] Madison to Jefferson, 24 October 1787, *Madison Writings*, 144.

[51] Ibid., 146.

[52] Wilson, *Works*, 184.

Wilson's main object was to lower expectations. Because political science is not as old as mathematical science, we should not expect the same kind of precision. In the *Federalist*, Madison made a much more ambitious and troubling argument. He opened by explaining that a person would "be sensible of this difficulty, in proportion as he has been accustomed to contemplate and discriminate objects extensive and complicated in their nature." This is to say that the critical question regarding the powers of the general government and the states would be misunderstood by readers who were unprepared to see complexity. That is, if Madison is to convince those most likely to be swayed by the charge that the new government is a "consolidation," Madison must make these simple men more sophisticated. Madison attempted this more difficult task by illustrating the ways in which knowledge is still incomplete. Just as philosophers have not yet agreed on how to distinguish the faculties of the mind, natural scientists had not yet agreed on the divisions in nature, even those as basic as what "separates the district of vegetable life from the neighboring region of unorganized matter." If the works of nature, in which all the "delineations" must be "perfectly accurate," appear indistinguishable, it must be because of "imperfections of the eye." Like the natural world, the classification of human institutions is subject to controversy, but, unlike the natural world, the imperfection is twofold. In addition to measurement error, there is imperfection in the institutions themselves. As a result, the "greatest adepts in political science" have not agreed on how to define the three "great provinces" of government, "the legislative, executive, and judiciary," or even the houses of the legislative department. So too with the extent of the common law in Great Britain and the jurisdiction of British courts. If the powers of government have yet to be defined, it is no surprise that words like "national" and "federal" remain disputed.[53] In fact, the more people are trained to see complexity, the more likely they are to recognize this enduring political problem.

In this reflection on the difficulties of taxonomy, Madison granted a central tenet of the anti-Federalist argument and turned it against them. Because it is impossible to distinguish the state from the national government, it is likely that delineation will be attempted by the more powerful of the two. Indeed, Madison all but conceded that future constructions would change the Constitution: "All new laws, though penned with the greatest technical skill, and passed on the fullest and most mature deliberation, are considered as more or less equivocal, until their meaning be liquidated and ascertained by a series of particular discussions and adjudications." It is these discussions, after all, that make those who consider the law more sophisticated in their judgments. But this only introduced a third way in which classification becomes impossible: "Besides the obscurity arising from the complexity of objects, and the

---

[53] Madison, *Federalist* No. 37, 225. For difficulties in marking one species from another, see Book III, chapter 4, of *Essay Concerning Human Understanding*, 463–65.

imperfection of the human faculties, the medium through which the conceptions of men are conveyed to each other adds a fresh embarrassment. The use of words is to express ideas." Even though the imprecision of words calls for new words, "no language is so copious as to supply words and phrases for every complex idea," so we must be aware that the imprecision of a word grows in proportion to the "complexity and novelty" of the object it defines. Madison drove this point home with a less than pious reference to sacred texts: even when "the Almighty himself condescends to address mankind in their own language," our "cloudy medium" of words render his efforts "dim and doubtful."[54] Just as discussions of the commands of God are likely to be dim and doubtful, discussion of the divisions between national and state authority will be rendered more difficult by the imprecision of words. Madison's concession first relied on the charges of the critics of the Constitution and then employed it against them: like the future broad constructionists those critics envision, they too may be victims of the indeterminacy of political words.[55]

After showing how words such as "federal" and "nation" are impossible to define, Madison moved to another difficulty, the Great Compromise. The Compromise was the result of "interfering pretensions of the larger and smaller States" regarding the question of representation. Madison was never happy with this compromise, so it is perhaps not altogether surprising that he departed from his cheerleading to note his displeasure.[56] But what is surprising is that Madison went further than he needed – and much further than any of his contemporaries – in showing the centrality of the compromise to the final document: more than a one-time deal, the compromise actually produced "a fresh struggle between the same parties, to give such a turn to the organization of the government, and to the distribution of its powers, as would increase the importance of the branches, in forming which they had respectively obtained the greatest share of influence." This is to say that the Great Compromise settled one question but opened others: the powers of the House and Senate, and perhaps other features where representation comes into play, were influenced by "extraneous considerations" rather than "theoretical propriety." What else Madison had in mind (perhaps the Electoral College, and the Senate's portion of executive powers) he never said, but it is worth pausing to note the clarity of Madison's confession of constitutional imperfection. Instead of narrowing the importance of the Great Compromise, Madison announced that it had infected the entire document.[57]

Another difficulty was born of regional differences and brought about more compromises. Again, Madison might have treated this difficulty as a

---

[54] Locke makes a similar point. See *Essay*, 490.
[55] Madison, *Federalist* No. 37, Scigliano, 226–27.
[56] David Brian Robertson, "Madison's Opponents and Constitutional Design," *American Political Science Review* 99 (2005): 225–43.
[57] Madison, *Federalist* No. 37, Scigliano, 227.

straightforward one, but instead, he complicated it by making a distinction between operating a government and creating a government.

> And although this variety of interests, for reasons sufficiently explained in a former paper, may have a salutary influence on the administration of the government when formed, yet every one must be sensible of the contrary influence, which must have been experienced in the task of forming it.

The former paper, of course, is No. 10, where Madison defended the extended republic on the grounds that the multiplicity of factions would help moderate the effects of faction. In that essay Madison had argued that the effects of factions must be controlled because the causes of faction were "sewn in the nature of men" and therefore irremovable.[58] By "enlarging the orbit" the extended republic would make it more difficult for a faction to achieve majority status and still be a faction, which is by definition adverse to rights or to the public good. But, however salutary this may be for administering a government, Madison wrote in No. 37 that a multiplicity of factions would have the opposite effect when forming a government. During normal politics, the extended republic solves a very old political problem (the people are disposed to vex and oppress each other), but during times of founding, it makes it worse. Although Madison did not say so in the *Federalist*, we know from a letter to Jefferson that Madison had in mind Congress's power over exports and imports as well as slavery. As he put it, "S. Carolina & Georgia were inflexible on the point of the slaves."[59]

Seen in this light, Madison's qualification of the application of the argument for the extended republic is a serious one because it suggests that not only will the extended republic fail to secure rights of minorities but also that it is likely to constitutionalize these failures. That is, even if the multiplicity of factions would work against any one faction that sought to undermine rights, that very multiplicity would work against rights in cases where rights have yet to be secured. And it is precisely in times of founding when such extensions of rights might occur. This distinction raises a troubling question: If the extended republic is dangerous to rights during times of founding, what is the alternative? If Madison's famous republican remedy for the republican disease does not work during times of founding, what does?[60]

Madison did not answer this question. Instead, he offered a strange account of the Convention of 1787 by appealing to religious faith. Given the success of the Convention, "any man of candor" would be "astonished," while the "man of pious reflection" would see the "finger of th[e] Almighty hand." Madison's invocation of the Almighty was perhaps meant to clear the rhetorical way for

---

[58] Madison, *Federalist* No. 10, Scigliano, 55.
[59] Madison to Jefferson, 24 October 1787, *PJM* 10: 214.
[60] In No. 49, Madison reference to "our constitutions" suggests that the state constitutions of the revolutionary period were free from this problem. Scigliano, 323–24.

the appeal to veneration coming in No. 49, but it nevertheless stands out in the pages of the *Federalist*. It is one of only two uses of the term in the entire work. As we have seen, the other also occurs in No. 37, but its point there was to remind readers that even God's words are imprecise, that is, to limit the importance of divine intervention in human affairs. The point can be further clarified with reference to the debates in the Convention. According to Madison's *Notes*, the word "miracle" was used only twice in the Convention debates. On one of those occasions, Alexander Hamilton asserted that "it was a miracle that we were now here exercising our tranquil & free deliberations the subject" and that it "would be madness to trust to future miracles."[61] Madison's use of the miraculous, it could be argued, was meant to show the uncertain, contingent, and generally shaky nature of the Convention, not to show its authoritativeness. More broadly, and without digging too deeply into Madison's faith, the invocation of the hand of the Almighty stands in stark contrast to Madison's other writings concerning the prospect of divine intervention. In 1825, for example, Madison observed that all too often the "finiteness of the human understanding" causes us to leap from effect to cause, from "Nature to Nature's God."[62] With this move to the final cause, Madison complains, "all Philosophical reasoning on the subject must terminate." Given the philosophic reasoning that Madison employs in No. 37, it is inconceivable that Madison expected his readers to put aside all philosophic reasoning because the work of the Convention was evidence of divine intervention.

Implications

Madison succeeded in persuading Randolph, and in preventing a second convention.[63] But his recommendation of constitutional veneration in No. 49 followed a remarkably tentative account of constitutionalism and of the Convention of 1787. The lesson of *Federalist* No. 37 is that the delegates to the convention faced two difficulties that were basically insurmountable. One was marking the boundaries of separation of powers while at the same time

---

[61] Madison, Koch, 216.

[62] Madison to Beasley, 20 November 1825, in Hunt, 9: 230. Another telling example of Madison's position on religious faith can be seen in his statement on proclamations of thanksgivings in "Detached Memoranda," *Madison Writings*, 766. See also Francis Corbin's statement to Madison that philosophers have to combat religion with "muffled Foils." Corbin to Madison, 25 December 1818, *Madison Papers Retirement*, 1: 398.

[63] Randolph ultimately supported the Constitution. In the Virginia ratification convention (June, 1788), Randolph explained that he believed the unconditional ratification of eight other states was reason enough for Virginia to ratify. This was Madison's strategy from the beginning, but, as Gutzman has noted, Randolph conceded to Madison as early as April that he disagreed with other critics of the Constitution and feared the result of a second convention (*PJM* 11: 25–6). It is also important to note that Randolph was instrumental in undercutting George Clinton's national call for such a convention. R. C. Gutzman, "Edmund Randolph and Virginia Constitutionalism," *Review of Politics* 66 (2004): 469–97.

resolving the ancient puzzle of the one, the few, and the many. The other was marking the line of partition between state and nation in a system that would divide sovereignty in ways that were still to be determined. This would have been difficult enough, given the "infinite diversity" of opinions on the subject, but the inescapable conclusion is that the delegates themselves – especially those from the small states – made these difficulties even more difficult by blending them together and confusing them with the struggle over representation between the small and large states.[64] The Senate, for example, would be the "great anchor" of stability, yet it would also be the repository for state equality. These conflicting objectives rendered each task of marking boundaries potentially incoherent and, in Madison's view, fundamentally flawed. Madison drove this point home by saying that the Connecticut Compromise only brought about a new struggle between the parties.

In this remarkable discussion, Madison went as far as to narrow the applicability of his famous discovery, the extended republic as a solution for faction. In particular, the problem of discussing imprecise forms with imprecise language seems to aggravate the enduring problem of faction. This is also to say that even if Madison argued that the extended republic would be able to protect against a majority faction denying rights during ordinary politics, Madison also acknowledged that a majority faction – and their representatives – might still be able to reinterpret the Constitution during times of extraordinary politics. This is to say that the extended republic – like separation of powers – is no magic bullet and was not in 1787.

It is true that this lesson, that constitution making is tough, would seem to make veneration even more desirable. This presentation, however, has argued that, for Madison, the benefits of constitutional veneration are mixed. Even if constitutional veneration can sometimes provide what deliberation cannot, there are serious reasons to be wary of it. We know, for example, that Madison believed that state equality in the Senate was a fundamental act of injustice that was caused by the unwillingness of some delegates to see beyond their local interests. The Senate, as a result, would be forever flawed. And, as the next chapter shows, Madison's argument for presidential removal powers reveals that Madison believed the principle of "stability," which he described in No. 37 as necessary ingredient of government, was tainted by its association with the equality of the states.[65] Because state equality in the Senate – unlike slavery – cannot be amended out of the Constitution (without the consent of the state losing its equal suffrage), ratification of the Constitution promised, perversely, that the "irregular course" pursued at the Convention would become one of the very things Americans would respect over time. On top of all of this, we learn from No. 37 that this compromise between the large and small states gave rise to a "fresh struggle" and thus to other unnamed compromises – or imperfections.

[64] The quoted phrase comes from Madison to Pendleton, 20 September 1787, *PJM* 10: 171.
[65] Madison, *Federalist* No. 37, Scigliano, 224.

The historical context of No. 49 supports this qualification of the argument for veneration. Read simply as an endorsement of constitutional veneration, the essay strangely dismantles an argument that was not on the table. Instead, when read as part of Madison's ongoing attempt to convince moderates like Edmund Randolph, it makes sense that Madison would be the first to bring up Jefferson and to do so in the context of discussing the requirements of republicanism. As author of the Declaration, and as the leading political figure among those who had not yet entered the public debate, Jefferson was perhaps the person most well positioned to argue that the new Constitution was insufficiently republican by offering a different definition of republicanism. That is, this preemptive and scathing critique of Jefferson – the only person referred to as an "authority" in the *Federalist* – helped Madison establish the Constitution's republican principles while at the same time closing the path for more deliberation. Because Madison knew that he could not close the discussion of republicanism in a way that would answer Jefferson and the most scrupulous republicans, while at the same time relieving those like Randolph who were most concerned with the deliberation of their constituents, Madison had to warn both sets of men against the excesses of the argument from deliberation. As a result he offered the argument from veneration, but not without providing another argument warning against its excesses.

3

Appeals to Elites

The Problem with Deliberation

As the last chapter argued, Madison offered the argument from veneration because of the very real possibility that moderates would be persuaded by calls for a second convention. This fear of a second convention was also related to Madison's turn to the Bill of Rights, a turn examined in detail in the next chapter. But this fear of a second convention is worthy of attention in its own right because it signals a problem with the standard accounts of Madison and Madisonian constitutionalism. Specifically, if Madison thought that a convention of specially chosen delegates would be unable to deliberate during times of founding, then on what basis did Madison think those very same individuals would be able to govern during times of normal politics? Put simply, if Madison distrusted elites during times of founding, what did he think of their capacity for deliberation during times of ordinary politics?

This question of deliberation during normal politics calls into question a fundamental pillar of Madisonian constitutionalism because it forces us to reconsider the nature of representation within Madison's constitutional thought.[1] Because it has long been held that a central tenet of Madisonian constitutionalism is that representatives would "refine and enlarge" the opinions and interests of their constituents, the question of deliberation is especially important. This point can be illustrated by pointing to Edmund Burke's well-known assertion of what is frequently called the trustee model of representation. In the

---

[1] Rakove makes the important observation that Madison in 1787 "never developed a clear or persuasive conception of how senators should be elected," and, as a consequence, he could not articulate how proportional representation "would preserve the elitist intimacy required for sober deliberation." Jack N. Rakove, *Original Meanings: Politics and Ideas in the Making of the Constitution* (New York: Knopf, 1996), 79.

most well-known passage of his speech at Bristol, Burke explicitly connected the strong theory of representation with deliberation:

> Parliament is not a congress of ambassadors from different and hostile interests; which interests each must maintain, as an agent and advocate against other agents and advocates; but parliament is a deliberative assembly of one nation, with one interest, that of the whole; where, not local purposes, not local prejudices, ought to guide, but the general good, resulting from the general reason of the whole.[2]

Burke clearly listed deliberation as one of the crucial functions of representation, and in so doing he presumed an important linkage between two important aspects of republican politics. In his view, representatives use their judgment to elevate policy beyond mere interest, but this judgment is shaped by deliberation with other representatives. Importantly, deliberation has been embraced by more than latter-day Burkeans, for "deliberative democracy" today has an impressive list of supporters.[3]

More than a historical detail for scholars of the ratification period, attention to Madison's understanding of relationship between policy making and deliberation can clarify Madison's larger understanding of representation. Because representation is connected to the larger question concerning the capacity of majorities to enact good legislation, this examination of deliberation can contribute to the renewed scholarly interest in Madison's understanding of the role and function of public opinion. If Madison did not believe that representatives would likely engage in deliberation, then we must revise our understanding of Madison's understanding of representation.

Throughout his life, Madison had many opportunities to lay out his understanding of what a representative should be. One important occasion has not, to my knowledge, received comment by scholars. It came in the form of a series of letters from his nephew, John Madison, when the elder Madison was Secretary of State in the Jefferson administration. The young John Madison wrote to reflect on the wide chasm between what he believed to be the requirements of representatives and the actual representatives he observed in the Virginia General Assembly. In his view, the General Assembly should be composed of men of "good morals" and "fine understanding," men who were "advocates for virtue" and possessed "universal wisdom." To that end, they should be men who "have devoted a considerable part of their time to the study of the principles of government," have "studied with unremitted zeal and ardour the dispositions of man," and "should know what is calculated to please and what

---

[2] Edmund Burke, "Speech to the Electors of Bristol," 1774, in *The Founders' Constitution*, vol. 1, ed. Phillip B. Kurland and Ralph Lerner (Indianapolis, IN: Liberty Fund, 2000; Chicago: Chicago University Press, 1987), 391.

[3] Amy Gutmann and Dennis Thompson, *Why Deliberative Democracy?* (Princeton, NJ: Princeton University Press, 2004). For a recent application, see Mariah Zeisberg, *War Powers: The Politics of Constitutional Authority* (Princeton, NJ: Princeton University Press, 2013).

will create displeasure." In short, they should possess the "virtue, justice & wisdom of Socrates." The problem was that the reality was much different. The younger Madison saw men who were "entirely ignorant of the nature of these laws" and who were "entirely ignorant of that system of government which is now in existence." As a result, the young John Madison's mind was filled with "horror" at his countrymen's inability to elect the "virtuous, just and w[ise?]."[4]

Curiously, there is no record of a response by Madison. With what must have been the clearest opportunity to think aloud about the nature of representation, Madison simply looked the other way. This silence is indicative of a larger silence, in that Madison's vast writings do not include all that many statements about the meaning and purpose of representation. Put differently, nowhere does Madison offer a statement as clear as the famous definition of representation given by Burke.[5] Nevertheless, as scholars have long recognized, the place and frequency of deliberation is a key to understanding Madison's political thought, and, as the following will argue, Madison's presentation of deliberation in the *Federalist* suggests that he was less than optimistic about the capacity of legislators for deliberation. That is, this chapter argues that just as Madison did not believe that deliberation among normal citizens or elites was likely during times of founding, Madison was also doubtful that deliberation would occur among elites during times of normal politics.

Representation and Deliberation in Madisonian Constitutionalism

Even with all of the scholarly attention lavished by respected scholars on the role that representatives would play in Madisonian constitutionalism, there remains a diversity of views on this subject. These various perspectives can be introduced with aid of the Alan Gibson's recent study of Madison's understanding of "impartial" administration.[6] In his helpful guide to the literature, Gibson shows that the scholarship on Madison has been divided between those who describe Madison as a pluralist thinker and those who describe Madison as an advocate of "disinterested" politics. Accordingly, the former group argues that Madison believed representatives would be advocates for narrow interests and the public good would emerge through compromises among the various interests. Thus in this view, and as Robert Dahl argued in 1956, features

---

[4] John Madison to James Madison, 24 June 1804, *Papers of James Madison: Secretary of State Series*, Vol. 7, ed., David B. Mattern, et. al. (Charlottesville: University of Virginia Press, 2005), 356–57. The question whether John Madison used "wise" is from the editors.

[5] I believe that Madison was aware of the distinction drawn by Burke. In an 1836 letter, discussed in Chapter 6, Madison says that the question of representation had divided "distinguished statesman," especially "in Great Britain, where such topics have been most discussed." Madison to _____, March 1836, Hunt 9: 607.

[6] Alan Gibson, "Madison's 'Great Desideratum': Impartial Administration and the Extended Republic," *American Political Thought: A Journal of Ideas, Institutions, and Culture* (2012): 181–207.

of Madisonian constitutionalism such as bicameralism and judicial review are necessary for Madison as ways to stop majority rule. In this view, then, Madison's argument presumes that any individual will be tyrannical if left unchecked and that representatives, as acting on behalf of majorities, need to be checked.[7]

In the view of the latter group, Madison believed that representatives in the extended republic would be able to rise above advocacy for narrow interests and be able to, in the famous words of *Federalist* No. 10, "refine and enlarge" the opinions and interests of their constituents. Gibson points to the famous scholarship of Gordon Wood, who argued that Madison and other supporters of the Constitution believed that good government could only be accomplished by men who could rise above the self-interested politics of the "middling" sorts.[8] Or, as Wood put it more recently, Madison in 1787 was not "as realistic and modern as often make him out to be" because "he clung to the great dream of the Revolution that virtuous politics might be possible in America."[9] A different example is the work of Joseph M. Bessette, who offers a useful corrective of Dahl's emphasis on Madison's anxiety about the tyranny of the majority.[10] In Bessette's view, Madison's constitutional plan was designed around the objective that deliberation would exist in governing institutions even if it did not in the people at large, and this deliberation would exist in part because of the quality of the people who would be selected to represent.[11] Others, such as Cass Sunstein, have similarly characterized Madison's position as resembling that of Burke.[12]

In Gibson's view, both of these explanations are wrong and the answer lies somewhere between the two. Specifically, with the pluralists, Gibson concludes that Madison never believed that individual representatives would display "heroic impartiality" presumed of those who emphasize the "virtue" of representatives. But, with Wood and advocates of the disinterested school, Gibson

---

[7] Robert Dahl, *Preface to Democratic Theory* (Chicago: University of Chicago Press, 1956).

[8] Gordon S. Wood, "Interests and Disinterestedness in the Making of the Constitution," in *Beyond Confederation: Origins of the Constitution and American National Identity*, ed. Richard Beeman, Stephen Botein, and Edward C. Carter II (Chapel Hill: University of North Carolina Press, 1987), 69–109.

[9] To be sure, Wood contrasts the Madison of 1787 with the Madison of the 1790s, who, in Wood's view, quickly abandoned this belief. Gordon S. Wood, *Revolutionary Characters: What Made the Founders Different* (New York: Penguin, 2006), 164–65.

[10] Joseph M. Bessette, *The Mild Voice of Reason: Deliberative Democracy and American National Government* (Chicago: University of Chicago Press, 1994), 6–39.

[11] Ibid., 36. The next chapter discusses in greater detail Madison's treatment of public opinion, but it should be noted that other scholars have a more positive assessment of deliberation by the public. One example is Bradley Kent Carter and Joseph F. Kobylka, "The Dialogic Community: Education, Leadership, and Participation in Madison's Political Thought," *Review of Politics* 52 (1990): 32–63.

[12] Cass R. Sunstein, "Interest Groups in American Public Law," *Stanford Law Review* 38 (1985): 38–48.

also concludes that the majority in Congress would be impartial because it would deliberate its way to the collective interest. Put another way, Gibson's middle ground agrees that that representatives would be more disinterested in Congress than they would in the state legislatures, but it does not presume that these individual representatives would rise to the standard articulated by Burke.

In addition to these two leading approaches and to the middle way offered by Gibson, there are other scholarly explanations. In a recent book and series of articles, Colleen Sheehan has argued that Madison believed public opinion was sovereign, and, in a subtle reading of Madison, argues that Madison believed that public opinion could be molded by leaders. Thus, for Sheehan, Madison's constitutional innovations were not aimed at achieving the right kind of representation. Rather, they were also aimed at creating a "deliberative and reasonable public opinion."[13] An alternative explanation is given by Bryan Garsten, who looks to Madison as a model for a robust and more ancient style of democratic deliberation. In Garsten's view, the problem with recent defenses of deliberation as fair discourse is that they grow out of a modern project, starting with Thomas Hobbes, to remove persuasion, which rests on individual judgment, from political life. Thus Madison resisted the alternatives of Hamilton and Jefferson, because according to Garsten, Madison saw that their alternatives, such as that of Hobbes, incorrectly started from a theory of a "unified sovereign." Thus Garsten finds the opposite of Gibson: Madison "regarded the dispersal of judgment as nonnegotiable; he did not advise parties to political disputes to alienate their judgment to an impartial arbiter." Garsten's Madison thus believes that "deliberation is best when it begins in self-interest."[14]

From these scholarly understandings of Madison, then, we might be able to predict an array of Madisonian answers to the young John Madison's question. One such answer would be that the younger Madison was exactly right. Burkean legislators are exactly what we need, and this is why we cannot trust state legislators but might be able to trust our national representatives, especially those in the Senate, because they will be selected from a deeper talent pool and, as a result, the representatives will be like those expected by the young John Madison. Another answer would be that John Madison was looking at the wrong problem. The real problem is that citizens need to be educated and uplifted so that they can recognize and then elect the wise and good. Yet another Madisonian answer might be that John Madison

[13] Colleen A. Sheehan, *James Madison and the Spirit of Republican Self-Government* (New York: Cambridge University Press, 2009). See also Larry D. Kramer, "'The Interest of the Man': James Madison, Popular Sovereignty, and the Theory of Deliberative Democracy." *Valparaiso University Law Review* 41(2006): 697–754.
[14] Bryan Garsten, *Saving Persuasion: A Defense of Rhetoric and Judgment* (Cambridge, MA: Harvard University Press, 2006), 203 and 209–10.

was somewhat confused. We cannot expect Burkean legislators to always be around, so instead we need to design institutions that will transform low and vulgar representatives into Burkean representatives. Yet another answer would be that John Madison was thoroughly confused. We cannot count on Burkean legislators because self-interest is so much stronger than virtue, so it is much safer to count on the lower motivations and channel these toward the public good.

Any of these answers are plausible, not least because passages from Madison's essays in the *Federalist* arguably sustain these various interpretations. But what is important to notice is that these various responses are at odds with each other and are mutually exclusive. If one is correct, the others must be wrong. Also worth noting is that the right answer depends largely on the weight placed on Madison's argument for the extended republic (*Federalist* No. 10) as opposed to the weight placed on Madison's defense of separation of powers (*Federalist* No. 51), a controversy that has been central within the Madison scholarship.

On this point about the centrality of *Federalist* No. 10, the argument of the preceding chapter is relevant. Madison made a surprising argument in *Federalist* No. 37. Namely, he conceded that the extended republic probably made faction even more dangerous during the Convention. If this is right, then it means that the discovery for which Madison is most famous is a discovery whose import is limited to particular times in politics. Put directly, Madison admits that the extended republic does not solve the problem of faction when governments are being created.

The Federalist on Deliberation by Elites during Times of Founding

Madison's qualification of the power of the extended republic is not the only surprising concession that emerges from this section of Madison's essays in the *Federalist*. As Gary Rosen has argued, in No. 38 Madison raised and answered a question left unresolved by the argument of the Declaration of Independence.[15] According to the Declaration, the people have a right and duty to alter and abolish a government that does not secure their rights, but the people are also "more disposed to suffer" than to go through with the ordeal of revolution and founding. Madison's remedy for this republican problem was straightforwardly less than republican: the many have to rely on the "safe mediation of the few – or one."[16] Just as the ancient founders had departed from the law to establish governments that could operate by deliberation and consent, the signers of the Constitution had made possible a republican government that could not arise by its own strength.

---

[15] Gary Rosen, *American Compact: James Madison and the Problem of Founding* (Lawrence: University Press of Kansas, 1999).

[16] Ibid., 124.

More than an acknowledgment of the difficulty that democratic government requires the intervention of the few, Madison used the examination of governments in antiquity to discuss the absence of deliberation during times of founding.[17] In No. 38, Madison brought up deliberation by name when he asked whether it was "a little remarkable" that in the ancient examples of government by "deliberation and consent" the "task of framing it" had "not been committed to an assembly of men," but rather "been performed by some individual citizen of pre-eminent wisdom and approved integrity." Madison pointed to seven examples and explained that it is not possible to know for sure whether each was "clothed with the legitimate authority of the people," but he noted that Draco and Solon seemed to have been asked by the people to reform the laws, and that in the case of Lycurgus, in which the proceedings were "less regular," the advocates for reform "turned their eyes" to Lycurgus rather than a "deliberative body of citizens." With the examples of Athens and Sparta, Madison sharpened his question: Why is it that the Greeks, a people so reputed for their love of liberty, "should so far abandon the rules of caution as to place their destiny in the hands of a single citizen?" One possible answer was that the problems of deliberation (what he calls "discord and disunion") exceeded the threat of treachery by a single person. Madison noted that even these Greek founders faced "difficulties" and had to resort to "expedients":

> Solon, who seems to have indulged a more temporizing policy, confessed that he had not given to his countrymen the government best suited to their happiness, but most tolerable to their prejudices. And Lycurgus, more true to his object, was under the necessity of mixing a portion of violence with the authority of superstition, and of securing his final success by a voluntary renunciation, first of his country, and then of his life.

Madison offered more praise for Lycurgus than he did for Solon, but what is also worth noticing is that Madison did not apply the Greek solution to his previous discussion about the unsuitability of the extended republic to acts of founding. Rather, Madison used the example to repeat his point from the previous essay, that any mistakes in the Constitution must be considered in light of the "defect of antecedent experience." That is, because previous governments resting on consent and deliberation traced their own origins to an act of tyranny rather than to an act of deliberation, the Americans had little guidance.[18]

After making this less than reassuring point, Madison spent the rest of the essay pointing out that there was no credible alternative to the new Constitution. As he showed in a lengthy catalog of anti-Federalist arguments,

[17] Burstein and Isenberg show the ways in which No. 38 and the following essays were written as a response to George Mason. They emphasize Madison's institutional answers, that the senate would not be too close to the executive, for example, rather than the more theoretical passages of these essays. Their account and my account can both be right. Madison was writing with moderates in mind, moderates who could be pulled away from Mason's more extreme position.

[18] Madison, *Federalist* No. 37, Scigliano, 229–31.

the critics of the Constitution were at war among themselves about the proper correction, even as almost everyone agreed that the Articles would not work. Madison likened the people under the Articles to a sick man: a sick man must accept a doctor's prescription even though there will be those who disagree about the measures prescribed, unless those who disagree can come up with an alternative other than doing nothing. This point reflected his concern in the letter to Edmund Randolph, discussed in the previous chapter, and built on the theoretical claims of No. 37: the lack of unanimity regarding an alternative, which itself must take the form of imprecise words, stems from the deliberative nature of criticism and seems to be irresolvable in politics. But why would Madison need to refer to the "irregular" foundings of the Greek republics in order to make this very practical point? Specifically, why open the question of the legitimacy of the Constitutional Convention if the main point of the essay is to show how there is no consensus about the ways to improve the Constitution? By explicitly calling our attention to the foundings of ancient governments of deliberation and consent, Madison went out of his way to ask the reader to wonder at the "astonishing" work of the Convention.

With these questions unanswered, Madison moved in No. 39 to take up two specific charges against the Constitution, that it was not "strictly republican" and that it was a "consolidation" of the states into one. The first is of interest. In order to answer the charge, Madison offered a definition of republicanism. He dismissed four modern possibilities (Holland, Venice, Poland, and England) mentioned by "political writers," because each failed to lodge power in the people. Oddly, Madison did not mention here any of the examples from antiquity that in No. 38 he had claimed were governed by deliberation and consent. Having forgotten about his ancient examples and having cleared modern examples cited by political writers from his path, Madison was free to offer a definition of the republican form:

> We may define a republic to be, or at least may bestow that name on, a government which derives all its powers directly or indirectly from the great body of the people, and is administered by persons holding their offices during pleasure, for a limited period, or during good behavior.

What is "essential," then, is that power derived from "the great body of the society," as opposed to a few or to a favored class. It is "sufficient" that elections and defined tenures be employed. This is to say that indirect elections and lengthy tenures may be republican, as long as power ultimately resides with the great body of the people. It is important to note that this definition emphasizes consent but not deliberation – a feature Madison had explicitly associated with republican governments in antiquity. This suggests that a government without deliberation can be republican as long as the people consent to it. Deliberation does not seem to be a necessary feature of the republican form.[19]

---

[19] Madison, *Federalist* No. 39, Scigliano, 240.

This point clarifies Madison's turn to the argument from veneration discussed in the preceding chapter. Deliberation is not a necessary ingredient of republican government precisely because deliberation is not always possible. Indeed, as the Constitutional Convention illustrated, it is not even likely during times of founding. As a result, veneration serves as a substitute by providing a democratic veneer to rule without deliberation. Because human reason is timid when left alone, and because men respect government when it is old and when it is respected by others, veneration provides what deliberation cannot.

To say deliberation is not necessary for republican politics, however, is not to say that it is impossible or never useful. As Madison explained in *Federalist* No. 37, the indeterminacy of words requires that laws be settled over time. This form of deliberation might take the form of elections, a series of precedents, or judicial decisions. For example, in the case of the Bank of the United States, Madison eventually decided that deliberation among the departments – and not the text of the Constitution itself – could settle the Constitution's sloppiness and justify his own reversal as to the meaning of the Constitution. As he later explained, defending himself against charges of inconsistency on the question of the national bank, the meaning of the Constitution can change from being unsettled to being settled, and this change seems to happen by way of normal politics under separation of powers and over time: "In the case of a Constitution as of a law, a course of authoritative expositions sufficiently deliberate, uniform, and settled, was an evidence of the public will necessarily overruling individual opinions."[20] Sometimes, deliberation can settle what mere veneration cannot.

The *Federalist* on Deliberation by Elites during Normal Politics

But what about deliberation by representatives during normal politics? Before we turn to what Madison did write in the *Federalist*, it is important to notice what he did not. After Madison used the word "deliberation" to describe the foundings of several ancient republics, he did not employ the word to describe either house of Congress. Given the standard understanding that Congress (and especially the Senate) would be the deliberative branch, this is a puzzling omission, and it is surprising that it has gone unnoticed by scholars. Is it a mere coincidence, or is it suggestive of Madison's understanding of the legislative power within the constitutional order?

In fact, the closest Madison came in the *Federalist* to using the word "deliberation" to describe Congress was his statement in No. 63 – assuming that Madison was indeed the author of No. 63[21] – that the "cool and deliberate sense

[20] Madison to C. E. Haynes, 25 February 1831, Hunt 9: 443.
[21] I believe that Hamilton, not Madison, wrote No. 63, but because my argument does not require it, I have chosen to make this point in a footnote. Robert Scigliano's edition names Madison as the author but offers two reasons for Hamilton's authorship. First, the author of No. 63 refers to

of the community" ought to prevail over "temporary errors and delusions."[22] In that essay, Madison argued that there ought to be a body of "temperate and responsible" citizens to "suspend the blow" until "justice, reason, and truth" can return to the public mind. There are good reasons, however, to doubt that this passage alone demonstrates that Madison thought the Congress would be deliberative. First, it is important to note that Madison wrote that it is the sense of the community – not the Senate – that ought to be deliberate. Second, even if we grant that this passage shows that the Senate is deliberative, the necessary implication would be that the Senate was supposed to be deliberative because the House would not be. If this is the case, then it would necessarily imply that the extended republic would not guarantee that members of the House were refining and enlarging the public view, at least not to the extent that Bessette's interpretation would suggest.

Two Objections

To be fair, there are two important objections that need to be addressed. First, there is the possible objection that Madison's writings in the *Federalist* do not constitute the whole of Madison's political thought. As Lance Banning has argued, the *Federalist Papers* might not accurately represent Madison, and emphasizing them alone – particularly a handful of essays – would distort Madison's more comprehensive understanding of the Constitution.[23] In a similar way, Colleen Sheehan would argue that the *Federalist* must be read in light of his party press essays of the early 1790s, essays that clarify Madison's understanding of the place of public opinion in constitutional politics.[24] Madison does, for example, write in his Helvidius papers that Congress was given the power to declare war because a declaration of war is "one of the most deliberative acts that can be formed."[25] Second, another possible objection would be

the "ancient republics" without the use of the distinction that Madison uses between a republic and a pure democracy in Nos. 10 and 14. Indeed, Hamilton seems not to have bothered with this distinction. Second, the author of No. 63 clearly revises the statement Madison makes in No. 14, that representation was invented in modern Europe, calling it "by no means precisely true." In addition to these very good reasons, I would add three more. First, the author of No. 63 is clearly skeptical of the theory of the extended republic presented in No. 10. (see p. 404). Second, Chapter 4's reading of Madison's case for responsibility shows a tension with Nos. 62 and 63. In those essays, Publius defends the stability of the Senate *and* explains the principle of republican responsibility, but in No. 37, Madison clearly writes that there is a necessary tension between republican responsibility and stability. Third, the author of No. 63 writes of the "cool and deliberate sense of the community," and Hamilton uses the phrase "deliberate sense of the community" in close proximity to "cool" in No. 71.

[22] Madison, *Federalist* No. 63, 403.
[23] Lance Banning, *Sacred Fire of Liberty: James Madison & the Founding of the Federal Republic* (Ithaca, NY: Cornell University Press, 1995), 1–10, 349–52.
[24] Sheehan, *Madison and Spirit of Republican Self-Government*, 15–30.
[25] Morton J. Frisch, ed., *The Pacificus-Helvidius Debates of 1793–1794: Toward the Completion of the American Founding* (Indianapolis, IN: Liberty Fund, 2006), 59.

the following: If Madison assumed that Congress would be deliberative, does it really matter that he did not use that word? Is it not the case that many passages in the *Federalist* imply or assume that Congress would be deliberative?

The first objection can be answered only by an exhaustive study of the thousands of pages in Madison's writings. This has been, so far, beyond the scope of any published study of Madison's thought. In the view of this author, there is very little evidence that Madison ever expected that members of either house of Congress would engage in deliberation. Indeed, the example involving the young John Madison is revealing: just when we might expect that Madison would offer a clear summary of his own views of the role of deliberation within representation, Madison either remains silent or demurs on the question. As will be discussed in Chapter 6, the closest Madison comes to offering a theory of representation was what might be his own "last letter," an 1836 letter composed for an unknown recipient. There, Madison noted the tension caused by the "moral" question of whether a representative should be bound by the instructions of his constituents, but, again, he did not take the opportunity to offer a ringing endorsement of the Burkean theory of representation.[26] Moreover, as Banning noticed, Madison "did not even mention the idea of a filtration of the people's will in his letter to Thomas Jefferson of October 24, 1787."[27] When Madison did comment on Congress, he most frequently complained of the shortcomings of its members. In this he was not very different from most other observers of Congress.

But what of his expectations in the beginning? Here, another fact is illuminating. Namely, Madison's omission of the word "deliberation" was not confined to his essays in the *Federalist*. Madison did not use the word to describe Congress in his speeches in either the Convention of 1787 (as recorded by him and published much later) or the Virginia ratification debates. The Convention debates are particularly revealing because other delegates, including the important James Wilson, *did* describe Congress as deliberative, but Madison did not. Madison did use the word, but when he did, he used it to either describe judges or to emphasize the *lack* of deliberation in the American people.[28] For whatever reason, Madison did not reach for the word when thinking about Congress.

Unlike the first objection, the second objection can be answered by concentrating on the argument in the *Federalist*. But in order to either answer this objection or to agree with it, it is necessary to settle on a meaning of "deliberation." Joseph Bessette writes that deliberation includes information, arguments, and persuasion. In a slightly different definition, scholars affiliated with theories of deliberative democracy argue that deliberation requires

---

[26] Madison to _____, March, 1836, Hunt 9: 607–10. For further discussion of the letter, see Chapter 7.

[27] Banning, *Sacred Fire*, 208.

[28] I performed a word search of Madison's *Notes* and of his speeches in the Virginia Ratification debates.

reason-giving (a policy requires an argument guided by the principle of reciprocity) and accessibility (the argument must be able to be understood by the party hearing it).[29] With these accounts in mind, we can say that deliberation in Congress would require three characteristics. First, deliberation implies slowness rather than quickness. Second, deliberation implies wisdom in that a deliberate policy would be a well-considered policy, as opposed to one that has not been subjected to the test of reason. Third, deliberation requires discussion among parties who place themselves in the positions of one another or at least intend to consider a policy from another's perspective.

The Amount of Deliberation: Speed

It is relatively easy to assess Madison's treatment of speed. It is clear from Madison's discussion of the size of Congress that he expected Congress would avoid the hasty legislation that plagued legislatures of the past. In the most thorough examination of this part of Madison's thought, Greg Weiner argues that time is the key variable in understanding Madison's otherwise confusing treatment of democratic majorities.[30] In his view, Madison was not especially worried about majorities as such. Rather, Madison was worried about impulsive majorities, so his reforms were aimed not at curbing majority rule, but rather at slowing down impulsive majorities. As Weiner puts it, "Madison's solution to the problem of impulsivity was to harness what he saw as the inherent power of time to dissipate passions."[31] Importantly, for Weiner, the point was not so much that time would lead to deliberation, and deliberation would solve the problem, but rather that a "cooling period" was a "necessary" and often a sufficient condition for "reasonable behavior."[32] Accordingly, for Weiner, "Madison's constitutional theory required majorities to cohere for long enough intervals to ensure they were guided by reason rather than passion."[33]

Weiner's argument aspires to end the debate about whether Madison was a democrat or not. Because his Madison dislikes the temporary moments when majorities make ill-advised decisions, his Madison can still like the majorities themselves. As Weiner put it, Dahl was wrong, because "the question is not who rules, but when."[34] But even if slowness is a necessary condition for deliberation, it is unlikely that it is sufficient. For Bessette and for theorists of deliberative democracy, it is necessary to have a certain kind of discussion. This involves a qualitative element that is not captured by the merely quantitative

---

[29] Gutmann and Thompson, *Why Deliberative Democracy?*, 95–124.
[30] Greg Weiner, *Madison's Metronome: The Constitution, Majority Rule, and the Tempo of American Politics* (Lawrence: University Press of Kansas, 2012).
[31] Ibid., 3.
[32] Ibid.
[33] Ibid., 51.
[34] Ibid., 52.

assessment of the amount of time that has passed. Historically, this quality of deliberation has been understood as involving assessments concerning the qualities of those participating in the deliberation as well as the qualities of the deliberation itself. By these standards, Madison's presentation of deliberation in the *Federalist* is less than convincing.

The Quality of the Deliberator: Wisdom

Any discussion of Madison's understanding of Congress must include his famous discussion of the differences between a pure democracy and a republic in *Federalist* No. 10. In that passage, Madison wrote that a republic would have representatives to "refine and enlarge the public view." In addition to being motivated by patriotism and the love of justice, this "chosen body of citizens" would have the "wisdom" to "best discern the true interest of their country." So it seems clear that Madison believed the extended republic would allow for legislators wise enough to see beyond "temporary or partial considerations" and deliberate or reason their way to the larger good. There is further evidence for the argument that Madison expected representatives under the Constitution to be wise. He explained in No. 57 that the first aim of "every political constitution" is to select the best "who possess most wisdom to discern, and the most virtue to pursue, the common good of the society."[35] As Madison put it in No. 56, this was especially true with regard to taxation, because a "skillful individual in his closet" could compose tax law for the whole nation.[36] In his presentation of the Senate, Madison wrote that "good government" requires "a knowledge of the means" by which the happiness of the people can be obtained.[37]

Bessette reads these passages to show that the Framers believed that much of the problem under the Articles of Confederation could be traced to the "deficiencies" of state legislators. For Bessette, the Framers believed that the relatively small size of the Congress combined with lengthy terms would promote reason, knowledge, and farsightedness. But, for present purposes, what is most striking is Bessette's claim that "there is at least as much discussion in the *Federalist* of the character and necessary virtues of political leaders as there is of the need to compensate for deficiencies in wisdom and virtue." Do Madison's essays share the characteristic that Bessette ascribes to the work as a whole?[38]

[35] Madison, *Federalist* No. 57, Scigliano, 365.
[36] Madison, *Federalist* No. 56, Scigliano, 361.
[37] Madison, *Federalist* No. 62, Scigliano, 398. It is important to note that in the discussion of skillful individual writing tax law in his closet, Madison goes out of his way to note that this individual would be armed only with his skill and the "local codes before him," and would not require "any aid for oral information" (361). In some "subjects of taxation," then, discussion seems to be superfluous (361), which would suggest a tension with the requirements of deliberation.
[38] Bessette, *Mild Voice*, 20–26, quotation at 20.

The answer is not clear. Even as Madison sometimes argued that republican government requires wise legislators, he also provided reason for readers to doubt the likelihood of such wisdom. In his argument against term limits, Madison wrote that "actual experience in the station" would provide a kind of knowledge. And, unlike tax policy, foreign policy could not be wholly "acquired in a man's closet" and instead required public information and "practical attention" in a legislature.[39] Even though it is not necessary to hang much on this point, at a minimum it qualifies the possible argument that the most knowledgeable representatives would be selected by pointing out that experience – like institutional structure – would inevitably shape the wisdom of the representative. Bessette acknowledges this point; as he puts it, "some part" of wisdom would be "brought into" Congress by way of the representatives who succeed in the election process, while "another part" would "result from the legislative process itself."[40] But this characterization does not describe fully enough the relationship between the parts. Even if the first (the wisdom of the elected representative) is a condition for the second (job experience), Madison clearly implied that it is still possible that the second can undermine the first. The problem is that wisdom in a representative is malleable, not always for the good.

Consider Madison's argument defending what his opponents considered to be the small size of the House. In a well-known passage in No. 55, Madison claimed that "passion never fails to wrest the scepter of reason" in "all numerous assemblies."[41] Here Madison went out of his way to say even a large assembly of men like Socrates would still be a mob. But the mention of Socrates in a way distracts from the broader point – this would be true in an assembly of "whatever characters," which is to say that it would be true of those with the wisdom, patriotism, and love of justice mentioned in No. 10. Madison simply asserted that wisdom is contingent on size in No. 55, but he explained his reasoning in No. 58. It turns out that, in large assemblies, "ignorance will be the dupe of cunning."[42] This implies that Congress will be composed of at least two sorts of men, both those who are ignorant and those who are cunning. Taken alone, this passage could mean that there will be ignorant and cunning men in *any* legislative body, that there is a threshold under which representatives will be neither ignorant nor cunning, or that the proportion of ignorant and cunning men increases as the size of the body increases. But read through the previous passage about Socrates succumbing to passion, it suggests that wise men may also be either ignorant or cunning – or both.

The difficulty can be stated this way. Madison's reasoning seems at first to be obvious: the first aim of a constitution is to select wise and virtuous

---

[39] Madison, *Federalist* No. 52, Scigliano, 346.
[40] Bessette, *Mild Voice*, 24.
[41] Madison, *Federalist* No. 55, Scigliano, 356.
[42] Madison, *Federalist* No. 58, Scigliano, 376.

representatives and the second is to keep them virtuous. But as we have seen in No. 58, Madison also worried that representatives may be both wise and cunning, so it is not enough for republican government to have wise legislators. The question, then, is whether wisdom can be directed toward the public good.[43] One possible answer to this question is suggested by Madison in No. 57, when he addressed the anti-Federalist claim that the representatives will represent the few rather than the many.

The Quality of the Deliberation: Interest and the Common Good

Perhaps the strongest quality of deliberation would be argument that transcends narrow advocacy for particular interest and is instead directed toward the common good.

This principle can be seen in Madison's famous definition of a faction as a group adverse to the "permanent and aggregate interests of the community." And it seems to grow out of the standard scholarly presentation of the difference between the Federalists and the anti-Federalists with regard to the meaning of representation. As Herbert Storing explained, the anti-Federalists believed a representative should be like, think like, and feel like his constituents, that his main goal is to be a delegate for constituent interest.[44] Accordingly, anti-Federalists wanted a larger legislative body, a shorter duration in office, and ineligibility for reelection. Because, the argument goes, Madison argued for a larger body, a longer duration, and eligibility for reelection, Madison therefore embraced the alternative theory of representation, that is, that representatives should be more concerned with the common good rather than with the more narrow constituent interests. Or, as Gordon Wood put it, the good representative should be "disinterested."[45] Wilson Carey McWilliams made the same larger point with a slightly different emphasis: the Federalists' understanding of representation grew out of a single principle: "Objective interests, objectively arrived at."[46] Bessette agrees that "the framers very much sought to create legislative institutions that would not be mere collections of advocates of narrow interests." Accordingly, Bessette concludes that the framers designed the electoral process to select men not "unduly tied" to local interests, and designed the institutions to "foster" a growing "attachment" to the national interest.[47]

The problem with this very standard presentation is that Madison could easily have articulated such an argument in the *Federalist*, but he did not.

---

[43] Madison calls attention to this problem in No. 49 when he stated – strangely – that philosophic reason teaches "reverence for the laws." Madison, *Federalist* No. 49, Scigliano, 323.

[44] Herbert J. Storing, *What the Anti-Federalists Were For: The Political Thought of the Opponents of the Constitution* (Chicago: University of Chicago Press, 1981).

[45] Wood, "Interests and Disinterestedness in the Making of the Constitution."

[46] Wilson Carey McWilliams, "The Anti-Federalists, Representation, and Party," *Northwestern Law Review* 84 (1990): 12–38.

[47] Bessette, *Mild Voice*, 27.

As a result, and as Alan Gibson has pointed out, there is a second school of thought with respect to Madison and the question of interestedness. As Gibson puts it, this school is best represented by Banning, and in this view, Madison's argument for the extended republic "would collapse if the legislature did not reflect the diversity in the extended republic." As Gibson further summarizes Banning's position, because the large republic was preferable to the small republic because it could "embrace such a variety of interests," it follows that these interests would be represented in Congress.[48] As we have seen, Gibson goes on to offer a third way as an alternative, arguing that Madison consistently looked to impartiality as the standard for representation. In Gibson's view, Madison had a "far richer understanding of impartiality and was much more ambiguous about the relationship of virtue and interest" than assumed by the two main schools.[49]

Gibson's point becomes clearer when Madison's *Federalist* essays are compared to Burke's speech at Bristol. As we have seen, Burke said more for the trustee theory of representation in a few paragraphs than Madison did in fifty pages. An objection to this point might be that it is possible that Madison did believe in something like a strong Burkean theory of representation but did not want to lay it out so clearly in the *Federalist* because he was trying to garner support for the Constitution. The objection is important because it focuses attention on the problem of what was not said in the *Federalist*, but the problem with it is that it fails to account for what Madison *did* write in the *Federalist*.

It is well known that Madison as Publius emphasized interest rather than virtue. In No. 51, he wrote that the interest of the officeholder must be connected to the rights of the office.[50] But it is worth pausing to see just how much of his argument hangs on the interest of the representative. In No. 57, Madison addressed the charge that the representatives will elevate the few over the many. As he put it, the charge is "perhaps the most extraordinary" in that it strikes at the principles of republican government[51]. He answered by listing five securities that representatives will remain true to their "representative trust":

1. The men who are elected will be "somewhat distinguished" by qualities that entitle them to election.
2. Because ingratitude is universally despised, it stands to reason that elected representatives will have at least "temporary affection" to constituents.
3. Because the vanity of elected officials is flattered by being the object of public choice, the representative will honor the form and process of representative government.

[48] Gibson, "Madison's 'Great Desideratum': Impartial Administration and the Extended Republic," 183.
[49] Ibid., 184.
[50] Madison, *Federalist* No. 51, Scigliano, 331.
[51] Madison, *Federalist*, No. 57, Scigliano, 365.

4. The prospect of reelection will support in representatives a "habitual recollection of their dependence on the people."

5. Representatives "can make no law which will not have its full operation on themselves and their friends."[52]

What is most striking about this list is that there is absolutely no discussion of the larger common good separate from fidelity to constituents. That is, Madison did not entertain the possibility that the public good might arise out of wise deliberation and be opposed to or different from that which is wished by the constituents. To put it differently, if deliberation implies wisdom, Madison went out of way to show how wise legislators will be less than deliberative insofar as they will be tied to their less wise constituents.[53]

In fact, Madison drove this point home. Before he introduced his fourth and fifth securities, he bluntly explained that the first three securities "would be found very insufficient without the restraint of frequent elections."[54] It is the prospect for reelection, not the previous motivations, which would ensure representatives would remain true to their constituents. Madison makes sure we appreciate the importance of this point by giving each security a name. "Duty, gratitude, interest and ambition itself, are the chords by which they will be bound to fidelity and sympathy to the great mass of the people."[55] With the securities thus named we can better understand their logic:

1. Duty – the men who are elected will be "somewhat distinguished" by qualities that entitle them to election.

2. Gratitude – because ingratitude is universally despised, it stands to reason that elected representatives will have at least "temporary affection" to constituents.

3. Ambition – because the vanity of elected officials is flattered by being the object of public choice, the representative will honor the form and process of representative government.

4. Interest – the prospect of reelection will support in representatives a "habitual recollection of their dependence on the people."

5. Interest – representatives "can make no law which will not have its full operation on themselves and their friends."

Given Madison's claim that the first three securities would be insufficient, it is clear that Madison elevated interest above virtues (duty and gratitude)

[52] Ibid., 366–67.

[53] On this point it is important that the author of No. 63 justifies the six-year term for senators, at least in part, as contributing a responsibility to the people over the long term. Seen from the perspective of No. 37, which emphasizes the tension between responsibility and stability, his justification suggests a concession toward constituent interest. It is only a different kind of interest. Madison, *Federalist* Nos. 63 and 37, Scigliano, 403 and 224.

[54] Madison, *Federalist*, No. 57, Scigliano, 367.

[55] Ibid., 368.

and even above passion (ambition). To ensure that we do not miss the point, Madison offered two reasons from interest and switches the order of ambition and interest in the list of names; ambition is fourth, and interest third.

It is possible that Madison's emphasis on interest does suggest a movement toward wisdom. In *Federalist* No. 10, he defined a faction as working against the "permanent and aggregate interest." While some passages explain how factions follow narrow interest rather than the permanent and aggregate interest, particularly the statement that the "most common and durable" source of faction is the "various and unequal distribution of property," the thrust of Madison's argument emphasizes the passions as the culprit. The problem is that self-love and reason have a "reciprocal influence" on each other, which means that our "opinions" are corrupted by our "passions." This is to say, whatever unity reason might discover between our self-interest and the common interest is obfuscated by our passions. Representatives and the extended republic moderate and dilute the effects of the unchangeable human trait.

By extension, perhaps, his elevation of interest over ambition in No. 57 suggests that wise and ambitious legislators will be made more rational through their calculations of self-interest. But if this true, it in turn suggests that wisdom properly understood – that is, when it is reformed by interest – is now tied to the will of the constituents. This is to say then that deliberation in the House is wise only insofar as it is directed by the interest in reelection. This implies not only that interest does what duty cannot but also that the representative will be connected to his constituents, which will necessarily comprise some geographic region smaller than the whole nation. Interest will bind the representative to the subnational, not the national, good. It is this emphasis on interest that places Madison's position somewhere between the anti-Federalists and Burke. But where?

It is worth noting two more points against the position that Madison believed Congress would be deliberative. The first takes us beyond Madison and requires more investigation to fully count one way or the other, but it is worth a mention. If the Framers wanted to make Congress deliberative, why did they remain neutral with regard to the rules of procedure in each house? Similarly, why did they not specify that House districts be at large and state-wide rather than leaving open the possibility of single-member districts? Either had the potential to institutionalize deliberation, yet the Constitution, and therefore Madison as Publius, is silent on each.

The second point is well known but not often discussed in this context. In his essays treating separation of powers, Madison went out of his way in earlier essays to show the limits of legislator. In No. 48, he argued that the legislative branch is the most dangerous branch and most prone of the three departments to bully the others.[56] In No. 49, Madison explicitly characterized legislators as the precise opposite of wise and virtuous: during an appeal to

---

[56] Madison, *Federalist* No. 48, Scigliano, 317.

the people, legislators would manipulate the ignorance and passions – not the reason – of the public.[57] It is possible, of course, that Madison believed that the appeal to the public would bring out the worst in legislators, who would not behave that way during times of ordinary politics. That is, legislators could be wise and virtuous up until the point they are asked to participate in a refounding. Even so, the fact remains that the institutional features discussed in the later passages of the *Federalist* would *not* be sufficient to guarantee wise and virtuous legislators, at least during these times.

The Right to Instruct Representatives

Madison had another opportunity to expand on his presentation in the *Federalist* when the first Congress debated the Bill of Rights. The context was discussion of what eventually became the First Amendment's protection of the right to assemble and petition. The wording from the committee was the following: "The freedom of speech and of the press, and the right of the people peaceably to assemble and consult for the common good, and to apply to the Government for redress of grievances, shall not be infringed."[58] Debate turned to the nature of representation when Thomas Tucker of South Carolina moved to add the right "to instruct their Representatives" to the amendment.[59]

The question of instructing representatives had a particular meaning, for members of Congress were well aware that it had been debated extensively in Great Britain and in colonial America. According to John Phillip Reid, colonial Americans had a more developed theory of instructions in part because the American argument for representation grew out of the fact that the Americans "thought instructions were more constitutional than did the British and much more binding on representatives."[60] Thus, for Americans, the right of the people to instruct their representatives "became a major weapon in the colonial Whig defense against parliamentary rule."[61] Further, instructions were woven within the democratic practice of New England governance. In Great Britain, however, the case for instructions was met by opposition, and it is this context that Burke offered his now famous account of representation. For Burke, as we have seen, representation does not require that the representative see instructions from his constituents as "authoritative." Rather, for Burke, representation implied that the representative would be independent.[62]

It is unsurprising, then, that the congressional opponents of the right to instruct used arguments that resembled Burke's account of representation. For

[57] Madison, *Federalist* No. 49, Scigliano, 325.
[58] *Annals of Congress*, House, 1st sess., 759.
[59] Ibid., 761.
[60] John Phillip Reid, *The Concept of Representation in the Age of the American Revolution* (Chicago: University of Chicago Press, 1989), 99.
[61] Ibid., 100.
[62] Ibid., 108–09.

example, Thomas Hartley of Pennsylvania argued that the people ought to trust the "honor and integrity" of the men they elect, and, in words much like those in the *Federalist*, Hartley argued that these men will sometimes have to protect the people against themselves: "When the passions of the people are excited, instructions have been resorted to and obtained, to answer party purposes; and although the public opinion is generally respectable, yet at such moments it has been known to be often wrong; and happy is that Government composed of men of firmness and wisdom to discover, and resist popular error." Thus, for Hartley, instructions were instruments of partisan passion and stood in the way of "honest reason and sound policy."[63] George Clymer of Pennsylvania went even further, arguing that the instructions were "destructive of all ideas of an independent and deliberative body." In particular, "they prevent men of abilities and experience those abilities that are in their power."[64] Likewise, Roger Sherman of Connecticut argued that instructions would destroy the object of representation, which was for one representative "to meet others from the different parts of the Union, and consult." If representatives were "to be guided by instructions, there would be no use in deliberation."[65]

On the other side, advocates of instruction argued that the right to instruct was a fundamental principle of republican government. According to John Page of Virginia, instruction and representations were "inseparably connected" in a "democracy," where the "great end [was] to form a code of laws congenial with the public sentiment."[66] And rather than trusting his own wisdom and experience, the representative should look to "the sense of the people on every occasion of magnitude."[67] Elbridge Gerry of Massachusetts added that representatives would be free to depart from the instructions, but that the instructions would serve notice that such departures would jeopardize their chances at reelection. More broadly, the point of declaring a right to send instructions would encourage people to do just that, and the people's opinions would serve as "useful information" for representatives.[68]

Madison appeared to take a middle path. In his view, the committee had been right to leave out the phrase because the right was either obvious or untrue. If the right meant that the people have the right to give advice to their representative or Congress as a whole, than that was obviously a right that was both true and already "provided for." But if the right was meant to bind the representative, even to go against the Constitution itself, then the right "d[id] not exist" because the Constitution had to be superior to the views of the constituents.[69] As to Gerry's argument from the sovereignty of the people,

[63] *Annals of Congress*, House, 1st sess., 761.
[64] Ibid., 763.
[65] Ibid.
[66] Ibid., 762.
[67] Ibid., 763.
[68] Ibid., 764–65.
[69] Ibid., 766–67.

Madison replied that "the people can change the constitution if they please," but "when the constitution exists, they must conform themselves to its dictates." This means that the assembly of people in parts cannot form a higher law than the assembly of the people in the whole – at least in the constitutional sense – by way of their representatives in Congress. More simply, Madison said he was against adding the phrase because it would subject the Bill of Rights to unnecessary criticism and arguments about "abstract propositions." The practical truth is that citizens would send instructions and representatives would decide whether they would be bound by them or not.

In this, Madison did not take the opportunity to lecture members of the House, including anti-Federalist Elbridge Gerry, about the meaning of representation. Nor did he simply point to his language from *Federalist* 10 that representatives would "refine and enlarge" the views of their constituents. To be sure, it is possible that Madison privately agreed with those who, like Roger Sherman, believed that instructions would hamper the deliberative function of representatives. But an equally plausible explanation is that Madison held misgivings about the likelihood of such deliberation but was reluctant to air those misgivings in the middle of a congressional debate about proposing amendments to the brand new Constitution. Whatever Madison's private views, his public statements are revealing in that they consistently avoid linking deliberation with the role of a representative. This was more than a haphazard omission. Madison referred to this event in one of his very last letters, written nearly forty years later.[70] He noted that Americans debated the question in the first Congress, and that these debates could be found in the "Register of Debates, imperfectly as they were reported," but he did not revise the records of what he said in 1789. Rather, there is a consistency between his treatment of representation in 1789 and 1834. In both, Madison avoided a clear endorsement of the strong theory of representation where representatives would refine and enlarge the views of their constituents.

In addition to providing Madison with more opportunities to reflect on quality of deliberation of Congress, the debates in the first Congress included two controversies that are useful in understanding Madison's political thought with respect to the problem of constitutional imperfection. Those two events are the debate on the usefulness of a bill of rights, as well as the debate on the power to remove executive officials.

[70] See Chapter 7.

4

Public Opinion before Parties

> "Defects themselves gain Strength & Respect by Time. Wd. it not then be better
> to expose fully, & in the Manner of wh. you are so capable, those Alterations
> wh. are necessary, or wch. wd in Theory render the Govt. more perfect. The First
> object shd. be to render the Theory as perfect as possible: if the Theory be such,
> the practice will be correspondent. Principles wh. are true in Theory, cannot fail
> in Execution of them."
>
> Reverend James Madison to James Madison, 1789[1]

There is perhaps no greater problem for Madison scholars than Madison's turn
to political parties. Within a year after Washington was inaugurated, and less
than three years after writing the definitive treatment of faction, Madison joined
Thomas Jefferson to create and organize the nation's first opposition party. This
turn set in motion the primary intellectual innovation of the decade, which was
the defense of public opinion as a legitimate source of authority. As scholars of the
period have recently emphasized, this assertion of public opinion as a legitimate
source of authority was initially resisted by the Federalist Party, and thus the two
arguments became intertwined with the two parties.[2] As Tocqueville noticed, one
party was the party of law and the other was the party of opinion.[3]

---

[1] Reverend James Madison to James Madison, 15 August 1789, *PJM* 12: 338.
[2] Colleen A. Sheehan, "Madison v. Hamilton: Battle over Republicanism and the Role of Public
Opinion," *American Political Science Review* 98 (2004): 405–24; Todd Estes, *The Jay Treaty
Debate, Public Opinion, and the Evolution Early American Political Culture* (Amherst:
University of Massachusetts Press, 2008).
[3] Alexis de Tocqueville, *Democracy in America*, trans. Harvey C. Mansfield and Delba Winthrop
(Chicago: University of Chicago Press, 2000), 166–70.

Portions of this chapter were previously published in 2008 as "The New Unitary Executive and
Democratic Theory: The Problem of Alexander Hamilton" in *American Political Science Review*,
453–65, and in 2012 as "Was James Madison Ever for the Bill of Rights?" in *Perspectives on
Political Science*, 59–66. Copyright © 2008 American Political Science Association. Reprinted with
the permission of Cambridge University Press.

It is surprising, then, that Madison scholars have not made much use of the period after ratification but before Madison's turn to political parties. In this short time, Madison was a member of Congress and took the lead in getting the new government established. This required settling old business, such as adding amendments to the Constitution, but it also required tough decisions about new business, such as creating executive departments to administer the new government. Both required members of Congress to put meaning to the words of the Constitution. So, for example, and as was discussed in the preceding chapter, the question of the right to instruct representatives carried with it rival understandings of the role and function of representatives. Likewise, creating the executive departments brought to the fore different understandings held by early Americans about the relationship between the president and Congress. In both cases, Madison put together the coalition in the House that eventually won two major legislative victories. One was the Bill of Rights and the other was the 1789 House debate on the removal power. The two happened simultaneously, and in each case, Madison believed that fundamental constitutional principles hinged on the outcome. While scholars have written on each of these questions, especially the Bill of Rights, there has been little work connecting the two to Madison's political thought and to his treatment of the problem of constitutional imperfection.

Given the argument of the previous chapter, it is worth noting as an aside that these events must have deepened Madison's concerns about the quality of deliberation in the House. As he surely noticed, even though the Congress had yet not divided between parties for and against Hamilton's Assumption Plan, there was a coalition that consistently voted against Madison during the two debates. On 24 September, when the House approved the final draft of the amendments to be proposed, fourteen members voted no.[4] Of these fourteen, ten voted as a consistent block during the three major votes on the removal power.[5] Of the remaining four, two joined the block on the most critical vote and another argued against Madison but recorded no votes.[6] The members of this block were surely anti-Federalists who formed a coalition in simple opposition. These votes reveal that there was very little compromise resulting from legislative debate. Indeed, Aedanus Burke was the only representative who voted with Madison on removals but against him on the Bill of Rights (or vice versa). Early on, Madison's letters show pleasure in the "Spirit of moderation and accommodation" of the debates in Congress.[7] After a few months,

---

[4] *Annals of Congress*, 1st Cong., 1st sess., 947.

[5] David J. Alvis, Jeremy D. Bailey, and Flagg F. Taylor, *The Contested Removal Power, 1789–2010* (Lawrence: University Press of Kansas, 2013). See the tables on pp. 118–21, especially table 4.4 on p. 121. Those ten include Coles, Gerry, Grout, Hathorn, Livermore, Mathews, Page, Van Rensselaer, and Sumpter.

[6] Theodorick Bland of Virginia supported the advice and consent position (*Contested Removal Power*, 28) but did not cast votes. Tucker and Jackson joined the block on the critical vote on 24 June.

[7] Madison to Edmund Randolph, 31 May 1789, in *PJM*, 12: 189. Madison to George Nicholas, 5 July 1789, in *PJM*, 12: 279.

however, his letters were filled with descriptions of these debates as "exceedingly wearisome" and "exceedingly difficult and fatiguing," and he blamed this on both the "dilatory artifices" of the "antifederal members" but also more generally on "the diversity of opinions & fancies inseparable from such an Assembly of Congress."[8] Nowhere did he observe that opinions and interests had been refined and enlarged by his colleagues in Congress.

But rather than offering more evidence for Madison's frustrations in legislative bodies, this chapter shows that, taken together, the debate on the Bill and Rights and the debate on the removal power can reveal much about Madison's understanding of the role of public opinion in republican government. In short, the removal debate reveals that Madison was well on his way to seeing the president as accountable to a national electorate, and this accountability would serve to promote the responsibility he wrote about in *Federalist* No. 37. But the debate on the Bill of Rights shows that Madison held back from making the fuller argument that the Constitution was defective because it lacked an account of public opinion and democratic leadership. Specifically, it shows that Madison probably did not believe that the Bill of Rights improved the Constitution by providing a text that would educate the people about the importance of their rights.

The Removal Power and Constitutional Silence

Madison's chance to apply the Constitution to a controversy over separation of powers came when the 1st Congress created the State Department. The legislation opened a question unresolved by the text of the Constitution: Who has the power to remove a department head? Some members argued that a department head could be removed only by impeachment. Others maintained that the power to remove was incident to the power to appoint, which meant that the Senate would have to give its advice and consent to presidential removals. Another argument was that Congress possessed the power to vest the power where it wished. Madison argued that the president alone has the power to remove, and his argument narrowly carried the day.[9]

There are two features of Madison's argument that are worth noting at the outset. The first noticeable feature is its apparent similarity with what would later be known as a Hamiltonian understanding of executive power. In defending the president's power to remove, Madison pointed to the differences between the vesting clauses of Articles I and II of the Constitution.[10] Because

---

[8] James Madison to Edmund Pendleton, 21 August, 1789, and James Madison to Edmund Randolph, 21 August 1789, in *Creating the Bill of Rights: The Documentary Record from the First Federal Congress*, ed. Helen E. Veit, Kenneth R. Bowling, and Charlene Bangs Bickford (Baltimore: Johns Hopkins University Press, 1991), 284.

[9] For a summary of the four positions and their importance in American political development, see Alvis, Bailey, and Taylor, *Contested Removal Power*.

[10] *Annals of Congress*, 1st Cong., 1st sess., 481.

the vesting clause in Article II speaks of "the executive power," while that of Article I speaks only of "legislative powers herein granted," it would seem that "[t]he question now resolves itself into this. Is the power of displacing, an executive power? I conceive that if any power whatsoever is in its nature executive, it is the power of appointing, overseeing, and controlling those who execute the laws." And as the "association of the Senate" in appointing was an exception, and "exceptions to general rules, I conceive, are ever to be taken strictly," the Senate's role in appointing was not a narrowing of the vesting clause's broader grant of the power to remove.[11] A few years later, Hamilton followed Madison's lead when defending Washington's Neutrality Proclamation against Republican critics. This time, the question was whether the Senate's participation in the creation of treaties affected the president's power to interpret or abrogate treaties:

> With these exceptions the EXECUTIVE POWER of the Union is completely lodged in the President. This mode of construing the Constitution has indeed been recognized by Congress in formal acts, upon full consideration and debate. The power of removal from office is an important instance.[12]

So it is curious that Madison employed the argument from the vesting clause before Hamilton – indeed, perhaps before anyone. At first glance, this point would seem to invite reexamination of Lance Banning's central thesis, that there was no change in Madison from the 1780s to the 1790s, because Madison in the 1780s was never a Hamiltonian.[13] That is, if Madison is actually the father of what we see as the Hamiltonian reading of Article II's vesting clause, then Banning's argument would have to be seriously qualified.

This step is not necessary, however, because it turns out that the question was also complicated on Hamilton's end. Ironically, Madison's embrace of presidential removal power marked a turn from Hamilton's published views on the question. As Madison was reminded, Hamilton had written in *Federalist* No. 77, "The consent of that body [the Senate] would be necessary to displace as well as to appoint," an argument that was quoted by William Loughton Smith in the House debates.[14] Scholars have long puzzled over Hamilton's statement, which would seem to deviate from his normally single-minded focus on increasing the power of the president. One possibility is that Hamilton was deliberately trying to make the presidency seem weaker than it was in order to pull moderates away from anti-Federalists. Another is that it was a sloppy error that Hamilton later corrected. But another possibility is that Hamilton's statement in the *Federalist* actually reflected Hamilton's view on the subject.

[11] Ibid., 516.
[12] Alexander Hamilton, Pacificus No. 1, in Harold C. Syrett, ed., *Papers of Alexander Hamilton*, 27 Vols. (New York: Columbia University Press, 1961–87), 15: 40.
[13] Lance Banning, *The Sacred Fire of Liberty: James Madison & the Founding of the Federal Republic* (Ithaca, NY: Cornell University Press, 1995), 13–107, 250–52.
[14] Hamilton, *Federalist* No. 77, Scigliano, 489.

There is evidence for this conclusion from the *Federalist* itself, as well as evidence from later in Hamilton's career.[15]

It is important to note that Madison believed there was a genuine difference between Publius and Madison on this question. When Madison summarized the rival positions, he stated that the position from *Federalist* No. 77 "seem[ed] to stand most in opposition to the principles I contend for."[16] The clue is one of Madison's main arguments for removals. In addition to pointing to the vesting clause, and in addition to pointing to the president's duty to execute the law, Madison also argued that the president must have the power to remove because the president alone was "responsible" for administration. Unlike Hamilton's efforts as Publius, then, Madison appealed to the democratic logic of "responsibility" to argue that the president alone must possess the power to remove in order to forge a "chain of dependence" between the president and the people. By looking at Madison's argument from responsibility, we revisit Madison's discussion of the natural tension between responsibility and one of the necessary ingredients of good government, stability. From his discussion of the problem of the Constitution and the removal power, we learn that for Madison there is such a thing as too much stability.

Madison's Case for Responsibility

As we have seen, Madison argued that the principle of separation of powers solved the puzzle of who has the authority to remove executive officials. As he put it, "the Legislature has no right to diminish or modify his executive authority."[17] But the problem is that the principle does not work without first determining the application. That is, how do we know if the power to remove is executive or legislative in nature? After all, as Madison reflected in *Federalist* No. 37, "Experience has instructed us that no skill in the science of government has yet been able to discriminate and define, with sufficient certainty, its three great provinces – the legislative, executive, and judiciary."[18] For Madison to persuade other members of Congress that the removal power was indeed an executive power, he would also have to find a method by which he and others could determine whether a power was executive in nature. The solution for Madison was the principle of responsibility. It is this political term, which

---

[15] For a review of the various scholarly explanations, as well as an examination of Hamilton's later positions, see Alvis, Bailey, and Taylor, *Contested Removal Power*, 57–61. See also Jeremy D. Bailey, "The Traditional View of Hamilton's *Federalist* No. 77 and an Unexpected Challenge: A Reply to Seth Barrett Tillman," *Harvard Journal of Law and Public Policy* 33 (2010): 169–84. For a consideration of the larger context in the *Federalist*, see Jeremy D. Bailey, "The New Unitary Executive and Democratic Theory," *American Political Science Review* 102 (2008): 453–65.

[16] *Annals of Congress*, 1st Cong., 1st sess., 516.

[17] Ibid., 481.

[18] Madison, *Federalist* No. 37, in Scigliano, 226.

Harvey Mansfield says Madison "apparently coined," which gets to the heart of the debate between Hamilton and Madison.[19]

During the first debate, on May 19, Madison explained that "one of the most prominent features of the constitution, a principle that pervades the whole system," is "that there should be the highest possible degree of responsibility in all the executive officers." Any measure "which tends to lessen this responsibility," and is not "saddled upon us expressly by the letter of that work," is contrary to its "spirit and intention." Responsibility in the executive power would be undermined by the Senate's sharing the removal power:

> If … he shall not be displaced, but by and with the advice of the senate, the president is no longer answerable for the conduct of the officer; all will depend on the Senate. You here destroy a real responsibility without obtaining even the shadow; for no gentleman will pretend to say, the responsibility of the Senate can be of such a nature as to afford substantial security.[20]

Madison's argument rested on two claims: that sharing the removal power would destroy executive responsibility, and that the Senate could not offer any responsibility to make up for the loss.

The first claim is straightforward. The participation of the legislative branch would undermine responsibility by destroying unity. As Hamilton had noted in the *Federalist*, a council of appointments in New York, comprised of the governor and three to five members of the Senate, had resulted in a system in which everyone agreed that the appointments were "improper" but nobody agreed as to who was to blame.[21] Madison applied the same logic to removals. By giving the Senate a share of the removal power, "you make the executive a two-headed monster … you destroy the great principle of responsibility, and perhaps have the creature divided in its will, defeating the very purposes for which a unity in the executive was instituted."[22]

The second claim, however, requires more elaboration, and if true, would shed light on the first. There are several explanations for this more difficult assertion that there is a difference in the quality of responsibility between the senate and the president. One possibility is the Senate's mode of election. By being more distant from the people – elected by state legislatures and holding staggered terms of six years – senators would be less concerned about public opinion and therefore less responsible. As Madison put it, the Senate was a "permanent body," which by its staggered or "particular mode of election" would be "in reality existing for ever." Appealing to lingering anti-Federalist sentiment, perhaps, Madison said that the Senate possessed a portion of "aristocratic power" and was therefore less trustworthy than the president. Or, to

---

[19] Harvey Mansfield, *Taming the Prince: The Ambivalence of Executive Power* (New York: Free Press, 1989), 270.

[20] *Annals of Congress*, 1st Cong., 1st sess., 395.

[21] Hamilton, *Federalist* No. 70, Scigliano, 453–54.

[22] *Annals of Congress*, 1st Cong., 1st sess., 519.

put it in the vocabulary of *Federalist* No. 51, the Senate's "mode of election" resulted in a particular "principle of action," one that was unsuitable for the removal power.[23]

There is another explanation, and it clarifies the preceding one. It is possible that Madison believed that the state equality of representation in the Senate made it less fit than the president to oversee national administration. That is, this explanation would say that it was likely that the Connecticut Compromise changed Madison's views on what was appropriate for the Senate and what was not. Madison alluded to this character fault of the Senate in a letter to Edmund Pendleton written on 21 June 1789.[24] In this report of the debate on the removal power, Madison summarized the "four constructive doctrines" articulated in Congress and provided the arguments for and against each position. When he got to the argument that the power to remove was incident to the power to appoint (Hamilton's position in the *Federalist*), Madison explained that it would have encouraged executive officers to find a party in the Senate and make themselves irremovable. More broadly,

> It transfers the trust in fact from the President who being at all times impeachable as well as every 4th. year eligible by the people at large, may be deemed the most responsible member of the Government, to the Senate who from the nature of that institution, is and was meant after the Judiciary & in some respects witht. that exception to be the most unresponsible branch of the Government.[25]

In this remarkable passage, Madison indicated both that the president is the most responsible officer and that the Senate is in some respects less responsible than even the judiciary, whose members hold their office for good behavior. This must mean that, for Madison, responsibility cannot be merely length of term and mode of selection because, by those terms alone, the judiciary would clearly be less responsible than the Senate and the House more responsible than the president. Instead, if responsibility includes the breadth of the electorate, then the fact that the president represents the people "at large," rather than the people in their state or local capacities, means that the president would be the most responsible. Senators, on the other hand, owed their existence to the "federal" compromise and thus could be considered as less responsible than judges nominated by the president. Or, as he put in it in the debate, "Shall we trust the Senate, responsible to individual legislatures, rather than the person who is responsible to the whole community?"[26] As was discussed in Chapter 2, Madison admitted in *Federalist* No. 37 that the compromise between large and small states gave rise to a "fresh struggle" in the Convention and influenced later debates.[27] It is possible that in 1789, with delegates like Smith seeking to

---

[23] Madison, *Federalist* No. 51, Scigliano, 332.
[24] Madison to Edmund Pendleton, 21 June 1789, *Madison Writings*, 465–66.
[25] Ibid.
[26] *Annals of Congress*, 1st Cong., 1st sess., 519.
[27] Madison, *Federalist* No. 37, Scigliano, 227.

interpret the Constitution according to its impact on state size, Madison was still fighting the good fight against state equality of representation.[28]

But more than an attempt to keep the partisans of state equality from expanding the power of the Senate, Madison's defense of presidential removal powers suggests that his understanding of responsibility in the executive included an account of the president as a national officer. In the debate on 16 June, Madison connected responsibility to presidential selection in order to explain why removals were executive in nature. To lay the groundwork for the constitutional argument, he first offered a principle: "I believe no principle is more clearly laid down in the constitution than that of responsibility. After premising this, I will proceed to an investigation of the merits of the question upon a constitutional ground."[29] But this time, to explain what might otherwise be too abstract, Madison prefaced his remarks with the details of presidential selection. He agreed with Smith's admonition that legislators should be guided by the "merit of the men" who will be president in the "ordinary course of things," rather than by the "splendor of the character" of Washington, since the "power here declared is a high one, and, in some respects, a dangerous one."[30] But, with that note of caution, Madison explained why there *would* be reason to trust ordinary presidents:

> When we consider that the First Magistrate is to be appointed at present by the suffrages of three millions of people, and in all human probability in a few years' time by double that number, it is not to be presumed that a vicious or bad character will be selected. If the Government of any country on the face of the earth was ever effectually guarded against the election of ambitious or designing characters to the first office of the State, I think it may with truth be said to be the case under the constitution of the United States.[31]

Madison's appeal to the suffrage of three million people is striking for at least two reasons. First, taken in the context of the argument for responsibility, it anticipated later claims by Jacksonians, described in Chapter 6, that the president represents a national majority. Second, it contradicted earlier statements

---

[28] For Madison's efforts at the Convention, see David Brian Robertson, *The Constitution and America's Destiny* (New York: Cambridge University Press, 2005), 132–49, 225–43. From William Maclay's notes we know that state size influenced the Senate debates. William Grayson, for instance, said, "The matter predicted by Mr. Henry is now coming to pass: consolidation is the object of the new Government, and the first attempt will be to destroy the Senate, as they are representatives of the State Legislatures." William Mcclay, *Journal of William Mcclay, United States Senator from Pennsylvania* (New York: D. Appleton, 1890), 108–14. Later, in 1834, referring to the partisan contest over Jackson's use of the removal power, Madison pointed out that the large states would be reluctant to augment the Senate's removal powers. Madison to John Patton, 24 March 1834, and Madison to Charles Francis Adams, 12 October 1835, Hunt 9: 534–36, 560–63.

[29] *Annals of Congress*, 1st Cong., 1st sess., 480.

[30] Ibid., 519.

[31] Ibid., 479–80.

by Madison. In his 1787 report on the Constitution to Jefferson, Madison pointed to the president as an example of the general government deriving some of its authority from the subordinate governments: "The President also derives his appointment from the States, and is periodically accountable to them."[32] Moreover, in *Federalist* No. 39, Madison described the president as both national and federal, in that presidential selection would take into account both the people and the states.[33] But in the removal debate Madison seemed to envision a national popular majority, even a popular majority that could be trusted. Though he added that the electoral college had corrected the "infirmities" of "popular selection," and that the possibilities of impeachment and the prospect of reelection would be a check on presidents, Madison explained that he "was not afraid" to place his "confidence" in a fellow citizen whom the people had chosen. Even though a national majority of millions of people could not guarantee a Washington in the ordinary course of things, it would usually find presidents who could be trusted with what would otherwise be a dangerous power.[34]

This curious appeal to the national popular majority as a safeguard against presidential tyranny might have been a rhetorical device to sweeten the argument for presidential power, but it was also central to his argument from responsibility and his larger attempt to instruct others how to determine whether a power was executive by nature. On the following day, Madison explained how removals would fit with presidential selection:

> If the President should possess alone the power of removal from office, those who are employed in the execution of the law will be in their proper situation, and the chain of dependence be preserved; the lowest officers, the middle grade, and the highest will depend, as they ought, on the President, and the President on the community. The chain of dependence therefore terminates in the supreme body, namely, in the people; who will possess, besides, in aid of their original power, the decisive engine of impeachment.[35]

Because it would be the "people" who hold the power, Madison probably used impeachment to refer to the option to choose another candidate at the end of four years, not to the formal impeachment process.[36] Unlike members of the Senate, the president would be able to claim a direct "chain of dependence" to the people and thus subject administration to the people's control.

[32] Madison to Jefferson, 24 October 1787, *PJM* 10: 211.

[33] Madison, *Federalist* No. 39, Scigliano, 244.

[34] This concern for the connection between the president and the electorate can also be seen in Madison's participation over the debate on presidential titles, where Madison argued that the real danger posed by exalted titles is that they would "diminish the true dignity of the first magistrate himself." Kathleen Bartolini-Tuazon, *For Fear of an Elective King: George Washington and the Presidential Title Controversy of 1789* (Ithaca, NY: Cornell University Press, 2014), 103.

[35] *Annals of Congress*, 1st Cong., 1st sess., 518.

[36] In his 16 June speech, Madison said that the president is "impeachable before the community at large every four years." *Annals of Congress*, 1st Cong., 1st sess., 480.

Madison seems to have believed that the national basis for presidential selection would ensure both that the removal power would be used safely and in accord with the national will. In this he seemed to rely on the famous argument that the extended republic would solve the problem of faction by rendering a national majority, the only truly dangerous faction under majority voting rules, so weak that it would be unable to trample minority rights or seriously damage the public good. At the same time, Madison seemed to prefer public opinion, by way of an electoral chain of responsibility, to administration by experts freed from the demands of electoral politics. He argued that if the president were required to seek the Senate's approval, then there would be too much "stability" in executive administration. By courting Senators whose longer and overlapping terms suggested a kind of permanence, executive officers would outlast their presidents and acquire their own authority and expertise. Administration need not worry about elections.

More than a narrow technicality, then, this pre-partisan difference between Hamilton and Madison concerned the balancing of stability and republican responsibility, a difficulty Madison discussed at length in *Federalist* No. 37. As was discussed in Chapter 2, Madison explained in No. 37 that one difficulty faced by the delegates to the Convention of 1787, and perhaps even one imperfection in the Constitution itself, was combining two properties necessary in any government – energy and stability – with the "genius of republican liberty."[37] The two "requisite" ingredients demanded that power be lodged in the hands of the one (energy) and the few (stability) for long periods of time, but the additional, American ingredient of republican liberty demanded that power be exercised by the many for a short period of time. The problem, of course, was that republicans feared the very thing over which they had no choice. But Madison and Hamilton differed in their solutions to the problem of republican demands.

Although Hamilton admired Madison's work at the Convention enough to enlist him in writing the *Federalist*, Hamilton may not have been persuaded by Madison's grand thesis. From Hamilton's notes of Madison's 6 June speech at the Convention, when Madison presented his extended republic argument to the Convention, we know that Hamilton believed that majority faction would survive the extended republic, because representatives would be just as susceptible to the same causes of faction as citizens are.[38] For Hamilton, the better solution was a well-composed Senate, which could check faction.[39] This trust in the Senate carried over into his understanding of executive energy, at least with regard to executing the law. To introduce his study of law enforcement, Hamilton mocked the "enlightened well wishers of republican government"

---

[37] Madison, *Federalist* No. 37, Scigliano, 223–25.
[38] Alexander Hamilton, Notes from 6 June, in Harold C. Syrett, ed., *Papers of Alexander Hamilton*, 27 Vols. (New York: Columbia University Press, 1961–1987), 4:165.
[39] Madison, *Notes*, 194.

and argued that they would have to revise republican government to accommodate energy in the executive.[40] At the same time, he worried that republican excess would undermine the stability he believed executive administration would need, explaining in *Federalist* No. 72 that the "intimate connection" between stability and duration included the concern that "every new President" would "promote a change of men to fill the subordinate stations."[41] By the time Hamilton finished his examination of executive energy, having warned about the dangers of having too frequent a change in presidents and having given the Senate a share of the removal power, he had explained that there was stability in the executive department too.

In this context, Madison's otherwise hyperbolic speeches in the House make more sense. To introduce his third and final speech, Madison said that the question of removals as involving "fundamental principles" and "liberty itself," for it would decide whether the government would "retain that equilibrium which the constitution intended, or take a direction toward aristocracy or anarchy among the members of the government."[42] It is no coincidence, then, that Madison defended presidential removal powers in the 1789 House debate by praising responsibility over stability. In response to Smith, who had quoted Hamilton, Madison said that Smith's doctrine would "give a stability to the executive department so far as it may be described by the heads of departments" that would be "incompatible with the genius of republican government."[43] Even before Hamilton offered his financial plan, it appears that Madison was worried that Hamilton's case for stability included an executive arm comprised of men who would be formally appointed and removed by the president with the advice and consent of the Senate but actually would have little to fear from national elections and thus serve for life. As he put it, if the Smith position won out, "Every individual in the long chain of which extends from the highest to the lowest link of the Executive Magistracy, would find a security in his station which would relax his fidelity and promptitude in the discharge of his duty."[44] If Hamilton had, as Madison reported proposed lifetime tenure (that is, during good behavior) for the president and Senators at the Convention of 1787, then the removal debate would have been an opportunity for Madison to connect the dots.[45]

---

[40] Hamilton, *Federalist* No. 70, Scigliano, 447.

[41] Hamilton, *Federalist* No. 72, Scigliano, 463.

[42] *Annals of Congress*, 1st Cong., 1st sess., 514.

[43] Ibid.

[44] Ibid., 515–16.

[45] Madison, *Notes*, 136. To be sure, Hamilton later claimed in a private letter that his proposal for tenure of good behavior was given under the understanding that proposals then were not considered "evidences of a definite opinion," but rather that "with a view to free investigation, experimental suggestions might be made." He also claimed that he had told Madison later in the convention that his plan would have no greater duration than three years. See *Papers of Alexander Hamilton* 26: 148. For an assessment of these problems, see Stephen Knott, *Alexander Hamilton and the Persistence of Myth* (Lawrence: University Press of Kansas, 2002).

The Madison Problem and the Bill of Rights

What Gordon Wood labeled the James Madison problem appears in the creation of the Bill of Rights.[46] In short, Madison was against the Bill of Rights
before he was for it. On 8 June 1879, Madison proposed in the House what
would become the Bill of Rights, and then shepherded his proposal through the
House, perhaps even more successfully than he had guided the Virginia Plan
through the Convention of 1787. According to the eminent Madison scholar
Jack Rakove, Madison was "not merely one participant among many or even
primus inter pares; he was the key actor whose purposes deserve scrutiny for
that reason alone."[47] Yet, only twelve months earlier, Madison had argued in
the Virginia ratifying convention that a bill of rights was unnecessary. This
change of heart has been documented by generations of Madison scholars,
and most have concluded that Madison was motivated primarily by political
expediency, and only secondarily – if at all – by a larger concern with the protection of rights or the function and design of the Constitution. However, in a
1998 article, Stuart Leibiger argued that even if there were stages in Madison's
thinking on the bill of rights, Madison eventually embraced a bill of rights on
abstract grounds. According to Leibiger, Madison believed that a bill of rights
would improve the Constitution, and, perhaps more important, provide what
Madison had always wanted in the Constitution but could not get from the
Convention.[48]

Leibiger's reopening of Madison's embrace of the Bill of Rights has its coun-
terpart among political scientists. In his seminal study of the anti-Federalists,
Hebert Storing concluded that Madison came to the side of a bill of rights for
reasons of politics, not because he thought a bill of rights was necessary in
its own right.[49] However, in 1997, Robert Goldwin argued in a book-length
account that Madison came to see the educative potential of a declaration of
rights.[50] The difference between Storing and Goldwin is important because
it illustrates how the historical question about Madison is intertwined with

---

[46] Gordon S. Wood, *Revolutionary Characters: What Made the Founders Different* (New York:
Penguin, 2006), 141–72.

[47] Jack N. Rakove, *Original Meanings: Politics and Ideas in the Making of the Constitution*
(New York: Knopf, 1996), 331.

[48] Stuart Leibiger provides a useful literature review in "James Madison and Amendments
to the Constitution, 1787–1789: 'Parchment Barriers'," *Journal of Southern History* 59
(1993): 441–68. According to Leibiger, scholars who agree with the conventional wisdom
include Ralph Ketcham, Robert Allen Rutland, Leonard W. Levy, Bernard Schwartz, Irving Brant,
and Kenneth R. Bowling. Bowling provides the typical account in "'A Tub to the Whale': The
Founding Fathers and Adoption of the Federal Bill of Rights," *Journal of the Early Republic* 8
(1988): 223–351.

[49] Herbert Storing, "The Constitution and the Bill of Rights," in *Toward a More Perfect Union:
Writings of Herbert Storing*, ed. Joseph M. Bessette (Washington, DC: AEI Press, 1995), 125.

[50] Robert A. Goldwin, *From Parchment to Power: How James Madison Used the Bill of Rights to
Save the Constitution* (Washington, DC: AEI Press, 1997).

a theoretical question, namely Madison's understanding of the character of the relationship of the Constitution and public opinion. According to Storing, Madison rejected the anti-Federalist argument that a bill of rights could serve as a "maxim of republican government." Storing writes,

> Madison drastically limited the kind of standard-setting, maxim-describing, teaching function of bills of rights that the Anti-Federalists thought so important. In the hands of Madison and the majority of the First Congress, the Bill of Rights became what it is today: not the broad principles establishing the ends and limits of government, not 'maxims' to be learned and looked up to by generations of Americans, not statements of those first principles to which a healthy people should, according to the Virginia Declaration of Rights, frequently resort; but specific protections of traditional civil rights.[51]

Goldwin agrees in part, for he concedes that Madison's principal objective was originally negative. By shepherding the Bill of Rights through Congress, Madison "saved" the Constitution from major structural changes. But Goldwin also argues that Madison changed his mind in one important respect. For Goldwin, Madison's October 1788 letter to Jefferson reveals that Madison had "finally came to the point of persuading himself that a bill of rights had a possibly useful function in a constitution for the United States," namely that it would create a force "potentially more powerful than any majority." This force, according to Goldwin, would be the "national sentiment" that would rally around a bill of rights. In sum, even if Madison believed the Constitution itself was the more sturdy foundation for liberty and embraced the bill of rights to satisfy public opinion, it is also true for Madison that the *support* for the Constitution was necessary for the Constitution to preserve liberty.[52]

But there is a more expansive version of Goldwin's position. As Goldwin puts it, Madison "knew something about public opinion that is vital to leadership in a democracy." And because Madison preferred what was proper over the "unwise measures the public was asking for," he was the "exemplar of the truer democratic leader."[53] For Goldwin, the point is that Madison did not merely follow public opinion. Rather, he knew that the Constitution needed the "devoted allegiance of the whole people" in order to be effective, so he found a way to be attentive to it while improving it.[54] With the reference to the whole people, Goldwin intends to show that Madison found a solution for the problem of tyrannical majority in the people's love of the Constitution.[55]

[51] Storing, "Constitution and the Bill of Rights," 125.
[52] Goldwin, *From Parchment to Power*, 99–101. Also, scholars have recently recognized the importance of the constitution as a written document. See, for example, James R. Zink, "The Language of Liberty: James Wilson on America's Written Constitution," *American Political Science Review* 103: 442–55.
[53] Goldwin, *From Parchment to Power*, 101.
[54] Ibid., 102.
[55] Ibid., 99.

Importantly, Sheehan expands Goldwin's conclusion by connecting it to her central thesis that Madison believed in "the sovereignty of public opinion."[56] This does not mean that Madison endorsed a blind following of public opinion, but rather that he was also concerned with forming it. "Thus, even before the formation of the new government (and before Hamilton unveiled any part of his program and prior to Jefferson's return to the United States), Madison applied his theory of public opinion to political practice." At the heart of this theory was what Sheehan sees as Madison's "stress on the importance of civic education and the need to form republican habits of mind and heart."[57] In her most recent book, Sheehan points to the Bill of Rights as evidence that Madison "looked to the laws to serve as schoolmasters in a republic."[58] Like Goldwin, she argues that Madison recognized that institutions were insufficient in the forming of citizen character and thus believed that a republican government could and should shape the character of its citizens.

This debate among political theorists about the educative potential of the Bill of Rights returns us to the historical question whether Madison was motivated mostly by political expedience, but it also broadens the historical question by forcing us to rethink expedience. To put it differently, the question whether Madison was ever for a bill of rights is really shorthand for a series of questions. First, was there a practical political objective that Madison believed would be solved by his supporting a bill of rights? Second, to what extent did Madison think that a bill of rights was necessary and on what grounds? Third, did Madison also want his later position to be seen as consistent with his prior position, or did he want to emphasize the change?

Possible Objectives

As Table 1 summarizes, there are five possible explanations for Madison's reversal. Before we turn to consider the evidence for each of these possibilities, it is important to comment on how these explanations interact with each other. It is true that none are mutually exclusive: any two of the five can coexist together, and all five can be true. Indeed, it could be argued that even Rakove, who is typically very decisive in his conclusions on Madison, finds evidence to support each of the five positions. But it is also true that only the last two explanations require us to believe that Madison saw the Bill of Rights as an *improvement* over the original Constitution. This means that if either, or both, of the fourth and fifth explanations are true, then none of the first three

---

[56] Colleen A. Sheehan, *James Madison and the Spirit of Republican Self-Government* (New York: Cambridge University Press, 2009), 108.

[57] Ibid., 13.

[58] Colleen A. Sheehan, *The Mind of James Madison: The Legacy of Classical Republicanism* (New York: Cambridge University Press, 2015), 78.

TABLE 1. *Explanations of Madison's support for the Bill of Rights*

---

1. *The standard explanation*: Madison switched his position in order to get elected to the first Congress, and then dutifully followed through on this campaign promise.
2. *Storing's explanation*: Madison halfheartedly accepted the Bill of Rights in order to satisfy well-intentioned opponents, and thus get the Constitution ratified and/or broaden the support for the ratified Constitution.
3. *Goldwin's soft explanation*: Madison changed his mind so that he could co-opt the writing of the Bill of Rights and thus "save" the Constitution from radical structural changes proposed by hard-core anti-Federalists.
4. *Leibiger's explanation*: Madison eventually perceived that the Bill of Rights would better secure rights by way of the judiciary.
5. *Goldwin's strong explanation*: Madison came to see the Bill of Rights as a valuable educative tool that would remind people of their rights.

---

explanations are sufficient explanations for Madison's change of heart.[59] But it also means, in turn, that if any or all of the first three positions are true, then neither the fourth nor the fifth can be a wholly satisfactory explanation of Madison's change.

The first explanation is the most cynical and the most straightforward. According to this view, Madison converted to the Bill of Rights primarily in order to get elected to Congress. The timeline would seem to support this view. Madison did not publicly endorse a bill of rights until late 1788, after he began planning his campaign to be elected to the House. That Madison had to campaign to be elected to the House is itself significant. Madison lost an election to the Virginia House of Delegates in 1777 largely because he did not provide alcohol for voters.[60] Later, in March 1788 he only reluctantly left New York to return to Orange the day before the election, later complaining that he had to "mount" the "rostrum" to give a "harangue" ("for the first time in [his] life") pleading with voters to be a member of Virginia's ratification convention.[61] Because Patrick Henry outmaneuvered pro-Constitution delegates in the Assembly, Virginia chose against Madison for Senator, instituted a strict residency requirement for members of the House, and drew district

[59] This explains, perhaps, why Goldwin uses his closing chapter to emphasize the fifth explanation rather than the third. Even as his title suggests an emphasis on Madison's saving the Constitution from radical structural changes, Goldwin closes by reflecting on the importance of the Bill of Rights as "the People Article": unlike the original Constitution, the Bill of Rights proclaims solemn truths that characterize a free people. Goldwin, *From Parchment to Power*, 176–84.

[60] Much of the following can be found in the notes of the James Madison Papers as well as in Richard Labunski, *James Madison and the Struggle for the Bill of Rights* (New York: Oxford University Press, 2006). See *PJM*, 12: 57. On the 1777 election, see Labunski, 32.

[61] Madison to Eliza Trist, 25 March 1788, *PJM*, 11:5. See Labunski, *Madison and the Struggle*, 46.

lines unfavorable to Madison and other pro-ratification candidates. As a result, Madison had to campaign in the district including his home in Orange County, which was considerably more anti-Federalist than eastern counties from which Madison might have been selected.[62] Because Henry and his allies had spread the word that Madison was, as Madison reported to Washington, "dogmatically attached to the Constitution in every clause, syllable and letter," Madison decided to spread the word that he was not opposed to amendments.[63] That Madison perceived the electoral importance of a bill of rights is indicated by the fact that he also told Washington that the question of his support of amendments would be the issue "most likely to affect the election."[64] Accordingly, Madison composed four letters meant to be distributed and published. As Richard Labunski documents, Madison crafted these letters with special attention to religious groups – especially Baptists – who would have been alarmed by Henry's charges that Madison was not in favor of an amendment protecting religious liberty. After his election, Madison credited his victory to his personally appearing in the district and to his distribution of his support for a bill of rights.[65] Thus, according to this explanation, Madison's switch should be seen as part of a no-holds-barred campaign to get elected.

If the first explanation emphasizes Madison's electoral strategy, the second considers political expediency from the perspective of ratifying the Constitution. Under this explanation, Madison came to advocate a bill of rights in order to get the Constitution ratified and to maximize its support. From this perspective, Madison believed the Bill of Rights to be unnecessary and harmless, but he needed to bring over to the ratification side well-intentioned critics of the Constitution who wanted specific protections of rights. According to Burstein and Isenberg, had Madison forgotten the promises regarding a bill of rights, he "would have alienated a large and influential contingent of principled moderates."[66] Another part of this explanation is the fact that the question of the Bill of Rights had become entangled with the more dangerous question of a second convention. The problem of second convention was connected with a milder, yet almost as dangerous, question, whether states could conditionally ratify the Constitution. Madison explained the problem as early as October 1787, in a letter to Washington: even if nine states ratified quickly, there was still the question of what would happen to the states that would not ratify.[67]

---

[62] Labunski, *Madison and the Struggle*, 120–46. On Madison's learning that the critical districts had been gerrymandered, see letters of 9 and 10 November written to him as well as Madison's letter to Randolph, 23 November 1788, stating that the location of Orange in the district will be determinative. *PJM* 11: 336–41; 362–63.

[63] Madison to Washington, 14 January 1789, quoted in Labunski, *Madison and the Struggle* 159.

[64] Ibid.

[65] See Madison to Randolph, 1 March 1789, quoted in Labunski, *Madison and the Struggle*, 174.

[66] Andrew Burstein and Nancy Isenberg, *Madison and Jefferson* (New York: Random House, 2010), 197.

[67] Madison to Washington, 28 October 1787, *PJM* 10: 225.

Madison soon knew that ratification would be difficult in New York and Virginia, and he hoped that those states would realize they had to ratify once nine other states did. All this changed when moderates starting talking about "conditional" ratification, ratification with the condition that there be a set of amendments to the Constitution. From Madison's perspective, these amendments could include dangerous structural changes, but the real danger was that conditional ratification would create two different levels of ratification. If states entered with different conditions of ratification, the foundation for the Union would have been irrevocably altered.

According to this explanation, then, Madison's hostility to a bill of rights was part of his larger effort to prevent a second convention. So in order to understand the conversion, we must first understand the character of Madison's initial opposition. Through most of 1788, Madison argued that a bill of rights was unnecessary and dangerous. But it was dangerous not only because, as Hamilton argued in *Federalist* No. 84, it was impossible to list every right.[68] Rather, it was dangerous because it opened the possibility of a mandatory or conditional second convention. From Madison's perspective, the first convention only narrowly escaped disaster by stringing together compromises that were odious and even unjust. A second convention could reopen these questions and, just as important, raise others.[69]

This explanation has some weight. As was argued in Chapter 2, it is because of the threat of a second convention Madison devoted *Federalist* Nos. 37–49 to reflect on what he called the "difficulties" of the Convention of 1787. Madison called this convention a "miracle," repeating the word he ascribed to Hamilton in the *Notes*, but only after going out of his way to reveal the flaws of the document.[70] Moreover, Madison went on to compare that convention with previous foundings, noting that prior regimes governed by deliberation and consent lacked deliberative foundings. Arguably, Madison intended the comparison to reveal to moderates – Edmund Randolph, for example – that the Convention of 1787 was marred by too much deliberation (or too little actual deliberation), but the point here is the proposal for ratification conditioned on later amendments opened the specter of another founding, and foundings were moments when the extended republic would not be a remedy for factions.[71]

---

[68] Alexander Hamilton, *Federalist* No. 84, 550. James Wilson made this argument in November 1787, when he asked, "who will be bold enough to undertake to enumerate all the rights of the people?" "James Wilson and John Smilie Debate the Need for a Bill of Rights," in *The Debate on the Constitution: Federalist and Anti-Federalist Speeches, Articles, and Letters during the Struggle over Ratification*. Part One, ed. Benard Bailyn (New York: Library of America, 1993), 808.

[69] Labunski, citing Veit and Levy, writes that the states had proposed at least seventy-five distinct amendments. *Madison and the Struggle*, 199.

[70] Madison, *Notes*, 216.

[71] This was discussed in the previous chapter. See also Gary Rosen's fine yet different account in *American Compact: James Madison and the Problem of Founding* (Lawrence: University Press of Kansas, 1999).

By summer, Madison came to the position that some amendments might be necessary to convince fence sitters. But before then there was, as Goldwin puts it, a major "breakthrough": in early February, Massachusetts had voted for ratification with a list of recommended amendments. This opened the possibility of a new alternative to conditional amendments and an alternative that Madison could accept. As he put it to Randolph in early April, "recommendatory alterations" would be the "only ground" to unite friends of the Constitution.[72] In June, Madison stated in the Virginia ratifying convention that he would support amendments, and to Rufus King, Madison explained that recommended changes were an "expedient" "necessary to conciliate some individuals ... who have certain scruples."[73] But it is clear that Madison himself did not at that time count himself among those individuals: only a few days earlier, Madison had argued in the Virginia ratifying convention that a bill of rights was unnecessary, making the familiar argument that every power not delegated to the national government was reserved.[74] It is also important to note that it was not clear then that the Massachusetts model of recommended amendments would prevail over the conditional amendments proposal. In July, for example, Madison had to convince no less than Alexander Hamilton that the conditional model would be unacceptable. Hamilton seemed to have been persuaded that conditional ratification would at least eventually result in Union "in toto and for ever." Instead, Madison pointed out that "any condition whatever must viciate the ratification" and urged Hamilton to ensure that the Massachusetts model prevail in New York. Madison even made a threat, telling Hamilton that New York will not be received into Union with conditional amendments because "compacts must be reciprocal."[75] Also, by August, Governor Clinton of New York had issued a call for a second convention, and Madison knew that the Virginia Assembly would be "warm" to Clinton's proposal (on 30 October the Virginia Assembly formally endorsed the proposal).[76] To make matters worse, North Carolina had surprised Madison by moving toward outright rejection or conditional ratification, and opponents in Pennsylvania had organized and assembled in a second, unofficial state "convention."[77] Given this steep decline in the prospects for ratification, Madison came to accept the

---

[72] Madison to Randolph, 10 April 1788, *PJM* 11: 18–19. Paul Finkelman emphasizes Madison's meeting with the Baptist minister, John Leland, who according to Finkelman would have been an example of a good man who was sincerely wanted a specific protection of religious liberty. Finkelman, "A Reluctant Paternity," 323–24.

[73] Madison to Rufus King, 22 June 1788, *PJM* 11: 167.

[74] Madison said, "There is not a shadow of right in the general government to intermeddle with religion." Speech on 12 June 1788, Virginia ratification debates, *PJM* 11: 130.

[75] Madison to Hamilton, 20 July 1788, *PJM*, 11: 189

[76] Labunski, *Madison and the Struggle*, 131.

[77] Madison to Jefferson, 10 August 1788, *PJM* 11: 225–27; Madison to Jefferson, 23 August 1788, *PJM* 11: 238–40; and Madison to Washington, 23 August 1788, *PJM* 11: 240–43. See also Pauline Maier, *Ratification: The People Debate the Constitution, 1787–1788* (New York: Simon & Schuster, 2010), 428–29.

Bill of Rights even before he positioned himself in October for his campaign. Thus, according to this explanation, Madison changed his mind in order to secure ratification, especially in New York and North Carolina.

The conclusion, then, that Madison was primarily motivated by political expedience rests on a combination of these first two explanations.[78] It can be summarized in the following way. Once Madison realized that the promise of later amendments was the only way to sway some states from the conditional amendment path, Madison granted that some amendments could be added. Accordingly, when he realized that his own selection to the House was not guaranteed, he spread the word that he was not opposed to amendments.

The third explanation, that Madison changed his mind in order to limit structural changes to the Constitution, moves us closer to an abstract defense of a bill of rights but can still be classified with the political expedience accounts. Under this explanation, Madison perceived that anti-Federalists would use the momentum for a bill of rights to make other alterations in the main body of the Constitution. Specifically, even as Madison and pro-Constitution forces successfully pulled moderates over to the side of recommended amendments instead of conditional amendments, they nevertheless put off the more inflammatory question of whether the amendments would renegotiate the powers between the state and national governments. Virginia, for example, ratified the Constitution but recommended twenty such amendments, including restrictions on Congress's power to lay direct taxes, a supermajority in the Senate for commercial treaties, and a prohibition of a standing army.[79] Accordingly, and as Goldwin puts it, Madison "saved" the Constitution from anti-Federalists by co-opting the amendment process early with the argument that the amendments should first concentrate on individual liberties rather than on the more divisive questions of power between the national government and the states.[80] Or, as Madison himself put it after the fact, it was best to have the amendments proposed and shaped by the "friends" of the Constitution rather than by its "enemies."[81]

If the first three explanations are alike in that each concludes that Madison changed his mind for reasons of political expedience, the next two argue that Madison eventually converted to a bill of rights on principled grounds. According to the fourth account, Madison came to believe that a bill of rights would better secure liberty. This explanation can take several forms. In its strongest and most interesting form, this account suggests that Madison foresaw that a list of rights could empower the judiciary and thus serve as the national check on the states that he had always wanted. This account thus borrows on what is commonly accepted about Madison's goals for the

[78] Finkelman is representative of this argument. See "A Reluctant Paternity."
[79] Labunski, *Madison and the Struggle*, 114.
[80] Goldwin, *From Parchment to Power*, chs. 6 and 7.
[81] Madison to Richard Peters, 19 August 1789, *PJM* 12: 346–48.

constitutional convention. Specifically, Madison believed that the states were incapable of protecting individual rights against powerful majorities within the states, and so his plan included a congressional veto over state laws "in all cases whatsoever."[82] So, according to this explanation, Madison perceived that the Bill of Rights could eventually serve as a check on majorities within the states that were prone to unjust legislation. In support of this explanation, and what is often not appreciated enough, is that Madison still believed that the Constitution was flawed after the convention, largely because it lacked this provision. In his famous post-Convention letter to Jefferson, for example, Madison devoted several pages to explaining why the negative over state laws was necessary even though he knew that Jefferson was not so enthusiastic about Madison's pet proposal.[83] Michael Zuckert has argued that Madison's constitutional plan makes little sense without this negative and that much of the logic of *Federalist* No. 10 relies on the existence of the negative.[84]

Strangely, Jefferson's reluctance might have provided a step in Madison's thinking. In his critique of Madison's proposed negative, Jefferson argued that Madison's "patch" was too big for the "hole," but he suggested that the power would be better in the hands of the judiciary, noting that "An appeal to a federal court sets all to rights."[85] Leibiger thus concludes that Madison came to see that "judicial review would make a federal bill of rights useful after unsound laws, even those backed by a majority, had gone into operation."[86] As Rakove points out, Madison's 8 June speech includes "one notable point he had not endorsed previously," namely that a bill of rights would enable federal judges to become guardians of rights.[87] Accordingly, Madison's original

[82] Madison, "Vices of the Political System," *Madison Writings*, 75–76; Madison to Jefferson, 19 March 1787 in *Madison Writings*, 64; and "Virginia Plan," *Madison Writings*, 89–90.

[83] Madison to Jefferson, 24 October 1787, *Madison Writings*, 149–52.

[84] Michael Zuckert, "Judicial Review and the Incomplete Constitution: A Madisonian Perspective on the Supreme Court and the Idea of Constitutionalism," in *The Supreme Court and the Idea of Constitutionalism*, ed. Steven Kautz, Arthur Melzer, Jerry Weinberger, and M. Richard Zinman, 33–70 (Philadelphia: University of Pennsylvania Press, 2009).

[85] Jefferson to Madison, 20 June 1787, *PJM*: 10, 63–66. It is important to remember that even if Madison supported judicial review in this sense, it does not mean he believed an appeal to the courts would be the appropriate remedy in separation of powers conflicts. There has been a renaissance of the view that Madison preferred "coordinate review" or "departmentalism" to the modern doctrine of judicial review. Consider Madison's Observations on Jefferson's 1783 Constitution: "No provision is made for the case of a disagreement in expounding them; and as the Courts are generally the last in making their decision, it results to them, by refusing or not refusing to execute a law, to stamp it with its final character. This makes the Judiciary Dept. paramount in fact to the Legislature, which was never intended, and can never be proper." Madison, "Observations on the 'Draught of a Constitution for Virginia," October 1788, in *Madison Writings*, 417. On departmentalism, see George Thomas, *The Madisonian Constitution* (Baltimore: The Johns Hopkins University Press, 2008).

[86] Leibiger, "James Madison and Amendments to the Constitution," 463.

[87] Rakove, *Original Meanings*, 335.

proposed amendments included the provision, "No State shall violate the equal rights of conscience, or the freedom of the press, or the trial by jury in criminal cases."[88] This provision was rejected by the Senate, but had Madison had his way, the Bill of Rights would have applied to the states from the very beginning. As Paul Finkelman puts it, Madison's preferred Bill of Rights "would have radically altered the federal structure of the new government."[89]

Like the fourth explanation, the fifth assumes that Madison believed that the Constitution would be improved by a bill of rights. But, unlike the fourth account, this explanation takes a step toward the Madison of the 1790s because it asserts that Madison conversion on the Bill of Rights can be understood as a conversion on the question of parchment declarations. Specifically, adherents of this view argue that Madison came to believe that bills of rights might help secure liberty by being educative documents. As has been noted previously, the major piece of evidence for this is Madison's October 1788 letter to Jefferson. In that letter, which marks Madison's turn to active support for a bill of rights in late 1788, Madison attempted to clarify his position to Jefferson concerning bills of rights. After offering several reasons why he did not view the question of a bill of rights "in important light," Madison went on to enumerate two ways a bill of rights might be of some use. One reason is parchment barriers might have some potency after all:

> The political truths declared in that solemn manner acquire by degrees the character of fundamental maxims of free Government, and as they become incorporated with the national sentiment, counteract the impulses of interest and passion.[90]

In this remarkable statement, Madison implies both that declarations can shape public opinion and that they can mitigate the causes of faction, passion, and interest. On this note, it is worth mentioning that Madison labels passion and interest as the causes of faction in the initial definition of faction in *Federalist* No. 10, but then a few paragraphs later includes opinion as a cause.[91] Read in light of his statement in No. 49 that the government should control and regulate the passions, this suggests that Madison could believe in the sovereignty of public opinion even as he believed that government should shape it.[92] Put in terms of the scholarly "Madison problem," this passage seems to connect Publius-Madison with Sheehan's Madison of the early 1790s. For Goldwin, this statement suggests a "major development in Madison's thought" in that it reveals that national sentiment, especially when bound together by patriotic love of the Constitution, could be more powerful than a tyrannical majority.

[88] Madison's Proposed Amendments, 8 June 1789. Labunski lists these in an appendix, 265–68.
[89] Paul Finkelman, "James Madison and the Bill of Rights: A Reluctant Paternity," *Supreme Court Review* 9 (1990): 304.
[90] Madison to Jefferson, 17 October 1788, *Madison Writings*, 418–23.
[91] Madison, *Federalist* No. 10, Scigliano, 54–55.
[92] Ibid., 325. On the 1790s Madison, see "Charters," *National Gazette*, 19 January 1792, in *PJM* 14: 191–92. See Sheehan, chapters 5–7.

By becoming *the* Bill of Rights, a bill of rights could create the "whole people," and by definition, the whole people would never be a faction.[93]

So which explanation is best? As noted earlier, it is possible that all the explanations are true. Better yet, it is possible that Madison believed each of them at different stages. Perhaps the most sensible explanation, then, is that Madison made the initial concession in order to accommodate moderates, and then found an argument that deepened his conversion. This is precisely what Liebiger and Goldwin would argue. Under their view, Madison arrived at a new position as his thinking matured. As Leibiger puts it, "it was a period of mutual learning, and James Madison's experience illustrates this process."[94] So, for Leibiger, the various explanations are better understood in terms of chronological stages. Madison began opposed to any amendments, because he feared a second convention. But as the logic changed from conditional amendments to recommended amendments, and then to having a ratified constitution, Madison returned his thinking to the problem of securing liberty. Accordingly, he looked for ways to improve the Constitution and formulated an abstract defense of bills of rights. Perhaps Madison looked for a new abstract principle because he had a new political problem.

A candidate, then, for the best summary of Madison's position comes from Madison's own outline of his 8 June speech in the House. There he wrote "Bill of Rights – useful – not essential."[95] But, as we have seen, the problem with this characterization is that it might not capture Madison's understanding of the Bill of Rights he actually got. That is, if Leibiger is right that the usefulness of a bill of rights would be to protect liberty in the states, then that is not what happened, not until the twentieth century at least. Moreover, this summary also reveals a tension within the logic of the fourth position. If it is true, as Zuckert has argued, that Madison believed the negative was essential, then why would Liebiger's more muscular Bill of Rights only qualify as useful but not essential? Perhaps we can better assess Madison's position when we ask the question in a slightly different way. Instead of asking whether Madison believed a bill of rights was necessary or even useful, it might be more helpful to ask if Madison believed a bill of rights would improve the Constitution.

Did the Bill of Rights Improve the Constitution?

As we have seen, Madison wrote Jefferson that a bill of rights might function as educative text. To my knowledge, there are only two other occasions where Madison suggested that a bill of rights could improve the Constitution. One is a November letter to George Tuberville, written three days after Virginia endorsed Clinton's call for a new convention and on the same day Madison wrote to

---

[93] Goldwin, *From Parchment to Power*, 71 and 99–102.
[94] Leibiger, "James Madison and Amendments to the Constitution," 443.
[95] As quoted in Labunski, *Madison and the Struggle*, 192.

Randolph declaring his intent to be considered for the House. Tuberville had told Madison that he saw "no impropriety" in New York's proposal.[96] In response, Madison claimed that even he had always thought there were some changes that he wished had been in the Constitution itself, that is, that there were amendments he wished had been "issued from the place in which it was formed." He explained that the question with these amendments was how to do it: because the first Convention revealed that a second convention would open too many questions and likely end in disaster, the answer was to go through Congress.[97] Another is Madison's 8 June 1789 speech in Congress. In it Madison argued that Americans had "something to gain" from a bill of rights. Specifically, abuses by government needed to be "guarded against in a more secure manner."[98] Because the real danger is not the government but rather the majority itself, a bill of rights could be useful as a check on majority opinion. Such a bill of rights might "impress some degree of respect for them, to establish the public opinion in their favor, and rouse the attention of their whole community."[99] If the letter to Tuberville supports the Leibiger account that Madison perceived the Bill of Rights as a way to accomplish what he could in the Convention itself, the speech in Congress would seem to corroborate the letter to Jefferson and support Goldwin's account that Madison believed a bill of rights would educate the people.

But these are the exceptions. By contrast, the vast majority of the more private post-conversion statements reveal deep ambivalence about the usefulness of a bill of rights. At a minimum, the majority of Madison's statements on the Bill of Rights do not confirm Leibiger's conclusion, that, "overall," "Madison spent more time discussing the abstract benefits of a federal bill of rights than he did elaborating on the political gains."[100] Rather, as the following examples show, it seems to be the case that Madison mostly talked about the necessity of conciliating the opponents to the Constitution, not how the Bill of Rights improved the Constitution. In a letter to the important moderate Edmund Pendleton, written only a few days after his letter to Jefferson extolling the benefits of maxims of republican government, Madison dropped his positive good account when he explained his own position. Instead, he argued a bill of rights would prevent disaster and would at the same time "do no harm."[101] Later in March, when Madison was engaged in the work of Congress, Madison wrote Jefferson that "some conciliatory sacrifices" would "extinguish the opposition."[102] Finally, there is the campaign promise itself, written in the letter to the Baptist minister George Eve. In it Madison explained that "circumstances had changed" such that amendments, "if pursued with a

[96] Ibid., 126.
[97] Madison to Tuberville, 2 November 1788, *PJM*, 11: 332–33.
[98] Madison, speech in Congress, 8 June 1789, *PJM*, 12: 199.
[99] Ibid., 12:204–05.
[100] Leibiger, "James Madison and Amendments to the Constitution," 462.
[101] Madison to Pendleton, 20 October 1788, *PJM* 11: 307.
[102] Madison to Jefferson, 29 March 1789, *PJM* 12: 38.

proper moderation," would serve "the double purpose of satisfying well mean-ing opponents, and of providing additional guards in favour of liberty." While Madison did suggest that a bill of rights would do some "additional" good, he did not say that he now believed these additional guards were necessary (or even effective), and, more important, the additional guards he had in mind did not make it into the final set of amendments.[103] It is telling that Madison did not talk about these guards in terms of being character forming. A better char-acterization of these post-conversion letters is that Madison's emphasis is on the change of political circumstances, not the improvement of the Constitution and not on the educative power of declarations.

Madison's most elaborate private summary of his position supports this point. It took the form of an August 1789 letter to Richard Peters.[104] Peters had sent Madison a long poem, using a cooking metaphor that there were too many cooks in the kitchen thus spoiling the "soup" of amendments.[105] In response, Madison extended the cooking metaphor from kitchen to the table, explaining that Congress was still in the "nauseous" project of amendments. He also changed the metaphor, saying that they were in "so deep" "that right or wrong some thing must be done." He then offered seven reasons for his turn to supporting a bill of rights.

1. Even though declarations on paper are less necessary than in other forms of government, they are useful in some degree.
2. Promises were made to those who had once insisted on conditional amendments, and these promises should be kept by honest men.
3. These promises were made so that friends of the Constitution would be elected instead of enemies of the Constitution.
4. If he and other friends of the Constitution had not proposed amend-ments, "the other side" would have proposed them within three days.
5. Amendments will "kill the opposition everywhere" and enable the government to proceed to important national measures that would otherwise fail.
6. If amendments are not added, the opposition will use the opportunity to call for a second convention.
7. Amendments are necessary to bring North Carolina into the union.

What is first apparent is that Madison described the work as a "nauseous" project, and he described it in terms of necessity rather than opportunity (right

---

[103] It is important to point that what Madison had in mind in terms of structural amendments did not happen, at least not in the Bill of Rights: "I think it will be proper also to provide expressly in the Constitution, for the periodical increase of the number of Representatives until the amount shall be entirely satisfactory; and to put the judiciary department into such a form as will render vexatious appeals possible." Madison to George Eve, 2 January 1789, *Madison Writings*, 427–29.

[104] Madison to Richard Peters, 19 August 1789, *PJM*, 12:346–48.

[105] On Peters's letter to Madison, see Labunski, *Madison and the Struggle*, 232.

or wrong, something *must* be done). But what stands out the most from this letter is that six of the seven reasons are reasons of political expedience. Only the first suggests that a bill of rights would improve the Constitution, yet, on closer inspection, even this is put rather weakly by Madison.

> 1. because a constitutional provision in favr. of essential rights is a thing not improper in itself and was always viewed in that light by myself. It may be less necessary in a republic, than a Monarchy, & in a fedl. Govt. than the former, but it is in some degree rational in every Govt., since in every Govt. power may oppress, and declarations on paper, tho' not an effectual restraint, are not without some influence.

This is at best a limited endorsement of a positive defense of a bill of rights. It begins with an outright lie, Madison's claim that he had always thought such a bill "not improper." It then makes a concession, that bills of rights "are not without some influence," but then limits that concession's applicability to republics. Throughout, Madison's tone is clearly dismissive. Even if they have some influence, bills of rights are still "declarations on paper" and "not an effectual restraint" alone. Moreover, as Storing noted and Goldwin conceded, his endorsements are circumscribed ("in some degree rational") and cast in double negatives ("not without some influence").[106] When the amendments were about to be approved by the House, Madison wrote to allies that the whole affair had been "extremely difficult and fatiguing" and "exceedingly wearisome."[107] He did not celebrate or say that the Constitution had been improved.[108]

Madison on the Constitution and Public Opinion

On one of the very days that Madison gave a speech in Congress on behalf of the Bill of Rights, his cousin the Reverend James Madison sent Madison a letter that included the quotation heading this chapter. Madison's cousin was both president of William and Mary and Episcopalian Bishop for Virginia. In his view, the Constitution was imperfect and needed to be fixed, in part because of what he believed to be problems in separation of powers.[109] Moreover, he

---

[106] Goldwin, *From Parchment to Power*, 149.

[107] Madison to Pendleton, 21 August 1788, and Madison to Randolph, *PJM*, 12: 348.

[108] To be fair, Goldwin suggests that the letter to Peters should not be taken as indicative of Madison's true position because Peters was a key state legislator in Virginia whose support would be needed for ratification of the Bill of Rights. Accordingly, Goldwin writes that Madison gave Peters "only such reasoning as Peters could use with other legislators and with constituents." In this, Goldwin concludes that Madison's letter to Peters was like Madison's letter to Jefferson in that each letter was "well suited to the recipient." But the same could be said of Madison's June 8 speech in the House; from one study of the period, we know that "the House galleries were packed with people." See Goldwin, *From Parchment to Power*, 153. For the description of the debate galleries, see Labunski, *Madison and the Struggle*, 187.

[109] In addition to the letter cited at the beginning of the chapter, see also Reverend James Madison to James Madison, 1 October 1787, *PJM*, 10: 185.

advised Madison that it was better to fix errors sooner than later because constitutional error can become fixed in the public mind. There is no record of a response by Madison, but, as will be discussed in Chapter 6, Madison repeated the Bishop's concern in the context of presidential selection. As was frequently the case with other correspondents, Madison let the Bishop's advice pass without comment.

But the congressional debates over the removal power and the Bill of Rights forced Madison to confront explicitly the problem of constitutional imperfection. The removal power debate is especially helpful with respect to understanding Madison and separation of powers. One result of this discussion is that it opens a line of inquiry regarding the Senate. It seems that Madison distrusted the Senate because he believed that it was not well constructed. Further, as David Brian Robertson's study of policy agency in the Convention of 1787 shows, the "political compromises" in 1787 "about 'who governs' tethered different institutions to different constituencies."[110] Madison believed that Senate was connected to the small states and would thus offer a home to those factions that had forever plagued small republics. At the same time, giving the Senate a veto over presidential removals would undermine the very guarantee that responsibility would bring to execution.

Madison's efforts in 1789 help clarify his understanding of executive power. Madison's argument was not merely about gathering executive powers under the broad contours of the vesting clause of Article II; it was also an attempt to find a way to determine what it means to say that a power was executive by nature. In this, there is the possibility that his position in 1789 can be accommodated with his 1793 criticism of Hamilton's defense of the Neutrality Proclamation. As Helvidius, Madison wrote that the "question of war or peace" was "confided" to the legislative department by the Constitution because the "laurels" of war inevitably find their way to "encircle" the "executive brow."[111] In both 1789 and 1793, perhaps, Madison was trying to connect the governmental function with his understanding of the proper blend of constitutional motive. This attention to *motive*, cast partly in terms of constituency, reveals that Madison anticipated and perhaps even brought about the connection between public opinion and presidential leadership that would be later made by Jefferson and Jackson. In this, Madison's case for presidential removal powers would seem to support Robertson's application of his argument about the institutions being associated with particular constituencies: "[T]he president, as agent of a national electorate, best represented Madison's original vision."[112] Likewise, Madison's speeches would seem to support the Banning and Sheehan argument that sees in Madison's partisan efforts in the 1790s were part of a consistent thread to, rather than a break from, Madison's attempts in the

[110] Robertson, *Constitution and America's Destiny*, 162.
[111] Madison, Helvidius, No. 4, *PJM* 15:108.
[112] Robertson, *Constitution and America's Destiny*, 162.

1780s to forge a constitutional union. The link would be that Madison's case for responsibility reveals a vibrant and necessary role for public opinion in executing the laws.

But Madison's turn to the Bill of Rights complicates this picture, and a lot depends on whether Madison believed the Bill of Rights improved the Constitution. If Goldwin and Sheehan are correct to conclude that Madison did believe in the utility of maxims of republican government, then there would be less distance between the Madisons of the 1780s and the 1790s. At the most basic level, we would have to acknowledge the similarity between Madison and the best of the anti-Federalists. In January 1788, Federal Farmer was the first to connect the maxims of republic government argument with the case for a bill of rights. Federal Farmer conceded that declarations do not "change the nature of things, or create new truths," but at the same time he argued that they "at least establish in the minds of the people truths and principles which they might never otherwise have thought of, or soon forgot." Moreover, because a truth is not useful unless it exists in the "minds of the people," a nation should take measures to ensure that its "leading principles" are recognized by the people. This is to say that rights can never be secure by a careful arrangement of powers alone; rather rights need to be understood and revered by the people.

> Men, in some countries do not remain free, merely because they are entitled to natural and unalienable rights; men in all countries are entitled to them, not because their ancestors once got together and enumerated them on paper, but because, by repeated negotiations and declarations, all parties are brought to realize them, and of course to believe them to be sacred.

Madison's October 1788 letter to Jefferson, then, suggests that even if Madison did not agree completely with Federal Farmer's concern for the character of the citizenry and his preference for the small republic, it is possible that Madison was not wholly unpersuaded about the necessity for cultivating a commonality of interests and passions among the citizens.[113] Under this view, Madison used the political opportunity to give the Constitution what Madison knew it lacked, namely an article outlining the character of a free people. In this, Rakove similarly points out that Madison went beyond the argument of Federal Farmer in that Madison believed the people needed to be reminded of rights in order for "republican citizens to govern themselves – to resist the impulses of interest and passions that were the roots of factious behavior."[114] That is, under this view, Madison thought that the structure of the Constitution was insufficient because the Constitution was inattentive to the republican habits and beliefs that make republican government possible.

---

[113] See Federal Farmer, No. 16, 20 Jan. 1788, in Herbert J. Storing, ed., *The Anti-Federalist: Writings by the Opponents of the Constitution* (Chicago: University of Chicago Press, 1981), 81.
[114] Rakove, *Original Meanings*, 336.

Madison's support for the Bill of Rights would seem to bring Madison closer to Jefferson than scholars have recognized. This is clearer when we consider Madison's second positive reason for a bill of rights. Even though a tyrannical majority is the real danger in republican government, there "may be occasions" during which "the evil may spring" from the "usurped acts of the Government" rather than the majority itself. On those occasions, "a bill of rights will be a good ground for an appeal to the sense of the community." Madison even went so far as to concede that a bill of rights would protect against "a succession of artful and ambitious rulers" who would try to subvert liberty through "gradual & well-timed advances."[115] Taken together, these two reasons were music to Jefferson's ears. Jefferson spent most of his life trying to institutionalize a routine recurrence to declarations of principle. For Jefferson, institutional design would always be incomplete until it addressed the problem of the people's capacity to recognize and resist tyranny. That is, rather than being eternally optimistic about the progress in the abilities of the majority, Jefferson in fact often worried about the decline in the people's understanding of their rights and in their willingness to forsake interest in order to pursue them. In this, Jefferson focused on a problem in constitutional government identified by Locke: although reason should lead the people to design and consent to a constitution, most seldom notice the call of reason and remain in their current state. Jefferson spent much of his life attempting to solve this problem by institutionalizing moments of refounding. Although these moments would be guided by declarations of principle, they would be revolutionary.[116]

The analysis here, however, has argued against this interpretation and instead has sided with Storing and others who conclude that Madison was never for a bill of rights. One possible consequence of this conclusion is offered by the natural law approach of Hadley Arkes.[117] Under his view, the Constitution matters less in what it says than in the principles on which it rests. This is to say that any particular provision of the Constitution must be understood with reference to the larger aim of respect for liberty and equality. For Arkes, this is especially true with regard to the Bill of Rights, which he sees as a mistake. As he puts

[115] Madison to Jefferson, 17 October 1788, *Madison Writings*, 418–23.

[116] See, for example, Jefferson's First Inaugural, where Jefferson recommends that the principles he stated in the inaugural should be the "creed of our political faith, the text of civic instruction." Merril Peterson, ed., *Thomas Jefferson: Writings* (New York: Library of America, 1984), 495. I explore Jefferson's concern with declarations of principle in *Thomas Jefferson and Executive Power* (New York: Cambridge University Press, 2007), chapters 4, 8, and 9. I make the case for Jefferson's view of decline in two book chapters: "From 'floating ardor' to the 'union of sentiment': Jefferson on the Relationship between Public Opinion and the Executive," in Francis Cogliano, ed., *A Companion to Thomas Jefferson* (London: Wiley-Blackwell), 184–98; and "Nature and Nature's God in Jefferson's *Notes on the State of Virginia*," in Christopher Nadon, ed., *Enlightenment and Secularism: Essays on the Mobilization of Reason* (Lanham, MD: Lexington Books), 231–40.

[117] Hadley Arkes, *Beyond the Constitution* (Princeton, NJ: Princeton University Press, 1992), 58–80.

it, James Wilson's famous argument that "everything not given is reserved" would be more protective of human liberty and dignity than any particular written guarantee. Rakove suggests a similar criticism: "By implying that traditional rights and liberties would be rendered insecure if they went undeclared, Anti-Federalists in effect suggested that the existence of these rights depended upon their positive expression."[118]

It is important to note, however, that Madison never really took this path, even though it was pointed out by Wilson. Instead, Madison most frequently said that a bill of rights was unnecessary because the Constitution already secured liberty. This means that securing liberty is a fundamentally a question of institutional design. This in turns means that character matters, but it matters most in terms of the officeholder. Yet even this character formation is recast in terms of "will" formation. As Madison wrote in the *Federalist*, this will guided is not by the virtues but rather by incentives, with the largest being connected to duration and eligibility for reelection. This brings us back to the nearly simultaneous debate about presidential removal powers, where Madison solved a constitutional riddle by giving an account of the function of the officeholder, and that function depended both on the job duties and on the constituency of the officeholder in question. When cast as electoral accountability to the whole nation, public opinion is important. But the example of the Bill of Rights also qualifies Madison's turn to public opinion. Even though the opportunity was there, Madison did not throw himself upon the argument that public opinion is everything.

There is another lingering question about Madison and public opinion in the context of the Bill of Rights. If Madison did not believe that bills of rights would be useful as "maxims" of republican conduct, why did he make that argument to Jefferson? While I know of no such account, the obvious extension of the political expediency argument would be that Madison wanted a plausible theoretical explanation for his switch because he believed that the argument from political expediency alone would not sit well with Orange voters in late 1788. But this only raises another problem: if Madison made this argument only to Jefferson, who was in France at the time, it would not have made its way into public discussion in time to help Madison's electoral chances. This suggests that the political expedience argument leaves unanswered yet another question. If Madison was mostly concerned with being elected, why did he not avail himself of the argument he made to Jefferson? That is, if Madison by late 1788 had come to believe that the Bill of Rights improved the Constitution, why did he write that letter to *only* Jefferson? Why not make it more public?

One possibility is that Madison was still in the process of changing his mind about the role of public opinion in constitutional politics and had not yet come to the conclusion that molding and shaping opinion was an important way to maintain republican government. Indeed, in his famous argument

---

[118] Rakove, *Original Meanings*, 324.

for the extended republic, he had powerfully argued that such attempts to form a particular character were based on the faulty assumption that it was possible to teach people to have particular passions. Because of the passion of self-love, these kinds of character formation enterprises had failed again and again over the course of history, at least in the context of republics. But it is undeniable that he embraced this very kind of opinion-shaping project, at least as a temporary expedient, when he helped create and legitimate the Democratic-Republican Party.

Another answer to this new question is that the letter should be read as part of the larger dialogue between Jefferson and Madison.[119] This dialogue includes their exchange over Madison's proposed changes to the Articles and what would become the Virginia Plan, as well as Jefferson's critique of the Constitution, and culminates in their exchange over Jefferson's "earth belongs to the living" letter. The next chapter revisits the exchange between Madison and Jefferson in the context of the early 1790s and Madison's turn to political parties.

[119] Finkelman argues that Jefferson's influence is unlikely. He points out that Madison suggested that he might support a bill of rights during the Virginia ratification convention, before he received Jefferson's crucial letter of 20 December 1787, the one insisting on a bill of rights. So, for Finkelman, it is incorrect to say that Jefferson "persuaded" Madison. Rather, he believes that Madison embraced the Bill of Rights for reasons of political expediency. Finkelman, "A Reluctant Paternity," 329.

5

The Turn to Public Opinion

"How devoutly it is to be wished, then, that the public opinion of the United States should be enlightened; that it should attach itself to their governments as delineated in the great charters, derived not from the usurped power of kings, but from the legitimate authority of the people; and that it should guarantee, with a holy zeal, these political scriptures from every attempt to add to or diminish from them."

– James Madison[1]

Even if Madison failed in giving the United States the constitution he thought best, he succeeded in terms of getting a better constitution proposed, ratified, inaugurated, and then safely amended. This was a tremendous accomplishment, and it required that Madison refuse to compromise on the essential features of what a constitution is, but it also required that he compromise on others that were essential to getting any constitution at all. This forced him to encounter not only the enduring and necessary imperfection of any constitution but also the unnecessary and contingent imperfections of the constitution that he got. During his first year in Congress, Madison was able to dominate the politics that emerged at the intersection of these two kinds of imperfections, at least with respect to the debate on the removal power and the Bill of Rights. But he was not so successful in the succeeding debates, and he lost on key policy questions such as the assumption of war debts, the national bank, and U.S. neutrality in relations with France and England.

Rather than accepting these losses as the necessary consequence of deliberation, or as settled by the compromise and consensus required to survive the separation of powers, Madison instead chose the extra-constitutional path of organized opposition. This choice was not inevitable, and it was perhaps the most critical event of the decade. It was a choice that probably cannot be

[1] Madison, "Charters," 19 January 1792, *Madison Writings*, 503–04.

understood without placing it in the context of Thomas Jefferson, whose return from France somehow happened at about the same moment of Madison's turn to parties. Together, the two founded what would become the most dominant political party, if only temporarily so, in American political history. More importantly, the two laid a foundation for partisanship by making the case for the legitimacy of public opinion. This move was no less important than the use of partisan organization in its implied transformation of the constitutional order, but it is relatively understudied in the scholarship of the political thought of the early republic.

Colleen Sheehan has done the most work in laying out the theoretical implications of Madison's turn in the early 1790s. In her argument, Madison believed that republican government presupposed that public opinion was sovereign, but it also required that government be designed in way that elevates and guides this public opinion. What is missing in her account is a clear linkage between Madison's political thought and his political actions. This point is not intended as a criticism. Rather, it is meant to acknowledge that her interest and research is aimed at uncovering Madison as a political philosopher. What is sometimes lacking, in my view, is a clear account of the extent to which her Madison differs from the Madison that scholars have constructed from the *Federalist Papers*. Indeed, Sheehan at times appears to read Madison backward, placing her 1790s Madison into the 1780s, and into Madison's efforts to write and then ratify the Constitution. As a result, it is sometimes difficult to square her Madison with scholarly accounts that emphasize Madison's well-known fear of unchecked majorities.[2] Part of the problem is that Sheehan wants to distinguish her Madison from Jefferson and therefore relies on the well-worn features of Madisonian constitutionalism that would seem to run counter to her analysis of Madison in the 1790s.

This chapter attempts to build on Sheehan's important work to provide a fuller picture of Madison's turn to the defense of public opinion as sovereign in republican government.[3] In particular, it prepares the way for the next chapter, which asks whether Madison's participation in the Revolution of 1800 should be seen as something like the appeal to the public as a solution to the problem of constitutional imperfection. Accordingly, this chapter examines Madison's turn to public opinion and to parties by placing that turn within the continuing story of Madison's alliance with Jefferson. This is necessary

[2] Sheehan's work will be discussed later in the chapter, but generally, see Colleen A. Sheehan, *James Madison and the Spirit of Republican Self-Government* (New York: Cambridge University Press, 2009), and Colleen A. Sheehan, *The Mind of James Madison: The Legacy of Classical Republicanism* (New York: Cambridge University Press, 2015).
[3] Others have emphasized Madison's efforts to shape public opinion. Bradley Kent Carter and Joseph F. Kobylka, for example, point to these efforts to characterize Madisonian deliberation as a "dialogic community," but I find Sheehan's account to be the most clarifying. Bradley Kent Carter and Joseph F. Kobylcka, "The Dialogic Community: Education, Leadership, and Participation in Madison's Political Thought," *The Review of Politics* 52 (1990): 32–63.

because, throughout this period, Jefferson continued to be on Madison's mind. At the very moment Madison wrote his letter to Jefferson explaining his conversion on the Bill of Rights, Madison was revisiting Jefferson's 1783 proposed Constitution for Virginia. And just as the debate over the assumption of war debts was escalating, Madison found himself responding to Jefferson's argument that the earth belongs to the living. By the time he was finished writing his defense of public opinion in his partisan essays in the *National Gazette*, he had qualified his own criticism of Jefferson's proposal and was willing to endorse at least a limited version of it.

Jefferson's 1783 Constitution

The preceding chapter discussed Madison's October 1788 letter to Jefferson. That letter is important because it includes Madison's clearest endorsement of the Bill of Rights as an educative text. But the unusual clarity of the argument in that letter raises another question. Why did Madison refrain making that argument as clear in public? Did Madison modify his position in order to satisfy Jefferson in some way? That is, does the letter say more about Madison and Jefferson than it does about Madison and the Bill of Rights? It is perhaps relevant that Madison had just spent a good deal of time thinking about Jefferson. At the urging of another friend in Kentucky, this one a former roommate in Congress, Madison revisited Jefferson's 1783 proposed constitution for Virginia to offer recommendations for constitution-makers in Kentucky. The former roommate was John Brown, who in a May 1788 letter asked Madison to write a plan of government to help guide members of a constitutional convention in Kentucky.[4] Madison responded that he would have complied with Brown's request had he received it ten days earlier (saying "nothing would give me more pleasure"), but he could not because he was busy preparing for business in Richmond (the Virginia ratification convention).[5] In August, Brown repeated his request and added another, asking Madison to send "some remarks upon Jefferson's plan of Govt."[6] Madison replied in September, explaining that he was in no hurry to send his comments because he assumed that the Kentucky convention had already met, but he wrote again in October, noting that he had just heard that the Kentucky convention had not yet met and would do so in November. He said he would "forward" his remarks on Jefferson's plan "by the next mail," but he did not sketch his own.[7]

As was discussed in Chapter 2, Madison had done something similar in 1785, for his old college friend Caleb Wallace. This time, however, Madison

4 John Brown to James Madison, 12 May 1788, *PJM*, 11: 42.
5 Madison to John Brown, 27 May 1788, *PJM*, 11: 60.
6 John Brown to James Madison, 26 August 1788, *PJM*, 11: 243.
7 Madison to John Brown, 26 September 1788, and Madison to John Brown, 12 October 1788, *PJM*, 11: 266 and 280.

did not make general suggestions but rather limited his comments to specific criticisms of Jefferson's proposed constitution for Virginia. With the letter to Wallace and *Federalist* No. 49, these 1788 observations were one of the three occasions when Madison offered a commentary on Jefferson's proposed constitution. Jefferson's 1783 constitution was possibly attracting a readership because Jefferson had attached it to his *Notes on the State of Virginia*. Further, as Dustin Gish and Daniel Klinghard have explained, Jefferson had recently arranged for the publication of the *Notes* in the United States, perhaps to correspond with and to influence the deliberations of the Convention of 1787.[8] Jefferson's book included his now famous proposal to call for a new constitutional convention whenever two-thirds of two of the three departments called for it. As was discussed in Chapter 2, Madison criticized this proposal in early 1788 in his *Federalist* No. 49, but he seemed to endorse it earlier in his 1785 letter to Wallace. Jefferson's *Notes* also marked Jefferson's ongoing efforts to make executive power compatible with constitutional government, and in this it revealed the maturation of Jefferson's views since his first proposed constitution in 1776.[9]

It should also be noted that it is possible that Madison sent these observations to Jefferson around this time, for Jefferson went out of his way to explain to Madison why his 1783 constitution did not include a bill of rights. In his important letter of 15 March 1789, which was written in response to Madison's October letter, Jefferson explained, "In the draught of a constitution which I had once thought of proposing in Virginia, & printed afterwards, I endeavored to reach all the great objects of public liberty, and did not mean to add a declaration of rights." So the difference between his 1783 constitution, which did not need a bill of rights, and the Constitution, which did, was that the latter "leaves some precious articles unnoticed, and raises implications against others." Perhaps Madison had sent his observations, then, noting that Jefferson had violated his own absolute call for a bill of rights. After all, in his first letter to Madison after having seen the Constitution, Jefferson had criticized the document's omission of a bill of rights, declaring that "a bill of rights is what the people are entitled to against every government on earth, general or particular, & what no just government should refuse, or rest on inferences."[10]

Madison's response also reveals that the Federal Convention of 1787 clearly influenced Madison, especially with respect to the Senate. In 1785, Madison

---

[8] Gish and Klinghard have argued convincingly that the publication of Jefferson's *Notes* was less haphazard, and that Jefferson was more deliberate in having the *Notes* published, than was previously thought. Dustin A. Gish and Daniel P. Klinghard, "Republican Constitutionalism in Thomas Jefferson's *Notes on the State of Virginia*," *Journal of Politics* 71 (2012): 35–51.

[9] Consider, for example, the difference between the vesting clauses for the governor in the 1776 and 1783 constitutions. Jeremy D. Bailey, *Thomas Jefferson and Executive Power* (New York: Cambridge, 2007), 55–60.

[10] Jefferson to Madison, 20 December 1787, *Thomas Jefferson: Writings*, ed., Merril Peterson (New York: Library of America, 1984), 916.

was especially concerned with including a Senate to reform the problems under the Articles of Confederation. In his words, a Senate would "give wisdom and steadiness to legislation," and "the want of these qualities is the grievance complained of in all our republics."[11] However, in 1788, Madison was less concerned with making sure that Kentucky have a Senate than with ensuring that the Senate be constituted according to the right principles. In particular, he objected to Jefferson's proposal to have senators represent districts on the grounds that a "spirit of locality is inseparable from that mode." The problem with single-member districts in the case of the Senate is that its members "lose sight of the aggregate interests of the Community" because they are influenced by the "interests or prejudices of their respective constituents." It would be better to make them "the choice of the whole Society, each citizen voting for every Senator." This would "impress on the minds of the Senators an attention to the interest of the whole Society."[12]

This was also true of Jefferson's proposal for a court of impeachments. In his 1783 constitution, Jefferson proposed a court of impeachments, comprised of members from each department of government and where each department could bring charges of impeachment against the other. Jefferson's proposal was clearly aimed at weakening the legislative department, but it also anticipated his coordinate theory of impeachments that he would more or less conform to throughout his life.[13] In his 1785 letter to Wallace, Madison endorsed this view: "It has been suggested that a tribunal composed of members from each Department would be better than either [giving it the executive or the judiciary] and I entirely concur in their opinion."[14] In 1788, Madison spent more time on this question, explaining that "a court of impeachments is among the most puzzling articles of a republican Constitution." After a lengthy discussion premised on the observation that it was "far more easy to point out defects in any plan, than to supply a cure," Madison concluded with a proposal for a court of impeachments that excluded the Senate: "Let the Senate be denied the right to impeach."[15] Again, caution is necessary when using Madison's view of what would be appropriate for Kentucky to understand what he thought was appropriate for the United States, but it is difficult to resist noticing that Madison in 1788 seemed less enthusiastic about the Senate than he was a few years earlier.

However, the most striking feature of Madison's 1788 observations on Jefferson's constitution is what Madison did not write. As was argued in

[11] Madison to Caleb Wallace, 23 August 1785, *Madison Writings*, 40.
[12] Madison, "Observations on Jefferson's Draft," *PJM* 11:286.
[13] Jefferson, "Proposed Revision of the Virginia Constitution," *Papers of Thomas Jefferson*, vol. 6, ed. Julian P. Boyd (Princeton, NJ: Princeton University Press, 1952), 301. For Jefferson's view of the impeachment power, see Jeremy D. Bailey, "Constitutionalism, Conflict, and Consent: Jefferson on the Impeachment Power," *Review of Politics* 70 (2008): 572–94.
[14] Madison to Caleb Wallace, 23 August 1785, *Madison Writings*, 43.
[15] Madison, "Observations on Jefferson's Draft," *PJM* 11: 291–92.

Chapter 2, *Federalist* No. 49 contains the most famous of Madison's commentaries on Jefferson's proposal for a new constitutional convention whenever called for by two-thirds of two of the three departments. There Madison argued that Jefferson's proposal for regular appeals to the people in the form of constitutional conventions would undermine the veneration of the Constitution necessary for constitutional government. Yet, in 1785, when Madison first commented on Jefferson's proposed constitution 1785, he recommended Jefferson's proposal for some kind of process for appeals to the people.[16] But in the 1788 observations he sent to Brown and perhaps Jefferson himself, Madison omitted any mention of Jefferson's proposal for institutionalized appeals to the people. This omission is all the more glaring in light of another comment about the judiciary. In the context of Jefferson's proposal for a council of revision, Madison noted that in all the state constitutions "& indeed in the Federal one also," there was no provision "for the case of a disagreement" in expounding the constitution. Given that courts "are generally the last in making their decision," they often have the advantage to "stamp" the law with its "final character." But this was wrong, for Madison, because it "makes the Judiciary Dept paramount in fact to the Legislature, which was never intended, and can never be proper."[17] This is an important comment for those interested in Madison's understanding of judicial review, but it must also be noted that Jefferson's proposal for constitutional conventions was a remedy for precisely those occasions when there was disagreement among the departments about the meaning of the constitution. Indeed, Madison's argument in *Federalist* No. 49 was made in the service of separation of powers conflicts, not constitutional change as such. In his final commentary on Jefferson's constitution, Madison was silent about appeals to the people, but he went out of his way to reject appeals to the judiciary as the proper method of resolving separation-of-powers conflicts over the meaning of the Constitution.

It is perhaps significant that Madison's silence about Jefferson's appeals to the people corresponds with the other major development for Madison in that same month. Significantly, Madison also wrote to Jefferson that a bill of rights could be useful as a way to educate the people about their rights. Perhaps Madison was undergoing a rethinking of what constitutional government could and should be, as the necessities of securing ratification had become less pressing. That is, with the Constitution more secure, it is possible that Madison was ready to walk back from his critique in No. 49 or at least possible that Madison thought Jefferson's proposal was no longer as big a threat as he did back in January and February. It is also likely that Madison was now concerned with finding common ground with Jefferson in order to firm up his membership in the club of influential supporters of the Constitution, and to implement his plan to recruit Jefferson to work in the national government. But whatever

[16] Madison to Caleb Wallace, 23 August 1785, *Madison Writings*, 45–46.
[17] Madison, "Observations on Jefferson's Draft," *PJM* 11: 293.

the case, these moments suggest a softening, either on philosophic or political grounds, of Madison. This would be tested, of course, in their next major exchange, which again involved a major proposal by Jefferson.

The Earth Belongs to the Living

Sometime in late January or early February 1790, Madison received Jefferson's now famous letter asserting that the earth belongs to the living.[18] Jefferson wrote it in September of the preceding year, but, for whatever reason, he held onto it for a few months and finally sent it in early January.[19] According to Burstein and Isenberg, Madison and Jefferson had just spent time together at Monticello between Christmas and New Year's Day.[20] Surely their conversation included Madison's urging Jefferson to accept Washington's nomination as Secretary of State, as well as Jefferson's experiences in revolutionary France.[21] But judging from the tone of Jefferson's letter, and from Madison's response, it appears that the two did not discuss Jefferson's theory when they were together. Perhaps when he was with Madison, Jefferson remembered that he had not yet sent it. It is also possible that Jefferson had already turned his attention to composing his important response to the citizens of Albemarle, which required unusual attention and which became what Dumas Malone labeled the best statement of his philosophy, and this prompted him to send the letter to Madison.[22] There is no indication that the two discussed Jefferson's proposal when they were together in the final week of 1788.

Jefferson's letter began with the premise, that the dead have no right to impose obligations on the living, to make an argument that he believed had not been previously made "either on this or our side of the water."[23] Specifically, he argued that no debt and no law should be passed from one generation to another, for "one generation is to another as one independent nation to another."[24] Importantly, this principle applied to constitutions, too, which meant that no constitution could be valid after nineteen years, the number he

---

[18] Madison to Jefferson, 4 February 1790, *Madison Writings*, 473–77.

[19] Jefferson to Madison, 6 September 1789, *Jefferson Writings*, 959–65.

[20] Andrew Burstein and Nancy Isenberg, *Madison and Jefferson* (New York: Random House, 2010), 203–04.

[21] Adrienne Koch, *Jefferson and Madison: The Great Collaboration* (Oxford: Oxford University Press, 1950), 99–100.

[22] Jefferson received the address from his neighbors in Albemarle on 16 January, and replied on 12 February. Dumas Malone, *Jefferson and the Rights of Man* (Boston: Little, Brown, 1951), 246–48. For an account of the difficult politics behind the address, see Bailey, *Jefferson and Executive Power*, 128–29, as well as Julian Boyd's notes for "Address of Welcome by the Citizens of Albemarle and Jefferson's Response," *Papers of Thomas Jefferson*, vol. 16, ed. Julian P. Boyd (Princeton, NJ: Princeton University Press, 1961), 171–78.

[23] Jefferson to Madison, 6 September 1789, *Jefferson Writings*, 959.

[24] Ibid., 962.

assigned to a generation using mortality tables. If a constitution "be enforced longer, it is an act of force and not of right."[25]

Madison's response lacked the quotable quality of Jefferson's letter and is not as famous, but it is well known. Unsurprisingly, he divided "the Acts of political Society" into several groupings: fundamental constitutions, laws irrevocable by the legislature, and laws revocable by the legislature. With respect to the first kind of acts of society, constitutions, Jefferson's "theory" seemed "liable in practice to some very powerful objections":

> Would not such a Government so often revised become too mutable to retain those prejudices in its favor which antiquity inspires, and which are perhaps a salutary aid to the most rational Government in the most enlightened age? Would not such a periodical revision engender pernicious factions that might not otherwise come into existence? Would not, in fine, a Government depending for its existence beyond a fixed date, on some positive and authentic intervention of the Society itself, be too subject to the casualty and consequences of an actual interregnum?[26]

Madison's answer here was clearly much like the critique of Jefferson's proposal to have a new constitutional convention whenever two-thirds of two of the three departments called for it. Although Madison did not use the word "veneration," he again argued that governments require a certain prejudice in the minds of the people and this prejudice comes about with time. In addition to these problems with the first class of acts, there were problems with the second class, those acts that are not revocable by the legislature. Here, Madison addressed Jefferson's application of the principle to debts contracted by the government. In his view, the problem was that some debts might be made on behalf of improvements, and "the improvements made by the dead form a charge against the living who take the benefit of them." Importantly, the example Madison gave was a "repelling a conquest," and indeed the "present debt" of the United States could be traced to that very example. So the problem with the application of the principle was that it underestimated the benefits passed down from one generation to another. The better principle would be to "see that the debits against the latter do not exceed the advances made by the former."[27] Madison called his criticism of the third set, laws that were revocable, "merely practical," but his criticism recalled the same fundamental issues brought about by the first two classes of laws. The problem was that factions would anticipate the end of the generational period, and there would be the "most violent struggles" between those who wanted to perpetuate the old debts and those who wanted to undo them. Moreover, the anticipation of the transition period would cause property to "depreciate its value" and "discourage the steady exertions of industry." Again, the problem was that factions

---

[25] Ibid., 962.
[26] Madison to Jefferson, 4 February 1790, *Writings*, 474.
[27] Ibid., 475.

would have more incentive to jeopardize rights – especially those of property – and they would be encouraged by the lack of respect for the law and for rights that ensues from generational constitution making.

A common reading of this exchange is that Madison "taught" Jefferson the principle of tacit consent. In the *Second Treatise*, John Locke explained that most people do not give their express consent to the constitution that emerges out of the social contract. Rather, they give their consent tacitly when they choose to live in civil society and enjoy its benefits over the insecurity of the state of nature.[28] Jefferson surely remembered this part of Locke, and had no need for Madison to remind him of it, for in his own letter he went out of his way to say that the "power of repeal" was not sufficient because of other reasons having to do with inevitably of corruption inside the government and inside the people. So the problem for Madison was not that Jefferson forgot tacit consent, but rather than Jefferson thought it was insufficient for genuine constitutional government. Indeed, Jefferson's doubts about constitutional government were surprisingly dark:

> The people cannot assemble themselves; their representation is unequal and vicious. Various checks are opposed to every legislative proposition. Factions get possessions of the public councils. Bribery corrupts them. Personal interests lead them astray from the general interests of their constituents; and other impediments arise so as to prove to every practical man that a law of limited duration is much more manageable than one which needs a repeal.[29]

So the problem for Madison was not that Jefferson did not know about the argument from tacit consent; rather, it was that Jefferson thought the right to repeal a law or constitution required too much from citizens because of the factious nature of normal politics. As a result, Jefferson believed that the revolutionary politics of founding was a better way to purify and elevate the otherwise corrupted opinions of the majority. What has not been noticed in this exchange is that Madison conceded for the second time that his famous solution for faction, the extended republic, would not work during times of founding. Because the extended republic makes the problem of faction even worse when a constitution is being framed, a frequent revision of the constitution would encourage factionalism and thereby render the extended republic less viable. As was discussed in Chapter 2, Madison had made this point in *Federalist*

---

[28] "And to this I say, that every Man, that hath any Possession, or Enjoyment, of any part of the Dominions of any Government, doth thereby give his tacit Consent, and is far forth obliged to Obedience to the Laws of that Government, during such Enjoyment, as any one under it." John Locke, *Two Treatises of Government*, ed., Peter Laslett (Cambridge: Cambridge University Press, 1960), 348.

[29] Jefferson to Madison, 6 September 1789, *Jefferson Writings*, 963. See also Jefferson to Madison, 28 June 1818, *Madison Papers Retirement*, 1: 295. For Jefferson's surprisingly dark assessment of public opinion, see "From 'floating ardor' to the 'union of sentiment': Jefferson on the Relationship between Public Opinion and the Executive," in *A Companion to Thomas Jefferson*, ed. Francis Cogliano, 184–98 (London: Wiley-Blackwell).

No. 37. Madison's point was that even though tacit consent was implicated by this consequence of the extended republic, it was still to be preferred over Jefferson's principle because of the practical consequences of the latter. Though tacit consent could not fix the injustice that flows from the politics of founding in the extended republic, it was safer to find ways to fix the "operation of this doctrine" than it was to throw it out by embracing Jefferson's principle. Moreover, Jefferson's principle would require too frequent a requirement of unanimity, either to the laws themselves or to the procedures for finding the voice of the majority. Given that Madison had just undergone a very difficult campaign for ratification, it is not surprising that the quiet politics of tacit consent seemed a more attractive option.[30]

This response to Jefferson has long been a central pillar in the scholarly edifice that this book has been calling Madisonian constitutionalism. It is clear from it that Madison was more concerned with stability than was Jefferson, and it is striking that Madison again appealed to the necessity of popular prejudice for the constitution.[31] It is also often noted that Madison's response was more practical and Jefferson's proposal more theoretical.[32] Sheehan differs with this standard account and, in line with her central thesis that Madison believed public opinion was sovereign, argues that the common reading "neglects Madison's explicit expression of agreement with the philosophic principles Jefferson set forth." What separated the two was not whether public opinion was sovereign, because both agreed "in the principle of popular sovereignty" and "the importance of the active participation of the people in republican politics." Rather, they disagreed about "how the sovereign authority of public opinion is best gathered and actively expressed in republican government." In her view, the exchanges reveal that the essential difference between the two is that Jefferson wanted to constitutionalize appeals to the people, whereas Madison wanted "to establish a political practice in which the settled decisions

---

[30] Madison to Jefferson, 4 February 1790, *Writings,* 476.

[31] Drew R. McCoy, *The Last of the Fathers: James Madison & the Republican Legacy* (New York: Cambridge University Press, 1989), 53–58; Greg Weiner, *Madison's Metronome: The Constitution, Majority Rule, and the Tempo of American Politics* (Lawrence: University Press of Kansas, 2012), 59–61; Richard K. Matthews, *If Men Were Angels: James Madison and the Heartless Empire of Reason* (Lawrence: University Press of Kansas, 1995), 256–65; and Jean M. Yarbrough, *American Virtues: Thomas Jefferson on the Character of a Free People* (Lawrence: University Press of Kansas, 1998), 117–22.

[32] Koch, *Great Collaboration,* 70–73; Burstein and Isenberg, *Madison and Jefferson,* 202–207. It should be noted that Gary Rosen argues that scholars have made too much of Madison's emphasis on Locke's principle of tacit consent, and proposes instead that Madison differed with Jefferson in that Madison believed that the consent was only necessary when government "proves itself either unable to secure the ends of the social compact or actively hostile to them." But Rosen makes this move to deepen what is basically the standard account, that is, that Madison's constitutionalism "may have lacked the grandeur of the political right of nature, defended by Jefferson in all its breadth, but it had the considerable merits of consistency and 'practicality'." Gary Rosen, *American Compact: James Madison and the Problem of Founding* (Lawrence: University Press of Kansas, 1999), 134 and 137.

of the people would control and direct the government." That is, in Sheehan's analysis, Madison rejected Jefferson's proposal because he did not want to set up the fundamental authority of the people as a challenge to normal legislative deliberation.[33]

The analysis here does not challenge the standard view of Madison's response as much as it recommends caution in overemphasizing the letter. Again, it should be remembered that the two appear not to have discussed the matter when they were together at Monticello, so it is thus hard to say how seriously either of the two took the exchange at the moment. Indeed, the editor of the Jefferson papers offers considerable textual evidence that Jefferson never intended to "press for adoption as a part of American legislation."[34] For present purposes, it is striking that Madison used the occasion to acknowledge for a second time that the logic of the argument for the extended republic would not apply during times of founding. Rather than solving the problem of faction, the extended republic might make it worse. Moreover, it also worth pointing out that over the next year, Madison brought up Jefferson's proposal twice in his correspondence with Jefferson. On both occasions, Madison poked fun at Jefferson, by observing that his proposal had no chance of getting encoded into law, perhaps driving home the point from *Federalist* No. 49 that Jefferson did not live in a nation of philosophers. But even more telling is that Madison's humor on both occasions assumed that the application of Jefferson's proposal would have improved the policy in question.[35] Indeed, Madison would return to Jefferson's idea in the next two years and publically endorse at least one application of it.

Assumption and the National Bank

The preceding chapter noted that Madison's assessment of deliberation in Congress declined over the course of his first year in the House of Representatives. In his letters in the early summer of 1789, Madison noted the slowness of business but seemed pleased by the spirit of deliberation. Over the next several months, the tediousness of the debates outweighed the virtues of deliberation, and eventually, Madison's criticism of deliberation in Congress grew sharper.

Part of the problem was that he was now on the losing sides of votes. By early 1790, after losing the vote on Hamilton's proposal for the national government to

---

[33] Sheehan, *Madison and the Spirit*, 139–41.

[34] See Julian Boyd's editorial note for "The Earth Belongs in Usufruct to the Living," *Papers of Thomas Jefferson*, vol. 15 (Princeton, NJ: Princeton University Press, 1958), 384–91.

[35] Madison to Jefferson, 14 February 1790, and Madison to Jefferson, 1 May 1791, in *PJM* 13: 41 and *PJM* 14: 15. In one instance, the point was that the Senate rejected a proposal to ascertain the "component classes of society" every ten years. Madison wrote that this would have provided the "kind of information extremely requisite to the Legislator, and much wanted for the science of Political Economy."

assume the war debts of the states, Madison was writing others that deliberation in Congress was critically flawed.³⁶ In a March letter to Benjamin Rush, Madison blamed the outcome of the debate on the assumption plan, which he called "radically immoral," on the mingling of opinion in New York and the debates in Congress. The correct policy might have won out, if what passed as the definition of a majority was "gathered from those philosophical and patriotic citizens who cultivate their reason, apart from the scenes which distract its operations, and expose it the influence of the passions." But this did not happen, and could not happen, for the simple reason that legislative deliberation necessarily has to take place in a geographic location. "Nothing is more contagious than opinion, especially on questions, which being susceptible of very different glosses, beget in the mind a distrust of itself." Because even representatives doubt their reasoning on public measures, "It is extremely difficult also to avoid confounding the local with the public opinion." As a result, Congress is prone to privilege "the united voice of the place, where they happen to deliberate."³⁷ Madison's suspicion that the Congress had the wrong view of public opinion was supported by a letter a few weeks later from Reverend Madison, assuring him that his arguments "have more Force, out of Doors, than within," because those were "not immediately concerned in the Debate" were more impartial than Madison's colleagues in Congress.³⁸ The Assumption debate proved, ironically, that Hamilton's criticism of Madison's theory of the extended republic was correct: legislative deliberation would have to happen in a particular place and this place would be subject to the problem of faction.³⁹

The same might be said of the debate on the national bank. But more than a difference over what constituted a just public policy, the bank debate was like the removal power debate in that it forced Madison to encounter the problem of constitutional imperfection. Because so much has been written about the debate over the constitutionality of the national bank, what follows is not an exhaustive treatment of Madison's view of that question.⁴⁰ Rather, it shows

³⁶ But see the earlier speech, on the location of the capital, where Madison complained that the arguments for one side had refused to disclose the general principles on which their arguments were based and had limited debate before all the facts could be given a hearing. Madison, Speech on 3 September 1789, *PJM* 12: 370–71.
³⁷ Madison to Benjamin Rush, 7 March 1790, *PJM* 13: 93–94. It is perhaps relevant that Madison misquotes the Constitution here, reading its Preamble to say a "more perfect justice" instead of a "more perfect Union."
³⁸ Reverend Madison to James Madison, 1 April 1790, *PJM* 14: 3.
³⁹ See Hamilton's notes for Madison's 6 June speech in the Convention. Alexander Hamilton, Notes from 6 June, in Harold C. Syrett, ed., *Papers of Alexander Hamilton*, 27 Vols. (New York: Columbia University Press, 1961–1987), 4:165. Sheehan likens Madison's statement to Rush to the modern concern for "inside the beltway politics," but she does not connect the argument in the letter to Rush to Madison's qualification of the extended republic in the party press essays. See Sheehan, *Madison and the Spirit*, 89–90.
⁴⁰ For a treatment of the questions raised by the bank, see Stanley Elkins and Eric McKitrick, *The Age of Federalism: The Early American Republic, 1788–1800* (New York: Oxford University

how Madison's participation in that debate differed from others' and how it clarifies other events in Madison's career.

The bank debate was different from the removal power debate in two key ways. One difference was that that the bank debate happened after the debate on the assumption of war debts, and therefore happened in the context of emerging political parties. A second difference was that Madison knew that the records of the Convention clearly demonstrated that Congress lacked the authority to incorporate a bank. Madison himself had proposed during the final days of the Convention that this power be granted to Congress, but it was rejected.[41] Accordingly, in his speech in Congress, Madison said "he reserved to himself the right to deny the authority of Congress to pass it," and his opinion on this matter was stronger, *because* "he well recollected that a power to grant charters of incorporation had been proposed in the general convention and rejected."[42] Given these differences, it is perhaps not surprising that Madison endorsed a method of interpretation that would help resolve problems such as this one, problems that derived from the necessity of constitutional imperfection. As he put it, "it is not pretended that every insertion or omission in the constitution is the effect of systematic attention." This could not be the case, for "this is not the character of any human work, particularly the work of a body of men." But even though the Constitution was flawed, it was still possible to derive a "rule of interpretation."[43] This rule consisted of several steps:

1. Interpretation cannot "destroy the very characteristic of the government."
2. Where meaning is clear, the consequences are to be admitted; where meaning is doubtful, the meaning can be tested by its consequences.
3. In "controverted cases," meaning can be determined from "reasonable evidence" concerning the "parties to the instrument."
4. "Contemporary and concurrent expositions" are acceptable examples of reasonable evidence.
5. When "admitting or rejecting a constructive authority," both the "degree of incidentality to an express authority" and its "degree of importance" are to be considered.

After laying out these rules, Madison next turned to the three places were supporters of the bank found constitutional authority. These were the power to

Press, 1993), 233–43; H. Jefferson Powell, *A Community Built on Words: The Constitution in History and Politics* (Chicago: University of Chicago Press, 2002), 21–30; and Gordon S. Wood, *Empire of Liberty: A History of the Early Republic* (New York: Oxford University Press, 2009), 143–45. For Madison's participation, see Jack N. Rakove, *Original Meanings: Politics and Ideas in the Making of the Constitution* (New York: Knopf, 1996), 350–55; Ketcham, *A Biography*, 319–23; Rosen, *American Compact*, 149–52; Sheehan, *Madison and the Spirit* 108–11; Burstein and Isenberg, *Madison and Jefferson*, 223–25.

[41] Madison, *Notes*, 638.
[42] Madison, Speech in Congress Opposing the National Bank, *Madison Writings*, 482.
[43] Ibid., 486–87.

lay and collect taxes, the power to provide for the general welfare, the power
to borrow money, and the necessary and proper clause. Madison then went on
to show why these clauses could not be read to authorize Congress to create a
bank. Madison's application of his rules is less interesting for us than the general thrust of the rules of themselves. This becomes more clear when we turn
to the defenses of the bank made by Alexander Hamilton in 1790 and by John
Marshall in 1819.

Broadly, both Hamilton and Marshall grounded their arguments on what
it is that governments do. In Hamilton's reasoning the problem disappears
once we concede a "general principle" that "is inherent in the very definition
of Government." This principle is "that every power vested in a Government
is in its nature sovereign, and includes the force of the term, a right to employ
all means requisite, and fairly applicable to the attainment of the ends of such
power; and which are not precluded by restrictions & exceptions specified
in the constitution; or not immoral, or not contrary to the essential ends of
political society."[44] In *McCulloch v. Maryland* (1819), Marshall would use
this same formulation, but offering it a more quotable way.[45] What is central
to both formulations is the two-part premise: first, that the powers of government have to be understood as means; and second, that these means must
to be understood with reference to the end of government itself, which is a
workable government. As long as these means are clearly connected to that
end, and as long as these means are not clearly forbidden, then the presump-
tion is that government has that power. In other words, once we concede that
the power belongs to sovereignty, the question is whether the Constitution
forbids the national government from having that power.[46] If it does not,
then it must be assumed that the Constitution implicitly grants it. To reason
otherwise would be to assume that the Constitution creates an unworkable
government.

[44] Alexander Hamilton, "Opinion on the Constitutionality of a National Bank," 23 February
1791, in *Alexander Hamilton: Writings*, ed. Joanne Freeman (New York: Library of America,
2001), 613.

[45] "We admit, as all must admit, that the powers of the government are limited, and that its limits
are not to be transcended. But we think the sound construction of the constitution must allow to
the national legislature that discretion, with respect to the means by which the powers it confers
are to be carried into execution, which will enable that body to perform the high duties assigned
to it, in the manner most beneficial to the people. Let the end be legitimate, let it be within the
scope of the constitution, and all means which are appropriate, which are plainly adapted to
that end, which are not prohibited, but consist with the letter and spirit of the constitution,
are constitutional." *McCulloch v. Maryland* (1819), in *The Founders' Constitution*, vol. 3, ed.
Phillip B. Kurland and Ralph Lerner (Indianapolis, IN: Liberty Fund, 2000; Chicago, Chicago
University Press, 1987), 258.

[46] My interpretation is different from Powell's in that Powell reads Hamilton as being optimistic about government being able to serve "the welfare of the community." I would say that
Hamilton is more interested in securing for the national government what he believed to be the
necessary components of sovereignty. See Powell, *Community Built on Words*, 28–29.

Madison's rules of interpretation have a much different emphasis. Most importantly, they are organized around the principle that the particular *kind* or *form* of government matters. The first rule asserts that the interpretation cannot destroy "the very characteristic of the government." The choice of the singular rather than plural form of characteristic assumes that there is some single characteristic of the government that distinguishes it from others. This is why the interpreter can look to the "meaning of the parties" and can have recourse to contemporary evidence. Both points assume that meaning of a constitution can be found more in its particularity than its likeness to what all other governments do or must do. It therefore matters that the Constitution is republican or not, and it matters whether the Constitution is national or federal or both.

This is a simple point of contrast between Madison and Hamilton, but it reveals a basic consistency in Madison's early treatments of constitutional imperfection. First, there is Madison's peculiar and single-minded focus on the process of ratification itself. As Chapter 4 showed, Madison stood apart from his contemporaries in making the argument that it is essential that every state ratified the Constitution on the same terms. Even Hamilton did not see the matter as clearly as Madison did, probably because for Hamilton what mattered most was that the government get up and running and because good government was more essential to winning the affection of the people than were the historical details of who ratified and on what terms. This point is revealed not only in Madison's insisting that each state ratify the same constitution on the same terms; it is also reflected in Madison's wanting to honor what he perceived to be the agreement with moderate anti-Federalists. In his view, they agreed to ratify the Constitution under the expectation that the Constitution would be given a bill of rights, so it was important to honor that understanding of the parties to the deal. This logic applied to the bank too. If Congress were to create a bank by appealing to some doctrine of implied powers, then the Constitution's opponents would say, rightly, that the Constitution's "adoption was brought about by one set of arguments" but "is now administered under the influence of another set."[47]

Second, there is the similarity with Madison's treatment of executive power. As we have seen in the removal power debate, a large part of Madison's argument was the assessment that giving the Senate a share of the removal power would give the government more stability than it should have. More precisely, this was a comment not only on the desirability of stability itself but also on one particular of the Constitution that emerged from the Convention. This Constitution, as Madison said again and again, had to accomplish the difficult task of balancing stability against republican principles. In his view, the removal power puzzle could be solved by remembering this fact of that Constitution. That point is reinforced but not replaced by Madison's appeal to separation of powers as the principle that should win out whenever meaning

---

[47] Madison, Speech in Congress Opposing the National Bank, *Madison Writings*, 489.

was in doubt. Again, the meaning of the Constitution depends in part on its particular characteristic.

Madison's attentiveness to the peculiarities of the Constitution also helps explain Madison's otherwise strange framing of his later arguments as Helvidius.[48] In response to Hamilton, who defended George Washington's 1793 proclamation of neutrality by again arguing that what mattered most was that a proclamation of neutrality was a "usual and proper measure" of government generally, Madison began his essays with the premise that it mattered *where* Hamilton found his evidence.[49] Specifically, Madison concluded that Hamilton drew his arguments from "British commentators" whose writings were colored by the fact that "the power of making treaties and the power of declaring war" were "royal prerogatives" of the British king.[50] This argument seems strangely *ad hominem* and best understood as part of the partisan rhetoric of the day until we remember that for Madison the particular characteristic of a constitution mattered a great deal in determining its meaning. Hamilton did not care so much about these distinctions because what mattered most, especially when constitutional meaning was unclear, was the essential characteristics of all good governments. Madison rejected this premise, and even went so far as to assert that both Locke and Montesquieu were "warped" by the example of England because he believed that it did not explain fully the particularities of "our government."[51] Even if the government should have a national bank, as Madison believed it should, the more important point for him was that the particularities of the Union, fully established at ratification, did not confer this power.

Party Press Essays

Colleen Sheehan has done more than any other scholar to demonstrate the importance of Madison's writings in the *National Gazette*. In her view, these writings were more than partisan tracts, for they grew out of Madison ongoing engagement with Enlightenment writings of the period, and by way of those writings, engagement with arguments going back to Greek antiquity. Moreover, Sheehan shows that Madison started this project in March 1791, perhaps even earlier, in a series of essays he called "Notes on Government." While scholars have long treated the 1791 "Notes" the same as the 1792 partisan essays in

[48] Much has been written of the exchange between Hamilton and Madison as Pacificus and Helvidius. See especially Benjamin A. Kleinerman, *The Discretionary President: The Promise and Peril of Presidential Power* (Lawrence: University Press of Kansas, 2009), 92–147; Elkins and McKitrick, *Age of Federalism*, 336–65. My own view can be found in Bailey, *Jefferson and Executive Power*, 81–94.

[49] Alexander Hamilton, Pacificus No. 1, in *Hamilton Writings*, 803. Madison, Helvidius No. 1, in *Madison Writings*, 539.

[50] Madison, Helvidius No. 1, *Madison Writings*, 545.

[51] Ibid., 540 and 537.

the *National Gazette*, Sheehan has shown that the 1791 "Notes" were more philosophic and less clearly partisan in tone than the 1792 work and, in her view, need to be given a "distinct status." She concludes that Madison's motivation for writing the Notes cannot be reduced to the partisan act of founding the Democratic-Republican Party. In her view, both works demonstrated Madison's democratic commitments because they reveal that Madison believed that public opinion was sovereign.[52] While Sheehan has done scholars a great service, both in her shrewd interpretative work and in her tireless historical investigation of the drafting of these essays, we need not accept her conclusion that Madison was engaged in high philosophy to appreciate the importance of both sets of writings. By March 1791, Madison had already lost on the assumption question and had already lost on the bank; indeed, February 1791 was probably the hottest month in terms of the debate on the bank.[53] By the time Madison published the essays in the *National Gazette* a year later, he was spending the vast majority of his time and intellectual effort in political debates that had become highly partisan.[54]

This point suggests that these essays were part and parcel of yet another act of founding, this time a political party. To assert themselves as a viable opposition to Washington and his administration, these partisans first had to defend opposition itself. This founding required a defense of public opinion that not yet been offered in American politics and therefore had not yet been offered in the modern context of a written constitution. Indeed, Washington's criticism of this opposition confirmed that Madison and his accomplices were innovators who had gone beyond the pale of what was acceptable, or "legitimate," to use Richard Hofstadter's famous phrase.[55] Madison might have guessed that this assertion of public opinion would define the politics of the decade, but he likely would not have seen that the legitimacy of public opinion as a source of authority would remain unresolved for well over a hundred years.[56] It also required that Madison provide his readers with a set of alternatives that would reveal the essential differences between the parties. As a result, Madison's essays in the *National Gazette* build up to a partisan climax, asserting that his party are the "real friends" of republican government, not "those who avow

---

[52] Sheehan, *Madison and the Spirit.*

[53] Madison's main speech against the bank was on 2 February, and Washington signed the bill on 25 February.

[54] Sheehan, *Mind of Madison*, 13–15.

[55] Richard Hofstadter, *The Idea of Party System: The Rise of Legitimate Opposition in the United States, 1780–1840* (Berkeley: University of California Press, 1970). Wood, *Empire of Liberty*, 203–04.

[56] Indeed, the contest between law and opinion endures as a feature of American politics. Consider, for example, debates concerning the election of 2000 or the nomination contest of 2008. For a discussion of this as an enduring discontinuity through Lincoln, see Jeremy D. Bailey, "Opposition to the Theory of Presidential Representation: Federalists, Whigs, and Democrats," *Presidential Studies Quarterly* 44: 50–71.

or betray principles of monarchy and aristocracy, in opposition to the republican principles of the Union, and the republican spirit of the people."[57] But in
making this charge, Madison had to provide an account of what politics in the
United States should be.

It would be easy to say that this required something different from his job
as Publius. That is obviously true, because in that case Madison's core job was
to convince New Yorkers to ratify the Constitution. As we have seen, Madison
quickly decided that it was best to defend that Constitution as it was written,
messy compromises and all, so he did not allow himself the luxury of entertain-
ing ideas of how to fix that Constitution. But more than requiring a different
task, the turn to partisanship also came at a time when he just participated
in several big debates in Congress about the meaning of the Constitution. In
forming a political party – that is, in determining what it would be that would
separate friends from enemies – Madison was able to articulate just what it
was that was most important about the Constitution and what was the way to
resolve to the problem of constitutional imperfection.

At the most basic level, then, what stands out from Madison's essays in the
National Gazette is that his party was the party of a *limited* government and
the party of public opinion. The turn to limited government is in some sense
obvious, but like the turn to opinion it marked a potential departure from the
argument presented in the *Federalist Papers*. To be sure, Madison's essays there
emphasize the republican credentials of the constitution, and these republican credentials assume that the new government would be a limited one. Yet
Hamilton had also written that the government must have certain powers,
and, more than that, that "these powers ought to exist without limitation."[58]
On top of that, Hamilton offered a principle that should guide "wise politicians" when they think about what it is constitutions should do. They should
"be cautious about fettering the government with restrictions that cannot be
observed." Hamilton's rational might have been appealing for someone like
Madison who from time to time reflected on the necessity of veneration, for
Hamilton wrote, "every breach of the fundamental laws, though dictated by
necessity, impairs that sacred reverence which ought to be maintained in the
breast of rulers toward the constitution of a country, and forms a precedent for
other breaches where the same plea of necessity does not exist at all, or is less
urgent and palpable."[59] It is significant, then, that Madison's turn included the
partisan dichotomy between limited and unlimited government. It was a turn
toward what would become Jeffersonian dogma – that the best construction
of the Constitution is the more limited one – and it presumed a rejection of
another in resolving the problem of constitutional imperfection. Rather than
siding with Hamilton and the belief that the Constitution must be capable of

[57] Madison, "The Union: Who Are Its Real Friends?" in *Writings*, 518.
[58] Hamilton, *Federalist* No. 23, Scigliano, 141.
[59] Hamilton, *Federalist* No. 25, Scigliano, 156.

anything, Madison cast his party – and therefore the Constitution itself – as being for limited government.

It is also significant that Madison characterized his party as being the party of public opinion. In the *Federalist*, Madison's treatment of public opinion was complicated by the fact that at times he treated majority opinion as one of the dangers to limited government while at others he treated opinion as an important incentive to the self-interested good behavior of officeholders. But in these essays, the complexity was different. In the first line of the essay given the title "Public Opinion," Madison declared that public opinion is the "real sovereign" in every "free" government, contrary, it would seem, to Bryan Garsten's assertion that Madison rejected the idea of a unified sovereign. But what complicated matters is that Madison also left room for public opinion to be shaped by the government. He accomplished this by making a distinction between fixed and unfixed opinion. When public opinion is fixed, it must be obeyed; but where it remains unfixed, there it can be influenced by the government. This distinction, Madison argued, "would prevent or decide many debates on the respect due from the government to the sentiments of the people."

Madison added a twist, however, by pointing to the Bill of Rights. He used it as an example of those things that influence the government by influencing public opinion. "By becoming part of public opinion," the Bill of Rights influences government. This comment would seem to provide more evidence that Madison believed the Bill of Rights was useful as an educative text, and it would fit perfectly with Madison's turn to public opinion in these essays. But that example, which was actually a set of constitutional protections proposed by the Congress, suggested ways in which government might influence opinion, not the other way around. This tension was not as evident in the version presented in his earlier "Notes on Government." There, Madison explained that the Bill of Rights "acquires efficacy as time sanctifies it and incorporates it with the public sentiment."[60] So, under this view, the Bill of Rights can help influence public opinion and therefore influence the government, but not at first. It can only do so after time passes and it becomes part of public opinion.

Next, Madison turned to the practical problem of determining public opinion. The problem with the distinction between fixed and unfixed opinion is that it presupposes that "real opinion" can be ascertained, and "the larger the country," the more difficult this is. In the large republic, the authority of government benefits from ease with which public opinion can be "counterfeited." Anticipating Tocqueville, and complicating his own presentation in the *Federalist*, Madison explained, "the more extensive a country, the more insignificant is each individual in his own eyes." Rather than commenting on the benefits of lowering the danger of majority faction, Madison instead noted: "This may be unfavorable to liberty."[61] Madison made this clear in the

[60] Madison, "Notes on Government," in Sheehan, *Mind of Madison*, 136.
[61] Madison, "Public Opinion," in *Madison Writings*, 501.

next paragraph, asserting that "whatever facilitates a general intercourse of sentiments" – such as "good roads," a "free press," and "a circulation of newspapers" – is "equivalent to a contraction of territorial limits" and therefore "is favorable to liberty."[62]

Madison gave these reflections on the problem of the extended republic a more constitutional cast in his essay, "Charters," where he returned to the more complex relationship between a written constitution and public opinion. Again, he repeated his point that public opinion is sovereign: "All power has been traced up to opinion." Even an "arbitrary government is controuled where the public opinion is fixed." This meant that republicans should wish, even "devoutly" wish, that opinion be "enlightened." But it also meant that republicans in the United States had "peculiar motives" – that is, motives limited to their particular experience – to support constitutional government in the United States. It is here where Madison addressed potential tension between constitutional government and public opinion. It is no surprise that constitutions – or a form of what he calls charters in this essay – played a key role. Whereas in Europe, "charters of liberty" had been bestowed by governments themselves, in the United States, the practice was for liberty to bestow "charters of power" on the government. This was a "revolution" in itself, for it meant that the new American charters proclaimed the "will," "authenticated by the seal of the people," and, as result, became the arbiter determining questions "between power and liberty." These charters of government thus represented the purest and most fixed form of public opinion, and, as such, were thus "superior in obligation to all others, because they give effect to all others." If these kinds of charters were to succeed, Americans would enjoy some of the credit.

But the peculiar motive for Americans was not only the fact that Americans "originated" the idea of a written constitution. Rather, Americans had a peculiar motive because the American charter is especially "complicated." This complication arises from the very thing that Madison had identified in *Federalist* No. 37 as the most difficult problem of all, the "partition of government

---

[62] Ibid. Madison's support for public opinion derived from newspapers was qualified, for he called it an "inauthentic medium." See his Speech on the Jay Treaty, 6 April 1796, *Madison Writings*, 571. It should also be pointed out that Madison relaxed some of the tension with his argument in *Federalist* No. 10 in the version Colleen A. Sheehan presents in her rendering of Madison's "Notes on Government." In that version, Madison writes that "whatever facilitates a general intercommunication of sentiments & ideas among the body of the people" "may favor liberty in a nation too large for free Gov[ernmen]t or hasten its violent death in one too small & so vice versa." In this version, Madison preserves his distinction between large and small republics and applies it to public opinion, saying that newspapers and other facilitators of public opinion are especially necessary in republics that are too large. This reveals that Madison was aware that his party press essays qualified his argument for the extended republic, and it reveals that Madison qualified the extent to which public opinion was good. For Sheehan, the solution is that Madison consistently sought a "middle ground between a confederation of individual sovereign states and a consolidated government." *Mind of Madison*, 103. For the version in the "Notes," see Madison, *Notes on Government*, in Sheehan, *Mind of Madison*, 127.

between the states and the union." This complication is combined with the complication of separation of powers; together, it results in a series of divisions of authority that defy a priori classification. As a result, the American charter requires "a more than common reverence for the authority which is to preserve order throughout the whole." Madison followed this with his frequently quoted plea that the charters be treated as "political scriptures" defended with a "holy zeal." But what stands out is not Madison's urging Americans to treat their Constitution as holy writ, but rather his acknowledgment that that kind of faith, a faith better described as zealotry, was necessary for the Constitution to succeed. More precisely, Madison's argument was not so much that every constitution requires veneration. Rather, his argument was that the American Constitution was so complicated that it required more veneration than usual.

It is not surprising, then, that veneration alone is not sufficient. In "Government of the United States," Madison returned to the difficulty of marking the partition between state and national governments. In it he wrote that it was easier to "separate, by proper definitions," the legislative, executive, and judicial powers than "to discriminate, by precise enumerations, one class of legislative powers from another class." When the powers are "of a more kindred nature, their boundaries are more obscure." But just because it is difficult, that does not mean it should be abandoned, because the alternative is either "schism" or "consolidation." Accordingly, "those who love their country" should instead look to guard the limits of the state and national governments. This requires more than veneration and holy zeal. Instead, it recommends "moderation in the exercise of the powers of both" and indeed an "abstinence" from powers that might "nurse present jealousies."[63] Again, Madison did not think veneration was sufficient.

There is yet another surprise, because these essays provide more evidence that Madison was not entirely convinced of his own critique of Jefferson's "earth belongs to the living" argument. In fact, just as he had in 1785 endorsed Jefferson's proposal to have a constitutional path for an appeal to the people, in 1792 he endorsed Jefferson's proposal to require that each generation pay its own debts. A few scholars have noted this change by Madison, but it remains relatively understudied.[64] The context was the essay "Universal Peace," where Madison took up Jean-Jacques Rousseau's proposal for a confederation of countries for the purpose of "arbitrating controversies."[65] Madison praised the French philosopher for wanting to find a permanent solution to the problem of war, since "every thing ought to be tried" to end what contains "so much folly, as well as wickedness." But he concluded that Rousseau's argument was deeply flawed. In Madison's view, Rousseau's problem was that he failed to notice that the causes of war could be "divided into two classes." One cause flows from

[63] Madison, "Government of the United States," in *Madison Writings*, 509.
[64] Sheehan, *Madison and the Spirit*, 138.
[65] Madison, "Universal Peace," in *Madison Writings*, 505–08.

the will of the government, but the other flows from the will of the people. The solution to the first was easy. "The government itself must be regenerated," such that hereditary powers would not hold the power to decide if there would be war or not. Because Rousseau had not "lived to see the constitutions of the United States and France," Rousseau was, like Locke and Montesquieu, still trapped within the horizon of monarchy. The new republics, however, had solved the first cause of war by making the will of the government "subordinate to, or rather the same with, the will of the community."[66] Rousseau erred because he did not see the republicanism principle in practice.

The second kind of war constituted a deeper problem and would not be solved by the transition from monarchy to a republic, because there would be wars that grew out of "the will of society itself." So, in typically Madisonian faction, Madison traced the enduring problem of war to the problem of majority faction. This time, however, Madison did not appeal to the extended republic or representation as the solution to the problem. Rather, the new problem would be solved by forcing the majority will to pay for its own wars:

> Here our republican philosopher might have proposed as a model to lawgivers, that war should not only be declared by the authority of the people, whose toils and treasures are to support its burdens, instead of the government which is to reap its fruits: but that each generation should be made to bear the burden of its own wars, instead of carrying them on, at the expense of other generations.[67]

So, for Madison, the key was to shift the authority for war to those who bear the burden, but this required the constitution maker to consider the tax burden from the perspective of differing generations. In this way, taxes would "keep the people awake." This was language taken out of Jefferson's often repeated concern that the people would eventually lose interest in watching over their government. Although Madison never credited Jefferson for this argument, it is nonetheless striking that Madison used it without qualification to criticize not only Rousseau but to continue his critique of policy under the Washington administration.

In fact, Madison went out of his way in this essay to show his support for Jefferson's theory by taking up the anticipated objection that wars bring benefits to generations beyond those who wage them. As we have seen, Madison had used this very argument to Jefferson, noting that the debts for "repelling a conquest" should be balanced against the likelihood that the "evils" of that conquest, if successful, would "descend through many generations."[68] This time, Madison answered this objection by saying that exceptions to the rule "could not be easily made," and if made, would have to be made "only" by "the parties interested" at the time. That is, Madison implied that the consent

---

[66] Ibid., 505–06.
[67] Ibid., 506.
[68] Madison to Jefferson, 4 February 1790, *Madison Writings*, 475.

of generation still not of age would have to enter into the decision to acquire debt in that generation's name.[69] More basically, the objection was based on a shaky premise: "the expense of necessary wars, will never exceed the resources of an entire generation."[70] Jefferson himself might have made this argument treating two generations as separate "parties" to a contract, but what is especially important is that Madison added one more. In Madison's view, the reason why the attention to generational debt would solve the problem of war is that it would clarify and elevate the very way the majority decides whether to go to war or not. "Avarice would be sure to calculate the expenses of ambition; in the equipoise of these passions, reason would be free to decide for the public good."

In some sense, there is no more Madisonian statement than this. It calculates the benefits of a process in policy making by weighing one passion against the other in the same way that, as Madison famously formulated, "Ambition must be made to counteract ambition."[71] But, in another sense, the statement is surprising in its departure from what we usually see in Madison. It suggests that public reason is possible during those moments when the passions normally associated with war (pride, glory, or fear) could be balanced by the passion of avarice. More than that, it suggests that inventions of political science such as representation and the extended republic are less necessary than the attention to how each generation calculates its interest in property. Generational consent, not separation of powers, appears to be the invention of prudence that is most effective in limiting wars waged by majorities.

Holy Zeal and the Passions

It is no wonder that Madison's turn in the 1790s has presented so much of a problem for Madison scholars and for Madisonian constitutionalism. As a critic of the Articles of Confederation and then as Publius, Madison warned of the dangers of majority faction. However, in the party press essays, Madison was more concerned with removing the obstacles to the majority. But there is an even more fundamental problem. In his famous tenth essay of the *Federalist*, Madison presented passion as one of the sources of faction, and it could even be argued that the entire argument presumes that factions are

---

[69] It is perhaps significant that Jefferson used the metaphor of generational debt when defending the Louisiana Purchase. In his letter to John C. Breckinridge, Jefferson likened the Purchase to "a guardian, investing the money of his ward" who must later say, "I did this for your good; I pretend to no right to bind you: you may disavow me, and I must get out of the scrape as I can: I thought it my duty to risk myself for you." Jefferson to Breckinridge, 12 August 1803, *Jefferson Writings*, 1139. See Bailey, *Jefferson and Executive Power*, 179–82.

[70] Madison, "Perpetual Peace," *Madison Writings*, 507.

[71] Madison, *Federalist* No. 51, in Scigliano, 331. Moreover, as Helvidius, Madison argued that the president could not have exclusive control of the treaty power because the president's ambition would be too attached to war. Madison, Helvidius No. 4, *PJM* 15:108.

permanent because passion, especially self-love, stands in the way of interest (understood in terms of reason).[72] But in these party press essays, Madison recommended that citizens defend a particular reading of the Constitution with a holy zeal.

This call for a holy zeal has two important implications. First, it offers yet another illustration of Madison wrestling with the problem of constitutional imperfection. The reason why holy zeal is necessary and even appropriate is because of the complicated nature of the Constitution. This complexity arises out of the enduring impossibility of marking clear lines in separation of powers and in federalism, but it is aggravated by the peculiar complexity of the Constitution, which derives in part from what Madison saw as its flaws. Second, in sorting out Madison's calls for zealotry and public reason, it is important to see that Madison's call for a holy zeal was eventually moderated by what at first glance seems to be a traditional Madisonian remedy, what he called the equipoise of the passions. Just as the great departments of government are held in their proper place by channeling the passion of ambition to give each department a will of its own, public opinion similarly needs to find the proper balance – an equipoise – from which its mandates can deserve to be seen as authoritative and sovereign. To the extent that scholars have noticed this important development in Madison's thinking, they have tamed it by linking it to Madison's occasional arguments that public opinion must be deliberative and settled for it to be authoritative. Thus Madison's holy zeal is made moderate enough to maintain Madisonian constitutionalism.

The argument here, however, goes deeper. The importance of Madison's turn to the equipoise of the passions is that the turn requires taking a Jeffersonian step. The equipoise of the passions is possible only when the people have been awakened by their own passions. Just as the revolutionary moment is possible only when the people are willing to risk their own material security, ordinary republican government sometimes requires that the people undertake the necessarily dangerous vigilance of their own representatives. More important, as the example of the prohibition of wartime debt for later generations shows, it is sometime necessary to institutionalize this awakened vigilance.

Madison's political party eventually defeated the Federalist Party by proclaiming the necessity of the vigilance of the people. Madison laid the groundwork for this argument in the early 1790s, writing that it should be the "patriotic study of all, to maintain the various authorities established by our complicated system."[73] Near the end of that decade, both Jefferson and Madison protested against the Alien and Sedition acts by asserting that constitutional government presupposed that citizens and elected officials watch over

---

[72] "As long as the connection subsists between his reason and his self-love, his opinions and his passions will have a reciprocal influence on each other." Madison, *Federalist* No. 10, Scigliano, 55.

[73] Madison, "Consolidation," in *Madison Writings*, 500.

and guard constitutional boundaries.[74] By 1801, Jefferson would use his First Inaugural to declare "the essential principles of our government," and the two held the two most important offices in the country, having won an election that Jefferson would famously call a revolution.[75] Madison's participation in that revolution offers the best opportunity to examine Madison's commitment to Madisonian constitutionalism.

---

[74] Madison, "Virginia Resolution Against the Alien and Sedition Acts," 21 February 1798, in *Madison Writings*, 589; Jefferson, "Draft of the Kentucky Resolutions," October 1798, in *Jefferson Writings*, 454.
[75] Jefferson, "First Inaugural Address," *Jefferson Writings*, 494.

6

Appeals to the People

Madison and the Revolution of 1800

"[T]he revolution of 1800 ... was as real a revolution in the principles of our government as that of 1776 was in its form; not effected by the sword as that, but by the rational and peaceable instrument of reform, the suffrage of the people."

Thomas Jefferson[1]

Even though there has been a resurgence of attention to James Madison, scholars have had surprisingly little to say about Madison during the period between 1800 and 1824. As discussed in the introduction, attention to Madison so far has mostly concentrated on Madison's efforts in the late 1780s and early 1790s to form, ratify, and implement the Constitution of 1787. Very little has been written about Madison's participation with Jefferson after 1800 to execute the Republican agenda they articulated in the 1790s.

To the extent that scholars have examined Madison in this period, the emphasis has been limited to several well-known events. The first is Madison's seeming switch on the question of the national bank. Here, scholars have noted that Madison eventually came to see the need for the national bank, perhaps because of the practical necessities revealed during the war, and came to accept its constitutionality. Accordingly, some scholars have pointed to Madison's statement that the bank's constitutionality was "settled" over time and have thus argued that what appears to be a contradiction is actually a consistency of a particularly Madisonian variety.[2] The second is the War of 1812. Presidency scholars have

---

[1] Thomas Jefferson to Judge Spencer Roane, 6 September 1819, in *Thomas Jefferson: Writings*, ed. Merril D. Peterson (New York: Library of America, 1984), 1425. In 1801, Jefferson used the word to describe the restoration of "our revolution." See Jefferson to John Dickinson, 8 March 1801, in *Jefferson Writings*, 1084.

[2] Gary Rosen makes this point most clearly, arguing that Madison accepted the bank because he perceived that "Constitutional veneration was more likely to be promoted by granting a degree of legitimacy to the occasional legislative excess." Gary Rosen, *American Compact: James Madison and the Problem of Founding* (Lawrence: University Press of Kansas, 1999), 172.

long pointed to this episode to conclude that Madison as Commander in Chief was less impressive than Madison as constitutional designer (1780s) or constitutional interpreter (1790s). Although scholars have increasingly become more attentive to Madison's refusal to curtail civil liberties during wartime, Madison's prosecution of the War of 1812 has not received high marks among presidency scholars and has been all but ignored by students of Madison's political thought (though, for some, it demonstrates the impracticality of Madison's understanding of executive power). The third is the Missouri Compromise. Here, scholars have noted that Madison sided with Virginia and the South rather than with the antislavery argument. Notably, Madison made it very clear that he would *not* embrace novel interpretations of the slave trade clauses to enhance any authority Congress held to regulate slavery. A fourth area of inquiry has been opened by J. C. A. Stagg's recent book, *Borderlines in Borderlands: James Madison and the Spanish-American Frontier, 1776–1821*.[3] Stagg explores Madison's diplomacy with respect to U.S. claims and ambition for Spanish-American territory. In Stagg's view, Madison's diplomacy helps resolve the rival interpretations of how the United States grew at Spain's loss by revealing the early republic in the context of international relations. From this perspective of Madison's tenure as secretary of state and president, Stagg finds "only one James Madison, not two."[4]

But these lines of research do not cast much light on what this book argues is the most central problem in understanding Madison's political thought over his career. That problem is this: Why did Madison choose Jefferson and why did he remain a Jeffersonian? This chapter explores that question in a more precise way by asking the following: What was Madison's view of the Revolution of 1800 and did it accord with that of Jefferson? To date, the answer to this question has been that Madison sided with Jefferson because Hamilton and the Federalist Party had attempted to subvert the Constitution with a dangerous faction of moneymen and monarchists. As correct as that answer is explaining why Madison and Jefferson joined together to form an opposition, it does not explain sufficiently why Madison *stayed* with Jefferson, so much so that Jefferson's last letter to Madison requested that Madison "take care of me when dead."[5] This alliance was not a foregone conclusion. Madison had broken with Hamilton and with Washington in the 1790s, and, as has been previously discussed, Madison had had his own differences with Jefferson. If the standard reading of Madisonian constitutionalism accurately characterizes

---

[3] J. C. A Stagg, *Borderlines in Borderlands: James Madison and the Spanish-American Frontier, 1776–1821* (New Haven, CT: Yale University Press, 2009). See also Garry Wills, *James Madison* (New York: Times Books, 2002).

[4] This is because "it is not enough merely to provide ever more detailed accounts of national politics in Washington alone," but the "alternative of trying to draw larger patterns from a rapidly proliferating number of local or regional case studies is probably not the answer either." This means that scholars need to return to foreign policy, which means that scholars must understand the executive who formulates those policies and then acts upon them. Stagg, *Borderlines in Borderlands*, 11–12.

[5] Jefferson to Madison, 17 February 1826, *Jefferson Writings*, 1515.

what Madison himself actually thought, and given the supposed difference between Madison's and Jefferson's aims for constitutionalism, it should be surprising that both agreed about the aims and scope of the Revolution of 1800. More broadly, did Madison believe that the election of 1800 was a revolution?

To be sure, whether there actually was a Revolution of 1800 has been a long-standing debate. In prior work, I have argued that there was in fact a revolution, that this revolution has been obscured by Henry Adams's conclusion that Jefferson was at least as Federalist as his predecessors, and that this revolution can be understood once we understand Jefferson's transformation of executive power.[6] Accordingly, we can see in Jefferson's presidency – especially Jefferson's democratization of the prerogative power, the creation of the de facto term limit, the use of declarations of principle, the defense of removal power, the Twelfth Amendment, and the impeachment of Justice Samuel Chase – the attempt to institutionalize revolution. Or, put differently, Jefferson used his administration to remake presidential power and in so doing remake the Constitution in his own image. But scholars have not really attempted to determine the extent to which Madison went along with these constitutional developments, or if he considered them important at all. This is in my view a missed opportunity because the question of the Revolution of 1800 reveals a linkage between constitutional veneration and the function of the executive in the constitutional order.

This chapter, then, has the immediate objective of examining Madison's understanding of the Revolution of 1800. In particular, it pieces together Madison's view of the relationship between executive power and constitutional imperfection by using Jefferson's executive and the Revolution of 1800 as a point of comparison. By understanding Jefferson's Revolution of 1800 as a practical solution to the problem of constitutional imperfection, we can trace Madison's perspective on the subject.

Jefferson's Transformation of Executive Power

Going back to Henry Adams, scholars have frequently concluded that Jefferson's presidency marked a reversal in Jefferson from his prior opposition to a strong executive. According to this standard view, Jefferson's actions as president show that Jefferson embraced the very Hamiltonian executive he and Madison had criticized in the 1790s. The leading piece of evidence for this conclusion is the Louisiana Purchase, because even Jefferson himself believed that he lacked the power to incorporate the territory by treaty and that a constitutional amendment was necessary. Supporting evidence includes Jefferson's aggressive and partisan use of the removal power, the embargo, and, to a lesser extent, Jefferson's treatment of the Barbary Coast pirates and

---

[6] Jeremy D. Bailey, *Thomas Jefferson and Executive Power* (New York: Cambridge University Press, 2007).

his occasional refusals to cooperate fully with the Marshall Court. According to Adams, Jefferson the president "stretched out his hand to seize the powers he had denounced."[7]

This view, however, has been challenged by recent scholarship, especially by Peter Onuf, Brian Steele, and myself.[8] I have argued that Jefferson's understanding of executive power in fact provides a way to understand key aspects of Jefferson's presidency as well as key aspects of his political thought. That is, Jefferson did have an understanding of executive power, and his decisions as president are best understood in light of that understanding rather than as departures or as hypocrisy. To put it differently, Jefferson had a plan for presidential power because he had a theory about the way the executive could help alleviate the problems of constitutional imperfection. Moreover, this understanding consisted of three key parts.[9]

The first was energy. Like Hamilton, Jefferson believed that an energetic executive was good for republican government. As a constitutional designer in the 1780s, he supported unity in the executive and independence from the legislative department, and as an advisor to Washington in the 1790s generally supported strong presidential powers. What separated Jefferson from Hamilton was not their disagreement about whether the executive should be strong, but rather what the source of the strength would be. In particular, Jefferson consistently resisted broad constructions of constitutional authority and instead looked to popular approval as the more secure foundation for executive authority. The presidency, then, offered the perfect match for Jefferson because its combination of unity and accountability, as described so elegantly by Hamilton in *Federalist* Nos. 70–71, offered a way to make an energetic government compatible with democracy. This opportunity was made all the more real by the partisan developments of the 1790s, initiated by Jefferson and Madison, which ultimately resulted in the acceptance of public opinion as a legitimate foundation for authority.[10] As Bruce Ackerman has

[7] Henry Adams, *History of the United States during the Administrations of Thomas Jefferson* (New York: Library of America, 1986), 174. For a fuller discussion of the scholarship on Jefferson's presidency, see *Jefferson and Executive Power*, 1–5.

[8] Peter S. Onuf, "Thomas Jefferson, Federalist" *Essays in History* 35, No. 20 (1993): 3–4; Brian Steele, *Thomas Jefferson and American Nationhood* (New York: Cambridge University Press, 2012).

[9] Bailey, *Jefferson and Executive Power*. See also Bailey, "Constitutionalism, Conflict, and Consent: Jefferson on the Impeachment Power," *Review of Politics* 70 (2008): 572–94; Bailey, "Jefferson's Executive: More Responsible, More Unitary, and Less Stable," in *Extra-Legal Power and Legitimacy: Perspectives on Prerogative*, ed. Clement Fatovic and Benjamin Kleinerman (Oxford: Oxford University Press, 2013), 117–37; Bailey, "From 'floating ardor' to the 'union of sentiment': Jefferson on the Relationship between Public Opinion and the Executive," *Blackwell Companion to Thomas Jefferson*, ed. Francis Cogliano (London: Wiley-Blackwell, 2012); Bailey, "The Revolution of 1800," in *A History of the U.S. Political System: Ideas, Interests, and Institutions*, ed. Richard A. Harris and Daniel J. Tichenor (Santa Barbara, CA: ABC-Clio), 66–77.

[10] Todd Estes, *The Jay Treaty Debate, Public Opinion, and the Evolution Early American Political Culture* (Amherst: University of Massachusetts Press, 2008).

documented, this was the crux of the election of crisis of 1800, which pitted Republican appeals to public opinion against Federalist appeals to the formal law.[11] Although this transformation would remain contested, it was formalized by the Twelfth Amendment's tightening of the connection between a potential mandate and presidential claims of authority.[12]

The second was a new understanding of executive prerogative. As a good deal of recent scholarship has demonstrated, the key difference between Hamilton and Jefferson was not whether there should be executive prerogative but rather what the source for executive prerogative should be. Again, the key difference – and a key consistency for Jefferson – was that Jefferson resisted reading prerogative into the Constitution and instead preferred to leave prerogative outside the Constitution. In this sense, Jefferson's handling of the Louisiana Purchase was less a departure from his principles and more a logical extension of what he had been doing and arguing for several decades going all the way back to his tenure as wartime governor of Virginia. Throughout his career, Jefferson defended what he perceived to be the necessary departures from the law, but he consistently avoided arguments that the law itself permitted those departures. Instead, he frequently argued that the officer who employs executive prerogative must "throw himself" on the people for their judgment.[13]

The third feature was a reliance on declarations of principle. Jefferson is known throughout the world today because of his authorship of the Declaration of Independence, but this was just one of many similar declarations Jefferson authored to influence and alter political events. Moreover, Jefferson brought this faith in declarations to his view of the executive. In place of novel interpretations of the law, which in his view clouded public judgment, Jefferson looked to these declarations to provide the principles by which the public would be able to judge energy in the executive, particularly with respect to prerogative. Hence Jefferson transformed the inaugural address from a formal acknowledgment of the transfer of power (and thus subservient to the oath of office) into a regular declaration of principles (and thus outside of and superior to the oath).

It is important to note that these three features add up to a discernible response to the problem of constitutional imperfection. Jefferson's notion of

[11] Bruce Ackerman, *The Failure of the Founding Fathers: Jefferson, Marshall, and the Rise of Presidential Democracy* (Cambridge, MA: Harvard University Press, Belknap Press, 2005).

[12] I make this argument in *Jefferson and Executive Power*, chapter 8. This argument has been expanded in a recent scholarship. See Robert E. Ross, "The Constitutional Development of Political Parties: A Theory of Emerging Structures and Reoccurring Patterns of Political Opposition," Doctoral Dissertation (University of Houston, 2014). See also Joshua D. Hawley, "The Transformative Twelfth Amendment" *William and Mary Law Review* 55 (2014): 1501–86.

[13] Bailey, *Jefferson and Executive Power*, 15–22, 28–64, and 171–94. See also Clement Fatovic, "Constitutionalism and Presidential Prerogative: Jeffersonian and Hamiltonian Perspectives," *American Journal of Political Science* 48 (2004): 429–44. For a discussion of the literature, see Bailey, "Executive Prerogative and the 'good officer' in Thomas Jefferson's Letter to John B. Colvin," *Presidential Studies Quarterly* 34, No. 4 (2004): 732–54.

energy in the executive took Locke's notion of an executive "always in being" and transformed it into a president who acts in "constant agency" on behalf of the people.[14] This means that in some way Jefferson's executive is lawless on behalf of the people, but it also means that the people's will is in some sense incoherent in the absence of executive action. For the purposes of comparison with Madison, the point is that Jefferson's understanding of executive power was predicated on the idea that extra-constitutional action was preferable to constitutional maintenance by interpretation so long as that extra-constitutional action was tethered to public judgment. But because that public judgment remains inchoate if left to itself, extra-constitutional action would itself be a form of executive leadership.[15] Jefferson's executive provides appeals to the people as the solution to constitutional imperfection by first making plausible the idea that the people can give their consent in the first place.

The Election Crisis of 1800 and the Extra-Constitutional Path

The election of 1800 offers one of the most jarring intersections of political theory and partisan practice in American history. It was both a botched election and an electoral revolution. As scholars have long noted, the election stalemate was a consequence of the Constitution's insufficiency with regard to political parties: the delegates to the Convention of 1787 did not anticipate that a national party would be able to organize around a slate of two candidates and thus failed to require Electors to distinguish between president and vice president in their two votes for president. Because the election dispute turned on the question whether it mattered that voters intended Jefferson rather than Burr to be president, the crisis opened a new path for the argument that the president is an agent of the people.[16] Because Federalists appealed to the letter of the law and Republicans appealed to the will of the people, the election dispute offers another good opportunity to consider Madison's understanding of the relation between the two.

In considering Madison's role in the election, it is important to remember that Madison was a committed and active partisan. In addition to founding and organizing the Republican party in the 1790s, Madison had taken specific steps to ensure Jefferson's election. In the Virginia legislature, he was on the committee that recommended the measure to shift Virginia's Electoral College votes from a district method to winner-take-all. Without this change, 1800

[14] John Locke, *Two Treatises of Government*, ed., Peter Laslett (Cambridge: Cambridge University Press, 1960), 348. Jefferson to George Hay, 20 June 1807, *Jefferson Writings*, 1179–80.
[15] See Benjamin A. Kleinerman, "Can the Prince Really Be Tamed? Executive Prerogative, Popular Apathy and the Constitutional Frame in Locke's Second Treatise," *American Political Science Review* 101 (2007): 209–22.
[16] For different takes on this point, see Garry Wills, *Negro President: Jefferson and the Slave Power* (Boston: Houghton Mifflin, 2003); Ackerman, *Failure of the Founding Fathers*, and Bailey, *Jefferson and Executive Power*.

would have been a repeat of 1796 – a victory for John Adams.[17] As party dealmaker, Madison worked to negotiate and execute a deal with Burr that Virginia's Electoral votes would also go to Burr, so that Burr could be vice president. Lastly, it must be pointed out that Madison cast an Electoral College vote.[18]

After the election, Madison's correspondence indicates that he followed and reported on the deadlock. From these letters, it seems that at first Madison was less anxious about Jefferson's chances than were others in his circle. Around 10 November, he responded to James Monroe's worry about an accidental tie with assurances that Jefferson would prevail:

> I can not apprehend any danger of a *surprize* that would throw Mr. J. out of the primary station. I can not believe that any such is intended, or that a single *republican* vote will abandon him. The worst therefore that could possibly happen would be a tie that wd. appeal to the H. of R. where the candidates would certainly I think be arranged properly, even on the recommendation of the secondary one.[19]

Six weeks later, Madison still held out hope that there would not be a tie, even though he had by then received Jefferson's 19 December letter reporting that Federalists "openly declare they will prevent an election, and will name a President of the Senate pro tem. by what they say would only be a *stretch* of the constitution."[20] This hope must have been quashed by Jefferson's letter of 26 December, which said that there was "no doubt" of a tie and that "The Feds appear determined to prevent an election, & to pass a bill giving the appointment to mr. Jay, appointed Chief justice, or to Marshall as Secy. Of state."[21] On 5 January, Madison wrote, "I have but little hopes, but from the prudence & decision of Burr himself."[22]

After it was clear that there was in fact a tie, and that Federalists had their own ideas about the way to settle the controversy, Madison suggested to Jefferson a resolution he believed would offer the right outcome but would also be legitimate from the perspective of republican theory.[23] As he saw it, the "course demanded by the crisis" was a "question of the first order." Specifically, because the new Congress would not meet for another eleven months, the question was whether it would be better "to acquiesce in a suspension or usurpation of the Executive authority till the meeting of [the next] Cong[res]s" or

[17] *PJM*, 17:416; Wills, *Negro President*, 68–69.
[18] *PJM*, 17: 416.
[19] James Monroe to Madison, 6 November 1800, and Madison to Monroe, ca. 10 November 1800, *PJM*, 17: 431, 435.
[20] Madison to James Monroe, ca. 27 December 1800, *PJM*, 448–9; Jefferson to Madison, 19 December 1800, *PJM*, 17:444–5.
[21] Jefferson to Madison, 26 December 1800, *PJM*, 17: 448.
[22] Madison to John Francis Mercer, 5 January 1801, *PJM*, 17: 452.
[23] Madison to Jefferson, 11 January 1801, *PJM*, 17: 454.

"for Cong[res]s to be summoned by a joint proclamation or recommendation of the two characeters hav[in]g a majority of votes for President."

Madison favored the latter option, the one that would have Jefferson and Burr issue a joint proclamation:

> The prerogative of convening the legislature must reside entirely in one or other of them, and if both concur, must substantially include the requisite will. The intentions of the people would undoubtedly be pursued. And if, in reference to the Constn: the proceedings be not strictly regular, the irregularity will be less in form than any other adequate to the emergency; and will lie in form rather than in substance; whereas the other remedies proposes are substantial violations of the will of the people, of the scope of the Constitution, and of the public order & interest. It is to be hoped however that all such questions will be precluded by a proper decision of nine states in the H. of R.

It is significant that Madison appealed to "prerogative" as a way out of the controversy and as an alternative to imaginative constitutional arguments by Federalists. And it is clear that Madison conceived of this solution as less than regular. But Madison's irregular solution is most revealing in that it twice refers "to the intentions of the people" *before* addressing whether the proceedings would be "regular" with regard to the Constitution. Accordingly, Madison writes that even though his solution would be less than regular with regard to the letter of the Constitution, it would fit within the substance and scope of the Constitution. Put differently, the Federalist plan to name Marshall or Jay president was arguably a regular fit to the Constitution's text, but it would violate its end. For Madison, then, determining and abiding by the will of the people was necessary to a correct understanding of the Constitution's end with regard to presidential selection.

If Madison's solution to the crisis of 1800 seems very distant from his critique of Jefferson in *Federalist* No. 49, it is because it was. The extent of this distance is revealed by four other parts of the context. First, and as has been mentioned, there is evidence that some Federalists were plotting to install someone other than Burr or Jefferson as president. In addition to the letter from Jefferson, Madison received letters from others reporting such plans.[24] Second, it is clear that Jefferson allowed the threat of military intervention to remain on the table. In his later *Anas*, Jefferson wrote that he told John Adams that any attempt by Congress to name a temporary president would "probably produce resistance by force."[25] At the same time as Jefferson's grave warning, the

---

[24] John Francis Mercer to Madison, 8 February 1801, and John Dawson to James Madison, 12 February 1801, *PJM*, 17: 462–64. From the editors of the Madison papers we know that there was a dinner for the retiring Oliver Wolcott reported in the *Gazette*, 7 February 1801. This dinner included a toast to C.C. Pinkney as the next president. Also, Ackerman has provided a new argument that one plan was to make John Marshall president, and that Marshall himself worked to make this happen. See Ackerman, *Failure of the Founding Fathers*, chapter 2.
[25] *Jefferson Writings*, 695.

Republican governors of Virginia and Pennsylvania had readied their militias, and, according to an account from a French visitor, a mob of persons "impatient" at the "obstinacy of the Federalists" made its presence felt in the tiny capital city.[26]

It is difficult to determine whether Madison agreed with Jefferson's threat of resistance by force. But it is certain that by March Madison knew that his friends had been leaving that path open. In a 18 February letter, Jefferson wrote Madison to plan for their travel together to Washington, but his report on the choice open to Federalists is most revealing:

> The Minority in the H. of R. after seeing the impossibility of electing B. the certainty that a legislative usurpation would be resisted by arms, and a recourse to a Convention to reorganise and amend the government, held a consultation on this dilemma, Whether it would be better for them to come over in a body, and go with the tide of the times, or by a negative conduct suffer the election to be made by a bare majority, keeping their body entire & unbroken, to act in phalanx on such ground of opposition as circumstances shall offer? We know their determination on this question only by their vote of yesterday.[27]

On 28 February, Madison wrote what comes closest to an approval of the Republican strategy, repeating the use of military metaphor:

> The result of the contest of the H.R. was generally looked for in this quarter. It was thought not probable that the phalanx would hold out agst. the general revolt of its partizans out of doors & without any military force to abet usurpation.

To be sure, Madison also observed that it was "fortunate" that the appeal to force had been "withheld," a result which provided "a lesson to America & the world," "given by the efficacy of the public will when there is no army to be turned agst. it!"[28]

Third, and perhaps more important, it is conceivable that Madison joined other Republicans in *hoping* for a new constitutional convention. On 5 February, George Jackson wrote Madison to assure him that there was "no Doubt" that "Jefferson will take the Presidential chair on the 4th."[29] The reason for Jackson's confidence was that Federalists had more to lose than did Republicans from an extra-constitutional appeal to the people:

> However the business is now fixt, And the Men of order and good government (as they call themselves) most give way or there will be no President, and let the Senate assume power if they dare. I very often tell some of them, take care of your Banks & paper currency. If you will not give us Jefferson for President, only

[26] Will, *Negro President*, 84–85; Ackerman, *Failure of Founding Fathers*, 88–89; and Daniel Sisson, *The American Revolution of 1800* (New York: Knopf, 1974), 422–27.
[27] Jefferson to Madison, 18 February 1801, *PJM*, 17: 467.
[28] Madison to Jefferson, 28 February 1801, *PJM*, 17: 475.
[29] George Jackson to James Madison, 5 February 1801, *PJM*, 17: 461.

Suffer an Interregnum to take place & see if your small states will ever get so much power in your hands again.

The negotiating point that Jackson emphasized – the power of the small states – is of supreme importance because it reveals how Madison might have connected partisan maneuvering to what he had always regarded as a larger constitutional flaw – state equality in the Senate. This flaw would have been all the more in the public mind because of the voting procedures in the House, in which each state had one vote. Perhaps, then, the reason for Madison's resort to this variant of an appeal to the people would not only be to ensure that Jefferson prevailed in the election but also to correct once and for all the constitutional flaw of state equality in the Senate. It is well known that Madison believed state equality in the Senate was a "sacrifice" of "theoretical propriety to the force of extraneous considerations."[30]

Fourth, as Ackerman points out, Albert Gallatin disagreed with Madison's proposal for Jefferson and Burr to call the new Congress into session. In the worst case, because it invited geographical factions to side with two competing Congresses, it risked "dissolution of Union." In the best case, the "complete success on our part" would come at the cost of departing from constitutional form and thus invite criticism. To put it differently, Gallatin advised that absent any "usurpation of power during the interregnum," it would be better to submit in order to maintain the constitutional high ground.[31] This point reveals that someone in Jefferson's inner circle argued that the best political path was the more constitutional path, but it also reveals that the person who gave that advice was Gallatin, not Madison.

This is to say that as Jefferson's presidency was just beginning, we can see that Madison had taken several important steps in solving constitutional difficulty. The most important fact is that in the election crisis of 1800, Madison's primary objective was ensuring that the correct candidate was awarded the office even if the process was less than regular. Moreover, this irregular approach would be guided more by the public will than it would be by clever constitutional argument.

Madison's Executive

As in the case of Jefferson, there has been a fairly standard account of Madison's presidency and of Madison's understanding of executive power. That account makes Madison more consistent than Jefferson, and, specifically, sees Madison as a consistent partisan of a weak executive.[32] Under this view,

---

[30] Madison, *Federalist* No. 37, Scigliano, 227.
[31] Ackerman, *Failure of Founding Fathers*, 83–84.
[32] One respected textbook concludes, "The decline of presidential influence was especially evident during James Madison's administration." Sidney M. Milkis and Michael Nelson, *The American Presidency: Origins and Development, 1776–2002.* Fourth Edition (Washington, DC: Congressional Quarterly, 2003), 108.

there is a line connecting Madison's passive handling of the presidency during the War of 1812 to his previous writings as Helvidius, and from these writings as Helvidius to his lack of attentiveness to the role of the executive when designing and forming the Constitution of 1787. In this view, Madison failed as president because he believed in a weak presidency.[33]

There has been, however, a kind of revisionist pushback against this negative assessment. In short, scholars who are perhaps worried about what they perceive to be an aggrandized executive in the last several decades have pointed to Madison as an example of constitutional sobriety during wartime. As Madison biographer Ralph Ketcham pointed out, Madison is the rather unusual wartime president who did not curtail civil liberties. Indeed, he had plenty of potential reasons to do so, and it is not so far-fetched to imagine that Andrew Jackson or Alexander Hamilton would have been less willing to let New England's resistance to the war go unanswered.[34]

Benjamin A. Kleinerman presents the clearest and most sustained of this revisionist interpretation of Madison and executive power. In Kleinerman's view, "Madison's presidency is tremendously successful precisely because he did not have to become a 'great' president in order for it to be so. Resisting the allure of greatness in order to comport with a republican constitutional order, Madison actively sought to transform the presidency into something much less active."[35] Importantly, Kleinerman distinguishes his account of Madison from others, especially that of Ketcham, by arguing that Madison's vision of the president differed not only from that of Hamilton but also that of Jefferson. That is, Kleinerman sees Madison as deliberately choosing a weak presidency because that president fit Madison's peculiar conception of executive power. In his prior book, Kleinerman argued that Madison represents a third way between Hamilton and Jefferson and in some ways foreshadows Kleinerman's preferred Lincolnian model of executive power. Kleinerman writes that Madison rejected Hamilton's recommendation to read prerogative into the Constitution on the grounds that any means required for the ends of government were already "implied by the very existence of government."[36] Although Madison believed that the Constitution was necessary to give sufficient energy to the government,

---

Ralph Ketcham, *James Madison: A Biography* (Charlottesville: University Press of Virginia, 1971), 585–86. It should be noted that Gary Schmitt reads Madison's argument as Helvidius as leaving considerable space for executive discretion. I think Schmitt overstates this point, but it is a useful reminder of the complexity of Madison's view of the executive. Gary Schmitt, "President Washington's Proclamation of Neutrality," in *The Constitutional Presidency*, ed. Joseph M. Bessette and Jeffrey K. Tulis, 54–75 (Baltimore: The Johns Hopkins University Press, 2009).

[34] Ralph Ketcham, "James Madison: The Unimperial President," *Virginia Quarterly Review* 54 (1978): 116–36.

[35] Benjamin A. Kleinerman, "The Constitutional Ambitions of James Madison's Presidency," *Presidential Studies Quarterly* 44 (2014): 9.

[36] Benjamin A. Kleinerman, *The Discretionary President: The Promise and Peril of Executive Power* (Lawrence: University Press of Kansas, 2009), 119.

he also believed that this energy "allows governmental power to be meaning-fully limited." So Kleinerman, like Rakove, interprets Madison's turn against executive power in the 1790s as "no important change" from his concern with legislative power in the 1780s. Rather than a change of principle, it was sim-ply a new application of the same principle to a new "threat."[37] This principle was that the constitutional government requires "landmarks of power," and Hamilton's emphasis on sovereignty and the ends of government threatened to obliterate the ability of the people to discern constitutional action from uncon-stitutional action.

Kleinerman uses this point to reflect on the place of public opinion for Madison and to make a subtle comparison with Jefferson. Kleinerman fol-lows Rosen and Sheehan to argue that Madison was concerned about the way public opinion, in its relationship to the constitution "as a foundational docu-ment," would be able to control the government.[38] On the one hand, this turn to public opinion is motivated by Madison's "realization that the institutional separation of powers Madison envisions in *Federalist* 51 does not work quite as well as he expected."[39] On the other – and this is a key step for Kleinerman – Madison resisted giving powers to the executive precisely because the president would be elected by the people. Pointing to Stephen and Ruth Grant's argu-ment about Madison in the constitutional convention, and to the fact that Federalists argued that the opponents of Washington were wrong to distrust the person who had been elected president, Kleinerman connects Madison's fear of democratic majorities to what Kleinerman sees as Madison's fear of elected presidents.[40] "To understand the whole of Madison's dispute with Hamilton, we must realize that, far from disputing a strong executive because he is insufficiently representative of the people, Madison disputes him because he is."[41] It is this wariness of democratic majorities that, for Kleinerman, confirms a fundamental difference between Madison and Jefferson. "It is because Madison continues despite or because of his republicanism to distrust democracy that, much like their disagreement about constitutional stability in Federalist 49, Madison's standard differs from his friend Jefferson's and resembles Lincoln's."[42]

Kleinerman's Madison, then, differs from Sheehan's Madison in that Kleinerman resists Sheehan's main argument that, for Madison, public opin-ion was sovereign. Instead, Kleinerman's Madison wishes to replace public opinion with constitutional fidelity. But, curiously, Kleinerman does not seek

---

[37] Ibid., 122.
[38] Ibid., 129.
[39] Ibid., 134.
[40] Ruth Weissbourd Grant and Stephen Grant, "The Madisonian Presidency," in *The Presidency in the Constitutional Order*, ed. Joseph M. Bessette and Jeffrey Tulis, 31–64 (Baton Rouge: Louisiana State University Press, 1981).
[41] Ibid., 137.
[42] Ibid., 143.

to reconcile his presentation of the Madisonian executive with Madison's well-known defense of the president's control over the removal power. This is a notable omission, because, as was argued in Chapter 3, Madison's treatment of the removal power has to do with the executive and with public opinion. Specifically, Madison linked presidential removal powers to an argument from democratic accountability.

Madison and Executive Power: Partisan Removals

As has been argued at some length, Madison's treatment of the removal power offers an underutilized opportunity to examine Madison's treatment of constitutional imperfection. In the first Congress, Madison had argued that the Constitution gave the president the power to remove. Interestingly, while legal scholars and presidency scholars have long been interested in Madison's role in the Great Debate of 1789, Madison scholars have not really paid attention to Madison's argument, even though Madison made the case that "responsibility" presumed an electoral "chain" between executive administration and the people.[43] Madison's preference of responsibility over "stability" as a way to understand the Vesting Clause of Article II marked an important, and pre-partisan, difference with Hamilton and an important clue in understanding Madison's rankings of constitutional priorities.[44] Indeed, at first glance, it would seem that this argument would provide critical evidence confirming the "democratic" interpretations offered by Banning and Sheehan.

It must also be mentioned that scholars who study removals tend to omit consideration of Madison's view after 1789. For example, Steven G. Calabresi and Christopher S. Yoo devote a chapter to each president, yet their five-page chapter on Madison only spends one page on his removal policies as president.[45] This might be expected, because, as Madison succeeded Jefferson in office, there was perhaps little opportunity for Madison to remove officials from office. But this misses the larger point. Madison's 1789 position was complicated when Jefferson expanded the power after winning the presidency. Although Jefferson in his First Inaugural famously called for conciliation between the parties, he soon set the precedent for a partisan use of the removal power.[46] On top of removing corrupt officeholders and midnight appointees

[43] For an introduction to the legal literature, see Steven G. Calabresi and Christopher S. Yoo, *The Unitary Executive: Presidential Power from Washington to Bush* (New Haven, CT: Yale University Press, 2008).

[44] Jeremy D. Bailey, "The Unitary Executive and Democratic Theory: The Problem of Alexander Hamilton," *American Political Science Review* 102 (2008): 453–65.

[45] Calabresi and Yoo, *Unitary Executive.*

[46] For an extended consideration of Jefferson's transformation of the removal power, see Bailey, *Jefferson and Executive Power*, chapter 6. The following discussion draws from J. David Alvis, Jeremy D. Bailey, and F. Flagg Taylor, *The Contested Removal Power, 1789–2010* (Lawrence: University Press of Kansas, 2013).

whom he believed had no rightful claim on the office, Jefferson removed Federalist officeholders in states where he believed Federalists held too large a proportion of the offices. When he removed Elizur Goodrich, collector at the port in New Haven, a group of New Haven merchants sent Jefferson a letter of protest. Jefferson responded with a public letter defending his removal policy on two grounds.[47] First, the victorious party had "an equal right" to a proportionate share of offices, and the recent elections were a fair way to determine what was proportionate. Because Federalists had for so long refused to share Connecticut offices with Republicans, removals would have to be especially remedial. Second, because administration must have the confidence of the people to be successful, it should reflect "the will of the nation." That is, because replacing Federalists with Republicans would invigorate administration by connecting it to the public will, partisan removals could be justified without appealing to proportionality.

As has been argued in a recent study of the removal power, Jefferson clearly relied on Madison's 1789 argument from responsibility, but he also changed that argument in important way.[48] Unlike Madison, Jefferson never pointed to the vesting clause or take-care clause to justify his position that the president held the removal power under the Constitution. Rather, Jefferson emphasized the part of Madison's argument that presidential removal powers would enhance responsibility. As was described in Chapter 3, Madison argued that giving the president the power would create a "chain of dependence" linking the president to the community. Similarly, to the New Haven merchants, Jefferson argued,

> If the will of the nation, manifested by their various elections, calls for an administration of government according with the opinions of those elected; if, for the fulfillment of that will, displacements are necessary, with whom can they so justly begin as with persons appointed in the last moments of an administration, not for its own aid, but to begin a career at the same time with their successors, by whom they had never been approved, and who could scarcely expect from them a cordial cooperation?[49]

This argument clearly corresponded with what was earlier described as the more accurate version of Jefferson's view of executive power: rather than grounding executive power in strained readings of constitutional text, Jefferson preferred to locate them in an understanding of the president's connection to public opinion. Importantly, Jefferson's reliance on party affiliation as a way to identify and sort public opinion was a potential change from Madison's more abstract defense of responsibility over stability.

---

[47] Thomas Jefferson to Elias Shipman and Others, 12 July 1801, *Jefferson Writings*, 498–500.
[48] Alvis, Bailey, and Taylor, *The Contested Removal Power.*
[49] Jefferson to Elias Shipman and Others, a Committee of the Merchants of New Haven, 12 July 1801, *Jefferson Writings*, 498–99.

These differences between Jefferson's response and Madison's prior argument raise two questions about Madison's view of constitutional politics. First, now that parties had entered the picture and Jefferson had defended removals on the basis of partisanship, did Madison adjust his understanding of the Constitution to include parties? Second, what did Madison make of Jefferson's assertion and transformation of presidential removal powers, particularly Jefferson's emphasis on the majority will?

The record does not provide a definitive answer. We do know that Madison participated in drafting Jefferson's reply to the New Haven Federalists, noting that Jefferson's response would require a "peculiar mixture of energy and delicacy."[50] We also know that Madison and Jefferson both criticized James Monroe for signing the Tenure of Office Act of 1820, which provided a fixed four-year term for some executive branch officials. Jefferson and Madison told Monroe they believed the law infringed on the president's removal power because it would invite the Senate to wield too much influence over removals.[51] Madison in particular worried that the law implied that Congress could limit the term to one year, which would have the result of transferring control over these officials to the Senate.[52] Finally, we know that Madison later endorsed the argument for presidential control over removals during the controversy over Andrew Jackson's removal policies. In that controversy, leading Whigs such as Daniel Webster and Henry Clay argued that the Decision of 1789 was wrong, and that a proper reading of the Constitution revealed that either the Senate should share the removal power with the president or that Congress may delegate the power where it pleases. Madison rejected these readings and remained convinced of the presidential position, arguing that the rival positions would "disturb the operation checks & balances" under the Constitution. To one such proponent, Charles Francis Adams, Madison argued that Adams's proposal to give the Senate a share of the removal power would have the "inconvenient" consequence of "throwing the Executive machinery out of gear" and thereby produce a "calamitous interregnum."[53]

Madison's critique of the Whigs sharpens the question at hand by adding the problem of Jackson to the problem of Jefferson. Jackson famously asserted a broad reading of executive authority and expanded the use of the veto power as well as the removal power. But, unlike Jefferson, Jackson's use was explicitly

---

[50] Following Henry Adams, I attributed this statement to Jefferson in *Jefferson and Executive Power* (162), but I have since only been able to find this phrase in Madison's letter to Nicholas. Adams, *History of the United States During the Administrations of Thomas Jefferson*, 152.

[51] See Alvis, Bailey, and Taylor, *Contested Removal Power*, 62–63.

[52] "If a law can displace an officer at every period of 4 years, it can do so at the end of every year, or at every session of the Senate, and the tenure will then be at the pleasure of the Senate, as much of the President, & not of the P[resident] alone." Madison to James Monroe, 28 December 1820, *Madison Papers Retirement* 2: 191–93.

[53] Madison to Charles Francis Adams, 12 October 1835, in Hunt, 9: 534–36.

partisan, as it was associated with the spoils system and with the new argument for the legitimacy of partisanship itself.[54] Yet another way it differed from Jefferson's – and this was noticed by Whigs like Webster – is that Jackson combined the argument from democratic accountability – what Madison called responsibility – with a muscular and even Hamiltonian rendering of constitutional authority under Article II of the Constitution.

Seen from this vantage point, Madison's late position on removals is of special interest and should be classified with precision. It is significant that Madison offered at least a qualified endorsement of Jackson by criticizing the Whig proposals to diminish the president's control over removals. But it is also significant that Madison stated, incorrectly, that Jackson had not actually defended removals by defending the spoils system, a system Madison also said needed to be corrected by amendment to the Constitution. What we do not know is if Madison agreed with Jefferson's expansion of Madison's own argument. On the one hand, I do not know of any statement from Madison endorsing the Jeffersonian gloss on Madison's original case for presidential removal powers. On the other, Madison seems to have changed the emphasis of his 1789 argument by talking less about the Vesting Clause and more about efficiency in the executive branch and separation of powers. Indeed, the arguments drawn from Article II seem to have dropped from his defense of presidential removal powers.

Extra-Constitutional Acquisitions of Territory: Louisiana and West Florida

Madison's acquisition of West Florida as president offers a potentially rich comparison point with Jefferson's Louisiana Purchase. The territory of West Florida, which ran along the Gulf Coast from New Orleans to just east of Mobile, had been disputed since the Louisiana Purchase. Spain said that it had never ceded that part of its territory to France, while the United States claimed that it had and that West Florida was part of the Louisiana Territory. In 1810, Madison's hand was forced, when, as Ralph Ketcham put it, "four-fifths of the perhaps twenty thousand inhabitants were Americans, and Spanish authority crumbled as France and then Great Britain threatened to occupy Florida and other territories under pretense of upholding their rival puppet governments of Spain." In June, Madison directed William Claiborne to send William Wykoff Jr. to organize Americans to request entry into the United States, and, in October, Madison issued a secret proclamation ordering military occupation. According to Stagg's account, one of the many inconveniences happened in the interval. Specifically, "West Floridians took steps of their own" and organized

---

[54] Again, see *Contested Removal Power*, chapters 2 and 3. See also Richard Hofstadter, *The Idea of a Party System*. See also Marc Landy and Sidney M. Milkis, *Presidential Greatness* (Lawrence: University Press of Kansas, 2000).

a constitutional convention, hoping to gain entry to the United States on better terms.[55] The problem for Madison was that under settled understandings
of international law, the United States could not negotiate with a territory it
already claimed it owned. That problem went away when Claiborne was dis-
patched to the area and arrived in December with the president's now public
proclamation and the authority to use military force.[56]

At first glance, Madison's acquisition would seem to be in the same ball-
park as the Louisiana Purchase. As scholars have long noticed, Jefferson's
purchase and incorporation of the Louisiana territory flew against Jefferson's
creed of strict construction – or, more precisely, the Louisiana Purchase was,
by Jefferson's own confession, "an act beyond the Constitution."[57] It is for
this reason that Jefferson, with Madison's help, drafted an amendment to the
Constitution that he believed would provide the necessary authority for the
treaty after the fact, an amendment that was never proposed. With respect
to Madison and West Florida, Burstein and Isenberg point out that Madison
had likely encouraged violation of the Neutrality Act's prohibition against
filibustering, a law Congress passed in 1794 after Washington's Neutrality's
Proclamation and the very law used to prosecute Aaron Burr.[58] More broadly,
Ketcham concludes that this was "government by proclamation," and was anti-
thetical to Madison's republican belief in executive deference to Congress.[59]
Indeed, there is evidence that Madison perceived a problem, and he looked
to his advisors and to Jefferson, expressing his concern about legal propriety.
To Gallatin, Madison wrote: "You will have seen the projected Constn: for W.
Florida & noted among other particulars, the power to the Temporary Govt. to
grant lands. Should it become necessary, for the Ex. to exercise authority within
those limits, before the meeting of Congs. I foresee many legal difficulties."[60] Of
William Eustis, Madison asked: "Will you turn your thoughts to the question,
what steps are within the Executive Competency, in case the deliberations of
the people of W. Florida should issue in an offer to place the territory under the
Authority of the U.S.?"[61]

Gallatin's response, however, reveals that in his view the Florida question
was unlike that of Louisiana in that the constitutional question hinged on a
statutory one. For him, the legal question was easy, because the laws regarding the incorporation of Louisiana had been "so worded as to include in the
districts of Orleans & Mobile whatever we may claim & possess." Accordingly,
"the law also which authorizes the President to take possession of Louisiana
will legally cover any other measures which policy may dictate in relation to

[55] Stagg, *Borderlines in Borderlands*, 60.
[56] Ibid., 70.
[57] Thomas Jefferson to John C. Breckinridge, 12 August 1803, *Jefferson Writings*, 1139.
[58] Burstein and Isenberg, *Madison and Jefferson*, 492 and 733 note 45.
[59] Ketcham, *James Madison*, 501.
[60] Madison to Albert Gallatin, 22 August 1810, *Madison Papers Presidency*, 2:500–01.
[61] Madison to William Eustis, 30 August 1810, *Madison Papers Presidency*, 2: 516–17.

that part of West Florida which lies between the Mississippi & the Perdido." Indeed, the legal question was not really the one that he saw as all that complicated. Instead, he advised, "But what ground ought generally to be taken consistent with justice, the rights and interests of the U. States, and the preservation of peace, is the difficult question."[62]

Madison eventually accepted this advice, but he seems to have at least acknowledged that the legal question could lead to different answers.[63] On 19 October, Madison wrote Jefferson that the crisis presented "serious questions, as to the Authority of the Executive, and the adequacy of the existing laws of the U.S. for territorial administration." Moreover, there was the additional question of whether he should wait to get direction from Congress: "And the near approach of Cong[res]s might subject any intermediate interposition of the Ex[ecutive] to the charge of being premature and disrespectful, if not of being illegal." But these legal questions had to be balanced by other considerations: "Still there is great weight in the considerations, that the Country to the Perdido, being our own, may be fairly taken possession of, if it can be done without violence, above all if there be danger of its passing into the hands of a third and dangerous party."[64] Less than two weeks later, Madison had decided that these questions were solved by Gallatin's reading of the statute. In his proclamation of 27 October, Madison explicitly cited congressional authority.[65] To William Pinckney on 30 October, Madison was matter-of-fact in his description of his action: "The occupancy of the Territory as far as the Perdido was called for by the crisis there, and is understood to be within the authority of the Executive. East Florida, also, is of great importance to the United States, and it is not probable that Congress will let it pass into any new hands."[66] With Gallatin, Madison believed the power had been delegated by Congress.

Difficulties remain. In the view of Burstein and Isenberg, Madison's appeal to statutory authority amounted to an appeal to Jefferson's extralegal acquisition of Louisiana to find a legal reason (the 1804 delegation by Congress) to get Florida.[67] But this presumes that for Madison Florida and Louisiana presented the same kind of constitutional difficulty. If Louisiana troubled Jefferson and Madison because the provision for incorporation exceeded the national government's power (not that the president's action infringed on congressional prerogatives), then it is hard to see how that problem would

---

[62] Albert Gallatin to James Madison, 5 September 1810, *Madison Papers Presidency*, 2: 526–27.
[63] Citing the letter to Jefferson, Stagg overstates the extent of Madison's doubts. See *Borderlines in Borderlands*, 73.
[64] Madison to Jefferson, 19 October 1810, *Republic of Letters*, 1648.
[65] "The acts of Congress, though contemplating a present possession by a foreign authority, have contemplated also an eventual possession of the said territory by the United States, and are accordingly so framed as in that case to extend in their operation to the same." See Madison, Presidential Proclamation, 27 October 1810, *Madison Papers Presidency*, 2: 595–97.
[66] See Madison to William Pinkney, 30 October 1810, *Madison Papers Presidency*, 2: 603–06.
[67] Burstein and Isenberg, *Madison and Jefferson*, 492.

not apply to Florida as well. The difference would have to be that the people being incorporated in the Florida case were mostly Americans, whereas the people being incorporated in the Louisiana case were not. As Stagg argues, a reason why Madison successfully acquired West Florida, and not East Florida or Texas, was that West Florida already had "a large enough number of American settlers."[68]

The second difficulty is that it is possible that Madison was incorrect about Congress's intentions. As Stagg has noted, Federalists in Congress disagreed with the action as a matter of policy, but they also disagreed with Gallatin's and Madison's interpretation of the law. In the Senate, debate mostly turned on the question of "how far the United States could be said to have had a good claim to West Florida under the 1803 Louisiana Purchase treaty and whether the president could still continue to negotiate with foreign powers over the status of a region that was now under the jurisdiction of the Orleans Territory."[69] This included long analyses of European treaties in the eighteenth century to determine whether Spain had in fact ceded the territory to France, as well as a long detour over whether Massachusetts Senator (and former Secretary of State) Timothy Pickering had violated Senate procedures when he read from a letter from Talleyrand, a letter that Pickering believed demonstrated that Talleyrand did not believe the Territory was included in the Louisiana Purchase. But the debate also included discussion of whether Madison's actions exceeded his constitutional authority. According to Pickering, Madison's proclamation was both an act of "legislation" and an act of "war." Consequently, it was self-evident that the president did not have the power under the Constitution, because the power was either legislative in nature or part of the war power, and Congress was given "exclusive" control over both. Moreover, it was "equally clear" that Congress had not delegated the power to the president because, in Pickering's view, under the terms of the law in 1803, any delegation of authority would have expired in 1804.[70] On the other side, Henry Clay countered Pickering's claim that the law had expired by saying a different part of the law had expired but the part dealing with the Floridas had not. As a result, "The President, by his proclamation, has not made new law but has merely declared to the people of West Florida what the law is."[71]

It is perhaps not a coincidence that Jefferson also offered a potential way to compare the two. Jefferson included West Florida in the hypothetical he used in his famous statement on prerogative in his letter to John B. Colvin, written in September 1810.[72] There, Jefferson introduced a hypothetical, weighing the

[68] Stagg, *Borderlines in Borderlands*, 207.
[69] Ibid., 79.
[70] *Annals of Congress*, Senate, 11th Cong., 3rd sess., 44–46.
[71] Ibid., 62.
[72] Jefferson to John B. Colvin, 20 September 1810, *Jefferson Writings*, 1231–34.

chance to purchase "the Floridas for reasonable sum" against the likelihood that "a John Randolph" would delay congressional action until Spain changed its mind about selling. To be sure, the hypothetical is not a perfect match because it included East Florida, which was the territory the United States did not claim it already held, and because the example might have been intended to say more about Louisiana in 1803 than about Florida in 1810. But what is important is that the hypothetical was designed to remove statutory authority as a source of authority for the action. That is, Jefferson went out of his way to wonder what he would do as president in the event that Congress stood in the way of the chance to acquire the Floridas. Jefferson's answer, which explicitly weighed the importance of "reverence for the law," was that the president should act to "secure the good of his country, and to have trusted to their justice for the transgression of the law."

Jefferson's Florida hypothetical is important because it reveals the distance between Jefferson and Madison. There is nothing in the record to suggest that Madison ever considered speaking of Florida in these broad terms. Whereas Jefferson was more than willing to push extra-constitutional prerogative as far it would go, Madison seemed reluctant to act on executive prerogative and then rely on the appeal to the people – or throw himself, as Jefferson frequently called it – by way of a constitutional amendment. Indeed, Stagg notes that Federalist arguments in Congress forced Madison's administration to publish "lengthy defenses of the American title to West Florida in the *National Intelligencer*," but these arguments were all about the claims the United States had to the territory, not lengthy or broad defenses of executive power.[73] Indeed, the defenses of the administration dismiss the constitutional argument on the grounds that the president can send troops to any of the "different parts of the same territory, it being included in our purchase of Louisiana."[74] Madison's handling of West Florida, then, corresponds with Kleinerman's argument that Madison deliberately distanced himself from the Jeffersonian understanding of executive power, but it also qualifies it in the sense that it appears that Madison was also willing to let congressional delegation stand in as a solution to vexing questions of constitutional authority.[75] But, as we will see, Madison did not always resist the appeal to the people as a solution.

---

[73] Stagg, *Borderlines in Borderlands*, 80–81. Stagg cites the 22 December and 29 December editions of the *National Intelligencer*.

[74] See "West Florida," quoting from the *Virginia Patriot*, in *National Intelligencer*, Washington, DC, 25 December 1810.

[75] It must also be noted that Madison defended Andrew Jackson's later controversial conquest of Florida in language that Jefferson had used to defend similar acts by others. To Monroe, Madison wrote that the "question between him & his country ought to be judged, under the persuasion that if he has erred, it was in the zeal of his patriotism, and under the recollection also of the great services he has rendered." Madison to Monroe, 13 February 1819, *Madison Papers Retirement* 2: 415. On Jefferson's language, see Bailey, *Jefferson and Executive Power*, 234–47.

Presidential Selection and Constitutional Imperfection Revisited

For early Americans, 1800 must have demonstrated that the Constitution could not anticipate every event. Indeed, the problem was so great that Americans did what they so rarely do – amend the Constitution. However, the Twelfth Amendment was more than the Aaron Burr Amendment. More than a solution for the determining who would be president and who would be vice president, the amendment was understood as an attempt to transform the constitutional order by more clearly connecting an electoral majority to the president.

Both Republicans and Federalists at the time knew that this would be result and calculated their political prospects as they discussed amending the rules for presidential selection. Perhaps the most important Federalist critic of the amendment was Connecticut Senator James Hillhouse. As I have argued elsewhere, Hillhouse perceived that the amendment would strengthen the president, and he accused supporters of the amendment of being blinded by "idol worship" of Jefferson.[76] What is also important to notice is that in the original 1804 debates, Hillhouse included an argument from veneration, an argument similar to Madison's argument in *Federalist* No. 49. Importantly, and in a speech that anticipated Lincoln's 1838 Lyceum address, Hillhouse linked his worry with an order-shattering executive to frequent changes of the constitution. In his view, "When a whole society has become acquainted with its constitution, changes in it are dangerous." This is because "every change you make renders the knowledge of it uncertain to the people." In No. 49, as we have seen, Madison argued that the opinions of individuals were unfixed, and thus needed to be fortified by others and by time. Here Hillhouse argued that "uncertainty" with respect to the Constitution is the same as "ignorance" of the Constitution, and, like Lincoln, he predicted that ambitious executives would flourish and wreak havoc precisely when the people are uncertain about the Constitution: "[A]fter successive changes, it is the time for an usurper; and then the *friend of the people* who had stolen away their hearts, under the pretense of stealing away their liberties, steals them away too."[77]

Even though Hillhouse lost, and the amendment was ratified, Hillhouse continued his campaign against the newly empowered presidency. In 1808, he published a pamphlet calling for new amendments to the Constitution. One of those amendments would have limited eligibility for the presidency to senators at the end of their terms, and would have rendered the final choice to a lottery, with the president being the senator who drew the "colored ball."[78] Later, as a member of the Hartford Convention of 1814–1815, Hillhouse was

[76] Bailey, *Jefferson and Executive Power*, 209.

[77] Annals of Congress, Senate, 8th Cong., 1st sess., 191.

[78] James Hillhouse, *Propositions for Amending the Constitution of the United States* (New Haven, CT: Oliver Steele, 1808).

undoubtedly influential in including reform of presidential selection in the Convention's proposed amendments. In particular, one amendment limited the president to one term and stipulated that there could not be two successive presidents from the same state.[79]

Hillhouse's arguments resurfaced when the controversy surrounding John Quincy Adams's election in 1824 forced Americans to revisit their understanding of the presidency in the constitutional order. As was the case in 1800 and 1804, when partisans debated the extent to which public opinion should matter when selecting the president, 1824 provided another chance to revisit the question whether the Constitution positioned the president as a representative of the national people. Even before the election itself, Madison found himself giving advice about reforming presidential selection by constitutional amendment. In response to a proposal from former U.S. Attorney George Hay, Madison offered his own language for a constitutional amendment. Madison especially wanted to end the practice of having the House vote by state delegation (equality) in the contingency election, which he thought violated the "Republican principle of numerical equality," and thought the idea of assigned Electors by districts might make the small states willing to go along. Importantly, Madison "liked best" the idea to reduce the number of candidates in the contingent election from three to two, in order to increase the likelihood of a majority support. But interestingly, Madison would have gone further. Madison's preferred plan would give each member of the Electoral College two votes, a first choice and second choice. The two votes would then be counted on two lists, so that if the first list did not produce a majority, the second list might, thus "furnish[ing] a double chance of avoiding an eventual resort to Congress." Madison's proposal here is of interest for two reasons. First, it shows that he would have gone further than did the Twelfth Amendment in providing the president with electoral independence. Second, it shows Madison did not think that constitutional veneration of a "settled" constitution was an unqualified good. In fact, he made the opposite argument. In his view, as the Constitution habituates citizens and politicians, "opinions and commitments formed under its influence may become settled obstacles" to constitutional change. Just as veneration for the Articles of Confederation might stand in the way of important reforms such as the negative on state laws, veneration for the Constitution itself might stand in the way of necessary reform.[80] Or, as the Reverend James Madison had told him in 1789, "Defects themselves gain Strength & Respect by Time."[81]

---

[79] George Cabot et al, "Report of the Hartford Convention," 1815, in Bruce Frohnen, ed., *The American Republic* (Indianapolis, IN: Liberty Fund, 2002), 447–57.

[80] Madison to Hay, 23 August 1823, Hunt 9: 147–55. Jefferson called the Articles a "venerable fabrick." Jefferson to John Adams, 13 November 1787, *Jefferson Writings*, 914.

[81] Reverend James Madison to Madison, *PJM*, 15 August 1789, 12: 338.

Veneration versus Innovation

Madison's qualification of veneration is even more pronounced once we realize that veneration was in the air. As we have seen, Hillhouse had appealed to it to oppose the Twelfth Amendment. Likewise, in the context of the election controversy of 1824, opponents to reforming presidential selection explicitly appealed to veneration as a reason to retain the Electoral College and the contingency election in the House. Before turning to this key debate about the value of constitutional veneration, it is necessary to summarize the amendments being proposed.

In the 19th Congress, there was an extraordinary debate about amending the Constitution to democratize presidential selection. There were many different proposals, but the two main ones were, first, to remove the Electoral College and institute a direct popular vote (Andrew Jackson would later propose a constitutional amendment removing "all intermediate agency" in selecting the president), and, second, to require the district method rather than winner-take-all in the states. The debates were entangled in the partisan conflicts of the day, especially by the question of Andrew Jackson and his defeat resulting from the "corrupt bargain" between John Quincy Adams and Henry Clay, but the parties were in the process of realigning, and the differing views on the role of the presidency contributed to that realignment. That is, the constitutional question in 1826 turned not only on the question of Jackson. Rather, it turned on the very principle that the Revolution of 1800 had made part of its centerpiece. Namely, the question turned on whether the president was supposed to be a representative of the people or whether representation in the federal government was a job only for Congress. In general, supporters of reform believed that John Quincy Adams's victory was illegitimate and that the Constitution was flawed in providing a constitutional path for someone to win the presidency by being favored by state delegations in the House rather than by the electorate at large.[82] The opponents to reform perceived that the reform would ratify the principle that the president represents the people, and, like the Federalist counterparts in 1800 and 1804, they argued that the original Constitution supposed a more limited role for the president. Moreover, they argued that the president should not and could not represent the people.[83] The contest of 1824 was like the contest

---

[82] See, for example, James K. Polk's argument that there should be no Electoral College and no contingency election in the House because "the people require no such agency." *Register of Debates*, House of Representatives, 19th Cong., 1st sess., 1647.

[83] Edward Everett was clearest in his critique, arguing that the president "is not a Representative of any part of the people, not even of those who choose him." Thomas Mitchell of South Carolina, who was a Jackson supporter, agreed with Everett and argued that no majority "could be united in favor of any one candidate." That is why the Constitution requires an "intervening body, by which their views might be previously collected, digested, and ascertained." *Register of Debates*, House of Representatives, 19th Cong., 1st sess., 1826, 1581, 1715, and 1717.

of 1800 in that it forced Americans to encounter the puzzle of presidential representation.[84]

In addition to these arguments about the representative nature of the presidency, there was also debate about the desirability of amending the Constitution. This debate turned explicitly on whether constitutional veneration was more desirable than "innovation." Henry Storrs of New York seems to have been the first in the House debate to bring up veneration as a reason to oppose the amendment. He prefaced his case against the amendment by imploring his colleagues "to approach this subject with the profoundest reverence of the Constitution," which was, in his opinion, the product of "patriots" who were "raised up by Providence," "highly gifted by nature," and "deeply versed in political knowledge." In his view, then, they should tread carefully as they were on "holy ground."[85] Andrew Stevenson of Virginia agreed, claiming that the Constitution was the work "of the most illustrious body of men that the world ever saw." Accordingly, he treated the Constitution with the "same feelings of veneration and awe" as he did with the "sepulcher of [his] fathers." Stevenson went on to defend veneration on grounds like those Madison laid out in No. 49, namely that this was not the time for "public experiments," which tend to "shake the public confidence in the stability of our free institutions."[86] Dutee Pearce also argued that the constitution should not "be affected by every wind" in public opinion because there would always be people dissatisfied politically and therefore desirous of constitutional change. As an example of this tendency, he pointed to the proposals of the Hartford Convention. In his view, if these and other proposals had actually succeed, the Constitution would become a "Mosaic pavement" of white and black stone.[87] Edward Everett of Massachusetts agreed with this point about stability and cited what he called an "acknowledge maxim of political prudence" – "that frequent changes of the laws, even in matters of ordinary legislation, are pernicious." He then said this point was even truer of the Constitution, which in the United States was "the only thing which the People of the United States have taken out of the grasp of this daily changeful legislation." Lacking the "perpetuities of the old world, political, social, and economic," the United States was in special need of a permanent Constitution.[88]

[84] There is an emerging literature about the development of the theory of presidential representation. For a discussion of this literature and for a discussion of the period from 1800 to 1864, see Jeremy D. Bailey, "Opposition to the Theory of Presidential Representation: Federalists, Whigs, and Democrats," *Presidential Studies Quarterly* 44 (2014): 50–71.
[85] *Register of Debates*, House of Representatives, 19th Cong., 1st sess., 1397–98.
[86] Ibid., 1532.
[87] Ibid., 1654.
[88] Ibid., 1573. In the Senate, Henry Edwards of Connecticut made the similar point that if Americans altered the Constitution "according to our impressions," it "would lose that respect and veneration it now has, and which it is desirable it should have." *Register of Debates*, House of Representatives, 19th Cong., 1st sess., 383.

Supporters of the amendment did not let the argument from veneration go unanswered, and some argued that veneration properly understood meant fixing the Constitution. Romulus Saunders from North Carolina said that he would not yield to anyone in his respect to framers of the Constitution, but, unlike Storrs, he would not "carry this veneration so far, as to suppose them divinely inspired, and that the humblest individual of that body possessed more information upon this subject, than all the politicians of the present day." Further, even though the Constitution had "stood the test of experience," "the infirmities of human nature forbid the idea of perfection in the Constitution." Not only did he believe that amendment of the Constitution was within reach; he also believed that members of Congress should "lend their aid" when "a majority of the American People require some modification."[89] Churchill Cambreleng of New York agreed, noting too that his "veneration for the Constitution could not be exceeded." Because he saw the Constitution as "a sacred inheritance," he "would touch it only to save it." Because the Constitution needed saving, the amendment was necessary.[90]

Others criticized the concept itself. Tennessee representative and future president James K. Polk also addressed the question of veneration, saying that he too had "reverence for [the government's] framers." But in his view their main contribution was establishing a system "where trembling subject does not bow submissively at the throne of power." Because the country in 1826 had "grown older in the knowledge of our Government" and had "learned from experience its defects," veneration should not stand in the way of change. In short, he could not "be blind its defects" and could not "idolize" the Constitution.[91] Another Tennessee Representative, Jacob Isacks, attacked veneration more directly, dismissing veneration as "idolatry" and as a diversionary tactic. In his view, the Framers were to be praised for establishing "the charter of our liberty" and not for creating a "charter of exemption from the weakness and wickedness of human nature." More broadly, Isacks argued that veneration stood in the way of progress: "Shall all the lights of science, of practical liberty, and experience be lost on us?".[92] Joseph Lecompte of Kentucky agreed, noting that "veneration of the Constitution" needed to give way when "the test of forty years' experience" had demonstrated that the Constitution was "defective in one very important point."[93] James Mitchell, from Tennessee, followed this frontal attack on veneration with one of his own. If veneration is to be preferred over innovation, then "all your institutions for education" – all the "common schools," "academies," and "colleges and universities" – would be "of no use or value." Indeed, in his view, the proponents of veneration believed

[89] Ibid., 1465.
[90] Ibid., 1552.
[91] Ibid., 1653.
[92] Ibid., 1708.
[93] Ibid., 1709.

that "the advantages of science had passed away" and that the framers were "models of infallible wisdom" and had benefited from divine "inspiration."[94]

It is difficult to determine the extent to which Madison followed these debates, but the irony of the situation must have not been lost on him. From the very beginning, Madison had consistently recommended amending the Constitution to connect the president more firmly to the national majority and to remove the disproportionate influence of the small states. But opponents to these reforms had consistently used Madison's own argument from veneration to counter these reforms. The record so far does not leave evidence one way or the other that Madison thought this appeal to veneration was appropriate or not, but there is no reason to believe that it changed Madison's own mind about the necessity and urgency of reforming presidential selection. Indeed, it is telling that Madison did not use the occasion to come to the aid of veneration by distinguishing its proper application from its improper ones.

Hillhouse and the Presidency Revisited

In 1830, Madison was given the opportunity to revisit these questions about the presidency within the constitutional order, when Hillhouse sent Madison a copy of his new proposals to amend the Constitution to fix presidential selection and to give the Senate a share of the removal power. These were revised versions of amendments he had proposed in 1808. As he explained to Madison, he continued to believe that the Senate was an underutilized institution:

> No nation on earth have an Organized body, so peculiarly adapted to such a selection. A senate appointed with an express reference to their being the Candidates for the two first offices in our government, and having six years experience in the discharge of executive duties, before they can receive such an appointment, would ensure a President both competent, and well qualified.[95]

Madison replied politely with criticism, noting that the question had always been connected to the contest between the large and small states and predicting that Hillhouse's proposal to choose the president by lot from the Senate would be a nonstarter for the large states. Importantly, Madison also argued that Hillhouse's plan would result in a less effective president because the president under that system would lack "evidence of national confidence": "A President not appointed by the nation and without the weight derived from its selection & confidence, could not afford the advantage expected from the qualified negative on the act of the Legislative branch of the Gov[ernmen]t."[96] Madison went on to argue that the proposal to give the Senate a share of the removal power would upset the "harmony" in the executive branch by making officials "independent" of the president.

[94] Ibid., 1722–24.
[95] James Hillhouse to James Madison, 10 May 1830. Founders Early Access, Rotunda.
[96] Madison to James Hillhouse, May 1830, Hunt 9: 366–70.

The irony of this exchange should not cover over its significance. Hillhouse was now casting his reforms as ways to fix the Constitution, and Madison was now defending *the* Constitution as it had evolved over time. That is, Hillhouse was no longer appealing to Madison's argument from veneration as he had in 1804, when Madison and Jefferson were the constitutional innovators. But Madison himself was not rigidly committed to the Constitution as it was. Only a few years earlier, Madison had endorsed amending the Constitution and his proposed change – like Hillhouse's very different proposal – revealed that the presidency had been very much changed, and with it the larger constitutional order. Madison's proposed reform in 1823, like those of Jackson's advocates in the next several years, would have completed what the Twelfth Amendment started and would have formalized what had been under way since 1800. Namely, the argument from presidential representation was let out of the bag, and it corresponded perfectly with the new need for a representative of the whole nation and with the emergence of public opinion as a part of republican politics. Madison was clearly on one side of this debate. This is to say that even though Madison did not embrace every aspect of Jefferson's understanding of executive prerogative, Madison was nevertheless a loyal foot soldier, a faithful son, and a central adviser in Jefferson's transformation of the political order – a transformation that Tocqueville would later call both revolutionary and inevitable.[97] This transformation necessarily included a fundamental reconstitution of the order Madison helped create in 1787 and the one for which he is remembered.

As the next chapter will show, the exchange with Hillhouse was not an isolated event. Madison was frequently sought out by others looking for approval of their own constitutional work. Some were innovators and others were preservers, but as a collective they forced Madison to explain his own view of the tension between his role as Father of the Constitution and his work as Jeffersonian revolutionary. Moreover, they highlighted the importance and interrelated difficulty of his remaining projects, protecting Jefferson's reputation and providing the authoritative account of the Federal Convention and the Constitution of 1787.

---

[97] Alexis de Tocqueville, *Democracy in America*, trans. Harvey C. Mansfield and Delba Winthrop (Chicago: University of Chicago Press, 2000) 168–69.

7

Appeals to Text and History

"Some men look at constitutions with sanctimonious reverence, and deem them like the arc of the covenant, too sacred to be touched. They ascribe to the men of the preceding age a wisdom more than human, and suppose what they did to be beyond amendment. I knew that age well; I belonged to it, and labored with it. It deserved well of its country. It was very like the present, but without the experience of the present; and forty years of experience in government is worth a century of book-reading; and this they would say themselves, were they to rise from the dead."

Jefferson to Kercheval, 1816[1]

At the risk of understating Jefferson's emphasis on a strict construction of the Constitution, the above quotation serves as a nice contrast to the sentence from Madison's 1792 essay "Charters" that was used to introduce Chapter 5. Whereas in that passage Madison recommended that public opinion defend its "political scriptures" with a "holy zeal," Jefferson mocked this kind of reverence as "sanctimonious" and regarded it as an obstacle to progress. This book, however, has offered evidence showing that it would be a mistake, however, to presume that Madison treated the Constitution as holy writ. This is especially evident in his work to preserve, shape, and use the history of the Convention.

Even with all of the attention lavished on Madison's tenth essay in the *Federalist*, it is possible that Madison's most important contribution was textual rather than conceptual. Were it not for Madison's *Notes on the Federal Convention*, our knowledge of the Constitution and its design would be left to mere speculation, drawn from the unattractive combination of unmoored abstract reasoning, linguistic acrobatics, and sketchy historical evidence. This point is itself revealing, for it demonstrates that Madison himself wanted the deliberation on the Constitution, messy as it was, to be available to future

[1] Jefferson to Samuel Kercheval, 12 July 1816, *Jefferson Writings*, 1401.

constitutional designers. Or, as Gordon Lloyd puts it, "Madison reported on an actual conversation over 88 days, six days a week, five hours a day, between up to 55 delegates from a variety of backgrounds."[2] Madison did so because he believed that the details of that conversation would be of value to those would-be founders who would eventually want to understand the American example. Madison said as much in 1830, noting that one obstacle to his own efforts in the 1780s was the "deficiency" in the historical record then regarding the "the process, the principles, the reasons, & the anticipations, which had prevailed" in the formation of prior confederacies.[3]

Madison's explanation of his motive makes an important and startling point. It shows that Madison believed that the lack of textual evidence available to him in the 1780s complicated his own project to reform the Articles and firm up the footing for Union. That is, the lack of textual evidence about foundings obstructed – or made less than perfect – that for which he is now best known as a political theorist, namely his contribution to the theory of confederacy. Nevertheless, why and how Madison did what he did to source the Constitution remains an understudied part of his political thought. Previous chapters have explored Madison's political thought and practice to cast light on how he believed deliberation would work within a constitutional framework. Madison's composition of his records of the Convention raises a different question about the role the Constitution itself is supposed to play in that deliberation. This chapter's primary goal, then, is to reorient scholarship toward investigating Madison's understanding of his own purpose in recording, organizing, and distributing his history of the Federal Convention of 1787. Given the staggering size of the scholarship on Madison and originalism, it would be surprising if there remains anything at all to be said. But I think this subject has been treated only obliquely, because the object of analysis has been the methodology of originalism, not Madison.

Before the chapter turns to Madison's publication of his records of the Convention of 1787, it places Madison in the ongoing debates about writing the history of the Revolution and the early republic. As Drew McCoy's unsurpassed study of Madison's retirement period masterfully shows, Madison spent the last two decades of his life using his reputation to correct what he perceived to be the excesses of the new generation of nationalists, states' righters, and adherents of popular sovereignty.[4] Part of this project required that Madison defend himself against charges of inconsistency over time, especially with regard to the national bank and the demarcation of national and state

[2] Gordon Lloyd, "Editor's Introduction," in *Debates in the Federal Convention of 1787 by James Madison, a Member*, ed. Gordon Lloyd (Ashland, OH: Ashbrook Center, 2014), viii.
[3] Madison, "A Sketch never finished nor applied," in *Madison Writings*, 840. Rakove dates this document as "1830?".
[4] Drew R. McCoy, *The Last of the Fathers: James Madison & the Republican Legacy* (New York: Cambridge University Press, 1989).

authority. From Madison's perspective, this required a new effort of conceptual clarification and re-education, but it also required that Madison ensure that the historical record accurately reflect his recollection of what happened. Madison was not the only Founder concerned with the historical record. In the 1820s and 1830s, Americans were revisiting 1776 and 1787 to make sure that those events were not forgotten but also to make sure that they were remembered in the proper way. Even as Madison was thinking about making his records of the Convention of 1787 *the* textual record for the Convention, he contributed to Jefferson's efforts to do the same for 1776.

The Principles of the Declaration

One example of Madison's attempt to get the historical record right is Washington's Farewell Address. In June, 1823, Jefferson forwarded to Madison a copy of a letter he had sent Supreme Court Justice William Johnson, a Jefferson appointee.[5] Johnson was writing what Jefferson described as a "history of parties" and had requested Jefferson's opinions on a number of events in the 1790s, including the dispute between friends of Alexander Hamilton and friends of George Washington regarding the authorship of the Farewell Address. Jefferson replied that Madison had written a draft for Washington at the end of his first term, but that when Washington issued the address at the end of his second term, "Madison recognized in it several passages of his draught." There were other passages, however, that both Jefferson and Madison recognized as "from the pen of Hamilton," and still others from Washington himself. Jefferson added that the confusion was that Washington probably asked Hamilton to form the parts "into a whole, and hence it may appear in Hamilton's handwriting, as if it were all his composition."[6]

Madison responded that posterity would recognize the importance of his own contribution to the Farewell Address, adding that the most significant revisions were not so much what was added but what was "omitted" by Washington and Hamilton. But he also asked Jefferson to tell Johnson not to include his role in the drafting of the address, and worried that its public appearance then (rather than later, under the inevitable "truth of history") would bring some "complaint" upon him. More interesting for this discussion, Madison added that the friends of Washington were doing Washington a disservice by making it a "question between him and Col. Hamilton." Most simply, the evidence would work against Washington, because it was "no secret" that Washington sometimes "availed himself of the friendship of others" when it came to writing. But, more generally, Madison believed that Washington's friends missed the point. "They ought to claim for him the merit only of cherishing the principles and views addressed to his Country, and for the Address itself the weight given

---

[5] Jefferson to Madison, 13 June 1823, *Republic of Letters*, 1861.
[6] Jefferson to William Johnson, 12 June 1823, *Republic of Letters*, 1863.

to it by his sanction." In other words, Washington should be praised not for whatever "literary merit" derives from being the "pen." Rather, he should be praised for using his reputation to support and dignify the ideas contained in the Address. This was not the first time Madison thought about the question of credit for authorship.[7]

In the 1810s and 1820s, Americans turned in earnest to discussing the history of the revolution in 1776 and the formation of the Constitution in 1787. One notable example can be found in the famous correspondence between Jefferson and John Adams. As the War of 1812 entered its second year, the two renewed their correspondence, rehashing their differences regarding the French Revolution, discussing the role of the natural aristocracy, and speculating on the grounds of belief. One key subject was their views of the Revolution of 1776. Adams pointed out that he believed the "general principles" by which the fathers achieved independence were twofold, namely Christianity and Anglo-American liberty.[8] Jefferson did not respond to this provocative comment, but it came up again. In 1815, Adams crystallized the question by asking, "Who shall write a history of the American revolution?"[9] Jefferson responded with a summary of various histories of the early republic, including Madison's project to record "the whole of everything said and done" at the Convention of 1787, but Adams quickly reformulated his question to mean the revolution in the minds of the people from 1760–1775, not the revolution itself, because in his view the latter was simply a consequence of the former.[10] Adams's reformulation suggests an important question about Adams' understanding of the principles of the revolution – which had changed in the 1760s, Christianity or Anglo-American liberty? – but more relevant for this study is that Adams's question about who would write a history of the revolution was soon answered in very different ways. Once again, New England and Virginia were feuding, this time over who deserved credit for independence.[11]

---

[7] Madison to Jefferson, 27 June 1823, *Republic of Letters*, 1867–1868. It is worth noting that Madison suggested the Farewell Address as required reading at the University of Virginia's school of law. It was included as one of six required texts, but it is also noteworthy that Jefferson said that he would not have thought of adding it. See Jeremy D. Bailey, *Thomas Jefferson and Executive Power* (New York: Cambridge, 2007), 227. For a summary of the events concerning the drafts, see Andrew Burstein and Nancy Isenberg, *Madison and Jefferson* (New York: Random House, 2010), 314–15.

[8] John Adams to Jefferson, 28 June 1813, in *The Adams-Jefferson Letters: The Complete Correspondence Between Thomas Jefferson and Abigail and John Adams*, ed. Lester J. Cappon (Chapel Hill: University of North Carolina Press, 1959), 339–40.

[9] Adams to Jefferson, 30 July 1815, *Adams-Jefferson Letters*, 451.

[10] Jefferson to Adams, 10 August 1815, and Adams to Jefferson, 24 August 1815, *Adams-Jefferson Letters*, 453 and 455.

[11] For a summary of the feud placed in the context of a collective desire to preserve the memory of the revolution, see Pauline Maier, *American Scripture: Making the Declaration of Independence* (New York: Knopf, 1997), 170–89.

The growing partisanship over the credit for the Revolution can be seen in a letter from Adams, written in 1818 to none other than James Madison. According to Adams, "There is a Strange, and invidious and pernicious question agitated in the Public," and that question was "Who was the Author the Discoverer, the Inventor of American Independence?"[12] For Adams, the question itself was flawed, for "we might as well enquire who were the Inventors of Agriculture, Horticulture, Architecture, Musick." But the flaws of the question notwithstanding, Adams had his own answer. In New England, he wrote, "the first Settlers brought Independence with them," and as a consequence, "Governor Winthrop, Jeremiah Dummer, Jonathathan Mayhew" might "claim the honor, with as good as Colour" as Patrick Henry, Samuel Adams, Roger Sherman, and, presumably, Adams himself. In response, Madison agreed that independence was "not the offspring of a particular man or moment."[13] Instead, the principle was latent in the principles of "self-taxation" held by the "forefathers." Events brought the principles out in stages – "Circumstances unfolded & perfected it." But Madison went further than Adams in crediting the men of 1776: "If the merit of Independence as declared in 1776 is to be traced to individuals, it belongs to those who first meditated the glorious measure, who were ablest in contending for it, and who were the most decided in supporting it." Interestingly, Madison named neither Jefferson nor Adams, but he did suggest that American independence did result from the few who best understood and articulated the principle. Even if Madison was too polite to name specific individuals who deserved the credit, his answer revealed that he differed with Adams in leaving some of the credit for the men who in 1776 made the case for independence.

Madison revisited this question a few years later, when he and Jefferson had a similar exchange in 1823. This time, the partisan question of the Revolution had been sharpened to include the status of the Declaration of Independence as well as its authorship. The newly sharpened question took on its predictable regional gloss when Timothy Pickering used a 4 July oration to charge that Massachusetts rather than Virginia should receive credit for the ideas of the Declaration. Relying on information provided by none other than John Adams, Pickering said that Jefferson and Adams met as a "subcommittee" to prepare the first draft of the Declaration, and he argued that the ideas were in James Otis's 1764 pamphlet, *The Rights of the British Colonies Asserted and Proved.*[14] Privately, Pickering had confided to Adams that the Declaration "does not contain many new ideas" and that it was instead a "compilation of facts and sentiments." Pickering went on to conclude that "the great merit" of any such compilation consisted in the "lucid and forcible arrangement of the matter."[15]

[12] John Adams to James Madison, 25 July 1818 *Madison Papers Retirement*, 1: 317.
[13] James Madison to John Adams, 7 August 1818, *Madison Papers Retirement*, 1: 341.
[14] Maier, *American Scripture*, 172; *Republic of Letters*, 1845.
[15] Timothy Pickering to John Adams, 2 August 1822. "To John Adams from Timothy Pickering, 2 August 1822," Founders Online, National Archives (http://founders.archives.gov/documents/Adams/99-02-02-7672 [last updated 12 January 2014]). Accessed 15 January 2015.

Jefferson had a different recollection, and in an August letter to Madison, Jefferson corrected what he saw as Adams and Pickering's mistake. According to Jefferson's recollection, there was no such subcommittee. Jefferson then mentioned that Richard Henry Lee had charged him as having "copied from Locke's treatise on government." Jefferson added that he did not "consider it as any part of [his] charge to invent new ideas altogether."[16] A month later, Madison wrote that he was glad that Jefferson had put his thoughts to paper. Meanwhile, according to James Morton Smith, Madison reviewed the evidence that Richard Henry Lee's friends were making on behalf of Lee, namely the ideas that came from Lee's proposal in the Continental Congress for independence, and it is possible that both Madison and Jefferson knew that a relative named Henry Lee was planning a biography of Richard Henry Lee. Madison then wrote to Jefferson assuring him that Richard Henry Lee's friends had overrated Lee's motion and had underrated Jefferson's draft. Importantly, Madison used the dispute over authorship as an opportunity to articulate what he saw to be the *objective* of the Declaration:

> The object was to assert not to discover truths, and to make them the basis of the Revolutionary Act. The merit of the Draught could only consist in a lucid communication of human Rights, a condensed enumeration of the reasons for such an exercise of them, and in a style & tone more appropriate to the great occasion, & to the spirit of the American people.[17]

By conceiving of credit in terms of the motive behind the Declaration, Madison thus expanded Pickering's concession that there was credit to be given for the "lucid and forcible arrangement of the matter." Importantly, Madison's version focused on the intention rather than merely on the style. This move was important, for Jefferson borrowed much of it two years later in his own letter to Henry Lee. In that letter, which has since become one of Jefferson's most famous, Jefferson answered Lee's questions about who first thought of the argument for independence:

> This was the object of the Declaration of Independence. Not to find out new principles, or new arguments, never before thought of, not merely to say things which had never been said before; but to place before mankind the common sense of the subject, in terms so plain and firm as to command their assent, and to justify ourselves in the independent stand we are compelled to take.[18]

Clearly, Jefferson borrowed from Madison's earlier letter, yet scholars have yet to comment on Madison's contribution to the famous response to Lee, perhaps because Madison's letter has not been included in the common single volume collections of Madison's writings. It appears that Jefferson's famous response

---

[16] Jefferson to Madison, 30 August 1823, *Republic of Letters*, 1875–1877.
[17] Madison to Jefferson, 6 September 1823, *Republic of Letters*, 1877–1878.
[18] Jefferson to Henry Lee, 8 May 1825, *Thomas Jefferson: Writings*, ed., Merril Peterson (New York: Library of America, 1984), 1501.

to Lee explicitly borrowed much of its logic from Madison, who had used Pickering's argument to make a broader a case for crediting Jefferson for the "object" of the Declaration.

The most obvious difference between the two is that Jefferson's rendering of the point is simply much better than Madison's. Madison's is adequate, yet Jefferson's soars. But there are at least three substantive differences that are worthy of attention. First, Madison's sounds surprisingly universal in that Madison refers to "human rights," whereas Jefferson's surrounding language appeals to "our rights" and an "American mind." This point parallels Brian Steele's recent argument that Jefferson's case for independence was always intertwined with his peculiar understanding of what made American nationhood distinct.[19] That is, Jefferson's rendering of Madison's language lends evidence to Steele's argument that Jefferson believed that America was different from the rest of the world.

Second, Madison's letter lacked Jefferson's credit to the American mind and to the "elementary books of public right." Madison's version also lacked the mention of specific philosophers (Aristotle, Cicero, Locke, Sidney, etc.).[20] Curiously, it is evident that Jefferson looked to Hume's *An Enquiry Concerning Human Understanding* for some of the language he added. In an argument against "abstract reasoners," Hume had written,

> It is easy for a profound philosopher to commit a mistake in his subtle reasonings; and one mistake is the necessary parent of another, while he pushes on his consequences, and is not deterred from embracing any conclusion, by its unusual appearance, or its contradiction to popular opinion. But a philosopher, who purposes only to represent the common sense of mankind in more beautiful and more engaging colours, if by accident he falls into error, goes no farther; but renewing his appeal to common sense, and the natural sentiments of the mind, returns into the right path, and secures himself from any dangerous illusions. The fame of Cicero flourishes at present; but that of Aristotle is utterly decayed. La Bruyere passes the seas, and still maintains his reputation: but the glory of Malebranche is confined to his own nation, and to his own age. And Addison, perhaps, will be read with pleasure, when Locke shall be entirely forgotten.[21]

---

[19] Brian Steele, *Thomas Jefferson and American Nationhood* (New York: Cambridge University Press, 2012).

[20] It is worth mentioning that, again, one of Madison's letters appears to be missing. From Jefferson's letter of 24 October, it is clear that Madison asked about whether Pythagoras or Copernicus was credited with having first taught that the sun was at the center of the universe. This question is likely an interesting continuation of the discussion of credit for authorship, but there is the possibility it has to do with recruiting faculty for the University of Virginia. See Jefferson to Madison, 24 October 1823, *Republic of Letters*, 1878–1879.

[21] David Hume, *An Enquiry Concerning Human Understanding*, in Eric Steinberg, ed., *An Enquiry Concerning Human Understanding, with A Letter from a Gentleman to his Friend in Edinburgh and Hume's Abstract of a Treatise on Human Nature* (Indianapolis, IN: Hackett, 1992), 2.

Jefferson's love of Locke and contempt for Hume is well known, but given the similarity in language and object of argument, it is difficult to imagine that Jefferson did not have Hume's passage in mind.[22] The praise of "the common sense of mankind" in conjunction with the mentions of Aristotle, Cicero, and Locke are probably not coincidental. But given all the scholarly attention to Madison's debt to Hume, why would Jefferson and not Madison be the one to remember Hume's language and the importance of the common sense of ordinary Americans?

Hume's language about returning mankind to the "right path" suggests a third and final point, one that might reveal a difference between Jefferson and Madison as well as answer the question above. In his First Inaugural, Jefferson offered a list of principles that would guide his administration but that would also serve as a constellation to guide Americans back to the right path when they strayed in moments of error or alarm. In his letter to Lee, Jefferson added to Madison's point (and to Pickering's) the idea that the assent of others had to be *commanded*, which suggests that its existence as common sense was either in doubt or insufficient. Although it has escaped notice, this was a point Jefferson made throughout his career. For example, Jefferson wrote that executive action was sometimes necessary to give "form and body" to public opinion.[23] This reflects, perhaps, a difference for Jefferson with Hume and perhaps with Madison with respect to the relationship between the Declaration and public opinion, for it reveals the role that Jefferson reserved for philosophy in shaping public opinion. Jefferson made this point clearest in his other famous letter on the Declaration. Often called his last letter, the letter to Roger Weightman revealed Jefferson's full ambition for the Declaration, that it would be a "signal" "to the world," "arousing men" to revolution and the establishment of the rule of natural rights.[24] Madison did not go this far. Though Madison expanded the question of authorship to include the broader and more important consideration of the objective behind the Declaration, he did not see the relationship between the Declaration and public opinion the same way Jefferson did. As was the case in the Bill of Rights, Madison simply lacked Jefferson's emphasis on the necessity of leadership.

One of Madison's last letters provides yet another comparison between the two Virginians. Like Jefferson, who devoted his last letter to the meaning of the Declaration, Madison gathered his energies in March 1836, only a few months before he died, to compose a substantive letter on the meaning of the Constitution. Like Jefferson, Madison believed his document was important

---

[22] On Hume, see Jefferson to John Norwell, 14 June 1807, and Jefferson to Major John Cartwright, 5 June 1824, in *Jefferson Writings*, 1176–77 and 1490–91. On Locke, see Jefferson to John Trumbull, 15 February 1789, in *Jefferson Writings*, 939–40.

[23] Bailey, *Jefferson and Executive Power*, 225–58. For a discussion of this point in the context of the First Inaugural, see pp. 132–50.

[24] Jefferson to Weightman, 24 June 1826, *Jefferson Writings*, 1517.

for the country's great "political experiment," upon which rested "hope of the world." But Madison's letter, which was (to be fair) written for a different objective, differed from Jefferson's in the sense that Madison's was not entirely future oriented. As was mentioned in Chapter 3, Madison here again focused on the puzzle of representation, but he also returned to the difficulties of the Convention. Strikingly, Madison returned yet again to the problem of the Great Compromise. As we have seen, Madison confessed in *Federalist* No. 37 that the compromise between large and small states led to a "fresh struggle" between the parties. Here, near death, Madison returned to that very problem:

> But it is equally true tho' but little adverted to as an instance of miscalculating speculation that, as soon as the smaller States, had secured more than a proportional share in the proposed Government, they became favorable to augmentation of its powers; & that under the administration of the Govt., they have generally, in contests between it, & the State governments, leaned to the former.[25]

Madison was surely trying to point out the irony of the small states construing the Constitution in the 1790s to enlarge national authority – when in the 1780s they were against it – but he also willfully pointed to a problem in constitutional meaning that he had strived to keep on the table since the weeks after the Convention of 1787. The Great Compromise did not settle the controversy over representation; rather, it spread the problem throughout the structure of the national government. That controversy was so unsettling that Madison spent what might have been his final intellectual efforts on it.

Sourcing the Constitution

Unlike Jefferson and Adams, Madison spent more time thinking about the historical record of the Convention of 1787 than he did about credit for the ideas of the Declaration. According to Drew McCoy, Madison in his retirement years "undertook the onerous task of organizing and preparing for eventual publication his voluminous cache of papers, including his comprehensive records of the debates at the 1787 convention."[26] But Madison's decision to compose his *Notes* remains understudied among Madison scholars. One potential reason is the textual difficulties involved.

One textual difficulty is that there are rival versions of the authoritative text. One version is the revised one, the one he left to his wife, Dolley Madison, hoping that she would be able to benefit financially. He had corrected it over time, and the Madisons approved it as the version they endorsed. The other version is what Max Farrand regarded as the "original hand written account in 1787." Farrand preferred this version, because, in his view, the revised version was likely corrupted by Madison's failing memory and partisan calculation.

---

[25] Madison to _____, March 1836, Hunt 9: 608–11.
[26] McCoy, *Last of the Fathers*, 73–74.

Adrienne Koch followed Farrand, siding with Farrand's "original" and against the later version, but she included footnotes directing readers to the later version. Moreover, according to Lloyd, "Koch's edition was, unfortunately the first to use the appellation *Notes* in the title, giving the impression that Madison's coverage is merely a bunch of jottings, scribbles, and abbreviations."[27] This is where the record has stood for a very long time, but Lloyd has recently recommended that that Koch's "*Notes*" be dropped from the title, concluding that the version James and Dolley Madison approved in the 1830s "is closer to what Madison wanted to leave behind than either Farrand's *Records* or Koch's *Notes*." But Lloyd also arrives at the "lamentable conclusion" that "there is no one indisputable authentic" version because Madison's posthumous version was marked up by the editors who published it in 1840.[28]

At the heart of the problem is the question of whether Madison ever finished his project. In an 1830 description of the work, "A Sketch Never Finish or Applied," Madison suggested his project was still in its early stages, a *sketch*.[29] According to Lloyd, "Sketch" was a new title he had given to something he had earlier called a "Preface to the Debates in the Convention of 1787," indicating that he wanted to underscore the unfinished nature of the work. Koch included Madison's "Sketch" as a preface for her edition, but Gordon Lloyd omits it; elsewhere Lloyd labels it a "rough and uneven draft, full of insertions and deletions."[30] Koch's including the "Sketch" thus emphasizes the point that Madison never really finished his records of the Convention, but it should also be said that Koch's including the later "Sketch" complicates her endorsement of Farrand's preference for the earlier "original" version.

In short, Madison's records of the Convention are problematic from the perspective of determining the authoritative record of the debates in 1787. But that is not the only problem. Another, to borrow Madison's own formulation, is determining Madison's "object" in compiling the work. What did Madison mean to accomplish in revising and perfecting his records of the Convention? One possibility is that he knew his wife needed the money. Another, quietly suggested by Farrand, is that Madison wanted to settle old scores and smooth over the contradictions of a life in politics. Another, preferred by Lloyd, is that Madison wanted to offer his version of Plato's *Republic*, but this time using an actual founding with real interlocutors. This question about Madison's intention for the work is sharpened and given urgency by another difficulty in understanding Madison's decision to return to 1787. This difficulty comes in the form of the prize-winning work of Jack Rakove and the methodology of original meaning.

---

[27] See Lloyd, *Debates in the Federal Convention*, v.
[28] Ibid., vii.
[29] *Madison Writings*, 828–42.
[30] I also rely on Lloyd for the point about the original title being crossed out. See Lloyd's very useful website on teachingamericanhistory.org.

Rakove and Original Meaning

In encountering constitutional imperfection, Madison found that one problem of constitutional politics is arriving at a method by which debates about the Constitution can be settled authoritatively. In addition to figuring out who gets the final say and determining where deliberation should take place, that task has other parts – should what it says be determinative, and if so, how do we determine its meaning? One common analysis, made famous by Rakove, is that Madison believed that determining the meaning of the Constitution required making a distinction between original intent and original understanding.[31] Under original intent, the interpretative goal is to understand what the lawgiver intended to accomplish in writing the law. In the context of the Constitution, that intention could be discerned from the available evidence from the debates in the Convention of 1787. Under original understanding, the interpretative goal is to understand the meaning of the Constitution from the perspective of those who ratified it. Accordingly, that meaning can be ascertained by reading the debates in the state ratifying conventions. Madison made this distinction during debate on the Jay Treaty in a speech that has been quoted often:

> But, after all, whatever veneration might be entertained for the body of men who formed our constitution, the sense of that body could never be regarded as the oracular guide in the expounding the constitution. As the instrument came from them, it was nothing more than a draught of a plan, nothing but a dead letter, until life and validity were breathed into it, by the voice of the people, speaking through the several state conventions. If we were to look therefore, for the meaning of the instrument, beyond the face of the instrument, beyond the face of the instrument, we must look for it not in the general convention, which proposed, but in the state conventions, which accepted and ratified the constitution.[32]

There is much to be seen here. Given the argument of this book, it is striking that Madison associated veneration with the view he classified as incorrect. But the big point is that Madison here clearly privileges the constitution ratifier over the constitution maker. As Rakove argued, this interpretative move was "entirely consistent with the great political and theoretical insight that had enabled Madison to persuade the Convention to follow his agenda," namely the supreme importance of a special ratification.[33] As was argued in Chapter 4, Madison believed that a clear and consistent ratification was a requirement for the Constitution and for the Union, so much so that Madison risked ratification itself by correcting those who were willing to allow some states to ratify the Constitution conditionally. Rakove's interpretation is compelling then,

---

[31] Jack N. Rakove, *Original Meanings: Politics and Ideas in the Making of the Constitution* (New York: Vintage Books, 1997).

[32] Madison, "Speech in Congress on the Jay Treaty," 6 April 1796, in *Madison Writings*, 574.

[33] Rakove, *Original Meanings*, 362. McCoy also cites a 1960 dissertation by Donald Dewey, McCoy 75.

because it would make sense that Madison would prioritize the act of ratification as providing *the* meaning of the Constitution.

Rakove's argument has the additional virtue of connecting other strands in the Madison scholarship. First, and most obvious, it is possible that Madison's focus on the ratifying agents makes Madison less elitist. In place of the delegates to the Convention, or demigods as Jefferson put it, it is the people themselves (still in the states, of course) who become the key agent of ratification. This turn, away from rule by "founding fathers," would seem to make Madison more democratic than the Madison presented by, among others, Robert Dahl. In this, it would also be consistent with his democratic turn in the 1790s and thus in line with the interpretations of Lance Banning, Colleen Sheehan, and, in a different way, Robert Martin.[34]

However, it should also be noted that Madison's emphasis on ratification as the key to constitutional meaning could also support the more conservative Madison described by Drew McCoy. In McCoy's account of Madison giving advice to those who were interpreting the Constitution, Madison generally recommended that interpreters look to the history of the ratification and not just to the text itself. "He believed that history must take priority over the arguments of present-day theoreticians who scrutinized text alone, because history provided, in addition to legitimacy, the only viable basis for stable government under the Constitution."[35] This, in turn, according to McCoy, meant that Madison's "fundamental concern for stability shaped other aspects of his approach to interpret the Constitution." In particular, Madison made a "strong case" for looking to precedent as another "touchstone" of constitutional interpretation.[36] So, in McCoy's view, Madison's decision to compose his record of the Federal Convention was of the same piece as his general method of looking to the broader ratification debates to determine constitutional meaning in that both were aimed at maintaining a stable and enduring constitutional order. Of Madison's retirement generally, McCoy finds that Madison saw new urgency in promoting stability: "Balance, restraint, and the discipline of personal and public passion were Madisonian – which is to say, enlightened eighteenth century – imperatives that appeared even more incongruous, hence all the more necessary, in the new, nineteenth century world that a younger generation of Americans now busied itself in making."[37] In McCoy's analysis, then, it is the continuity in Madison's thought that is most important. It is

---

[34] But Gary Rosen points out an important qualification here that Madison was more worried about legislative constructions than he was about those by the judiciary, so, unlike some modern-day originalists, Madison did not give to the legislative branch the wider latitude associated with the Federalist interpretation of the necessary and proper clause. Rosen, *American Compact*, 167–68. Robert W. T. Martin, *Government by Dissent: Protest, Resistance, & Radical Democratic Thought in the Early American Republic* (New York: NYU Press, 2013), 115–46.

[35] McCoy, *Last of the Fathers*, 78.

[36] Ibid., 79–82.

[37] Ibid., 65.

Madison as Burke or Hume, concerned with creating and preserving a constitutional heritage, bound by precedents and culture. To borrow Jim Ceaser's terminology, McCoy's Madison looks to history, not nature.[38]

Although Rakove sees that Madison's turn to original understanding meshes well with Madison's emphasis on ratification, Rakove concludes that it was fundamentally inadequate as a way to determine constitutional meaning. Madison's argument about the treaty power relied on two pieces of evidence: the debates in the state conventions and the amendments proposed by those conventions. In the first case, according to Rakove, Madison "ignored" Federalist arguments that implied the limits on the treaty power had to do with the president and the Senate, not the House. In the second case, as Rakove puts it, Madison "never explained how criticisms of the Constitution could be transformed into its meaning when the opposite inference was more logical."[39] That is, for Rakove, if anyone in 1795 and 1796 had the more originalist understanding of the treaty clause, it was the Federalists, not Madison.

Complicating matters is the fact that Madison's speech on the Jay Treaty was not his first or last word on the subject. As Rakove points out, Madison's appeal to original understanding was inconsistent with Madison's own prior attempts to appeal to original intent during the 1791 controversy over the bank. There, as was discussed in Chapter 5, Madison looked to the text of the Constitution itself as well as to evidence from 1787 and 1788. But in addition to looking to ratification debates, Madison also noted that the power to incorporate a bank had been considered and rejected by the delegates at the Convention. Madison did not then seem to privilege the state conventions over *the* Convention.[40] This is all correct, but what Rakove does not point out is that Madison returned to this approach and employed it again and again throughout his life. Rather than settling on a preferred method, Madison continued to wrestle with the problem of the Convention as a source of authority for constitutional meaning, and he varied in his preferred method for determining the meaning of the Constitution.

Appeals to the Convention

We have seen that Madison claimed in his "Sketch" that his record of the Convention was never finished. But he made a second claim, that it was never applied, which raises another problem. At one level, the meaning is clear.

[38] James Ceaser, *Nature and History in American Political Development* (Cambridge, MA: Harvard University Press, 2008). This would be an appropriate analogy, for, as Ceaser shows, the Whigs of the 1830's turned to history as a way to moderate what they saw as the likely excesses of arguments from natural rights.

[39] Rakove, *Original Meanings*, 363.

[40] Ibid., 353. Rakove sees these historical appeals as "no more than a distraction" in the debate. His object is to trace the origins of such appeals. My object here is to note Madison's shifting positions.

Madison intended to release these records after the deaths of all of the delegates to the Convention, and he resisted requests by friends and political allies to publish his notes during his lifetime. One opportunity came in 1817, when John Quincy Adams contacted him at James Monroe's urging. Adams was leading a coalition in Congress to publish the journal of the convention debates, and Adams wrote Madison seeking his blessing and seeking information, information regarding votes and the details of the plans offered by Pinckney and Hamilton. What is most noticeable about Madison's responses is how perfunctory and chilling they were; Madison limited his answers to as few words as possible. As to Adams's question regarding the larger merit of the project, Madison replied coldly that the convention decided the journal would be subject to the discretion of a future congress and that Adams himself would know better as to whether releasing the Journal would have a "useful tendency."[41] As McCoy notes, Madison's reticence was challenged again, when Robert Yates published his own records of the Convention. From Madison's perspective, this was especially problematic. Robert Yates had attended the Convention as a delegate from New York, but he left the Convention early and returned to New York after it had become clear that the Convention would create a more powerful national government than he and New York Governor Clinton wanted. During the ratification debates, Yates sided with the anti-Federalists. Madison called Yates's records incomplete and even "mutilated" – and indeed, they had been edited by Edmund Genet – but did not think it reason enough to release his own notes.

But if Madison meant to say that he "never applied" his own sketch, then that would be obviously false. McCoy shows that Madison from time to time put aside his reluctance to enter public controversies and instruct younger politicians "how they should approach the general task of interpreting the Constitution."[42] In fact, Madison frequently relied on his recollection of the Convention of 1787 to attempt to resolve constitutional controversy. Much has been made, for example, of Madison's evolution on the question of the bank. In the early 1790s, Madison and Jefferson made the question of the constitutionality of the bank a centerpiece of their opposition to Federalist politics, but, as president, Madison recommended and then approved the creation of the Second Bank of the United States. Scholars have made much of this change, with one group pointing to the bank as an example of inconsistency, and another group seeing it as an example of greater consistency with Madison's constitutional theory.[43] In 1831, Madison wrote that the "inconsistency [was]

[41] John Quincy Adams to Madison, 15 December 1817, *Madison Papers Retirement*, 1: 173–75; Madison to John Quincy Adams, 23 December 1817, *Madison Papers Retirement*, 1: 179–80; John Quincy Adams to Madison, 22 October 1818, *Madison Papers Retirement*, 1: 367–69; and Madison to John Quincy Adams, 2 November 1818, *Madison Papers Retirement*, 1: 372.
[42] McCoy, *Last of the Fathers*, 74.
[43] For Greg Weiner, for example, the bank illustrates Madison's commitment to majority rule, so long as it is moored by the passage of time. See Greg Weiner, *Madison's Metronome: The*

apparent only," "inasmuch as [his] abstract opinion of the Constitution" had not changed. Rather, his assent to the bank "was given in pursuance of my early and unchanged opinion, that, in the case of authoritative expositions sufficiently deliberate, uniform, and settled, was an evidence of the public will necessarily overruling individual opinions."[44]

The truth is that Madison often contradicted himself on whether the intention of the members of the Convention or the understanding of those at the state ratifying conventions was to be used. In 1817, and in the context of internal improvements, Madison argued that understanding of the people who ratified the Constitution was more important that the intent of the men who wrote the document.[45] Likewise, in his "Detached Memoranda," which Rakove dates around 1819, Madison faulted George Washington for trying to understand the Constitution by looking to the Convention debates of 1787. The context was again the Jay Treaty, and Madison returned to the same formulation he had made more than two decades ago:

> If the meaning of the Constitution was to be looked for elsewhere than in the instrument, it was not in the General Convention, but the State Conventions. The former proposed it only; it was from the latter that it derived its validity and authority. The former were the Committee that prepared the Bill, the latter the authoritative Bodies which made it a law, or rather through which the nation made its own Act. It is the sense of the nation therefore not the sense of the General Convention, that is to be consulted; and that sense, if not taken from the act itself, is to be taken from the proceedings of the State Conventions & other public indications as the true keys to the sense of the nation.[46]

So, again, the source of Washington's error was that he looked to the General Convention for constitutional meaning, rather than to the people who gave life to the document. But in the very same Detached Memoranda, Madison *also* pointed out that Washington departed from sense of the Convention by signing the bank bill. Specifically, Madison wrote that Washington was perplexed because, on the one hand, he was disposed to "favor a liberal construction of the national powers," but, on the other, he "had witnessed what had passed in the Convention which framed the Constitution, and he knew the tenor of the reasonings & explanations under which it had been ratified by the State Conventions."[47] So it is true that Madison here mentions both, but

---

Constitution, Majority Rule, and the Tempo of American Politics (Lawrence: University Press of Kansas, 2012). See also Ketcham, *James Madison*, 603–07; Rosen, *American Compact*, 169–77; and Garry Wills, *James Madison* (New York: Times Books, 2002), 75–77.

44 Madison to C. E. Haynes, 25 February 1831, Hunt 9: 442–43.

45 For this view in the context of internal improvements, see Madison to St. George Tucker, 23 December 1817, *Madison Papers Retirement*. See also Madison to Henry Lee, 25 June 1824, *Madison Writings*, 803.

46 "Detached Memoranda," *Madison Writings*, 750–51. Rakove assigns "1819?" as the date for this document.

47 "Detached Memoranda," *Madison Writings*, 749.

what is noteworthy is that Madison includes Washington's knowledge of the Convention debates in his summary of where Washington went wrong on the bank. In other words, Madison in 1819 preserved the very inconsistency that Rakove saw in his efforts in the 1790s. In the case of the bank, constitutional meaning could be found in the Convention, but in the case of the Jay treaty, constitutional meaning ought not be found there.[48]

The bank was not the only policy issue that brought Madison to find constitutional meaning in the perspective of the Convention itself. Another was slavery. As the Missouri crisis escalated, Madison justified his own position about the expansion of slavery by referring to the intent of the men who wrote the Constitution. For example, Robert Walsh wrote Madison in 1819 to ask about the meaning of the word "migration" in Article One, Section Nine of the Constitution. Walsh explained that he had written Madison, because "no one can know as well as you do, what were the views & intentions of the framers of the Constitution in regard to the extension or rather the restriction of negro-slavery." Madison responded with a precise definition, explicitly referring to both the intentions of the delegates at the Convention and the understanding of participants at the state conventions as evidence for his position.[49] A few weeks later, Madison used his memory of the Convention debates to advise the sitting president. In a letter to James Monroe, Madison appealed to his status as authority on the Convention debates to take sides against those in 1820 who wanted to limit the spread of slavery by passing laws in Congress:

> I have been truly astonished at some of the doctrines & declarations to which the Missouri question has led; and particularly so at the interpretation of the terms "migration or importation &c." Judging from own impressions, I should deem it impossible that the memory of any one who was a member of the General Convention could favor an opinion that terms did not then exclusively refer to migration & importation into the U.S.[50]

Thus Madison tried to guide Monroe during the Missouri crisis by informing him what the meaning of the Constitution was, meaning that could be easily accessed in the memory of any of the men who, unlike Monroe, attended the Convention in 1787. A few days later, Madison wrote again to say that he did not think Congress has the power under the Constitution to restrict slavery in certain territories, and this view arose both from his "habit of a guarded construction against Constitutional Powers" and his belief that slavery would be more favorable for slaves (both in terms of its conditions and in the prospect

[48] In retirement, Madison also said that the participants in the state conventions also presumed that Congress could not incorporate a bank. Madison to Spencer Roane, 2 September 1819, *Madison Papers Retirement* 1: 502.
[49] Robert Walsh to Madison, 11 November 1819, *Madison Papers Retirement*, 1: 548–49; Madison to Robert Walsh, 27 November 1819, *Madison Papers Retirement*, 1: 553–59; and Madison to Robert Walsh, 11 January 1820, *Madison Papers Retirement*, 1: 584–85.
[50] Madison to James Monroe, 10 February 1280, *Madison Papers Retirement*, 2: 6–7.

of emancipation) if slavery were diffuse rather than concentrated. Madison did not tell Monroe that the Convention debates were out of bounds as a source for constitutional meaning.[51]

Another policy was internal improvements. Even when he wrote that the view of those who ratified the Constitution was more important than those who proposed it, Madison sometimes conceded that his own views were based on his "knowledge of the views of those who proposed the Constitution."[52] In 1817, in response to Monroe's specific requests for advice about the difference between the internal improvements Madison vetoed and the Cumberland Road passed under Jefferson, Madison responded about why he believed the Cumberland Road was different and less problematic than the policy under consideration in 1817. But he also added his concerns about the general looseness with which the constitutional limitations on the powers of Congress were being discussed. This time he worried about the "serious danger" of "precedents" aiding an "unwarrantable latitude of construction." Specifically, the problem was that these precedents were being used in ways that "can not be supposed" to have been expected "in the view of their authors" both as to the "bearing contended for, and even where they may have crept" by way of legislative "weariness" and a general lack of watchfulness.[53] Here Madison had in mind the legislative intent of prior Congresses, but in 1824, Madison looked to the legislative intent of the Convention to explain his view of this ongoing policy controversy. In a letter to Edward Livingston, Madison noted his disagreement with Livingston's broad reading of the Constitution and pointed to the Convention's explicit rejection of the power to make canals. He explicitly mentioned "my recollection that the authority had been repeatedly proposed in the Convention, and negative, either as improper to be vested in Congress, or as a power not likely to be yielded by the States." With respect to canals, he added that had that power been included in the Constitution, "it would have been impossible to overcome the opposition" to ratification. He also noted that even Hamilton had conceded that canals were probably not within Congress's power.[54]

Madison's inconsistency could have arisen because Madison perceived that the emphasis on the state conventions was flawed. As Rakove points out, it has the problem of privileging what did not make into the Constitution rather than what actually did. Also complicating matters is that the distinction between the two acts is blurry, thanks in part to Madison. For example, in

[51] Ibid., 2: 16–17. It should be noted that Madison also referred Monroe to the state ratifying conventions in New York and Massachusetts, but that was for a separate point about the North's acquiescence in the three-fifth compromise.
[52] Madison to Henry St. George Tucker, 23 December 1817, *Madison Papers Retirement*, 2: 181.
[53] Madison to James Monroe, 27 December 1817, *Madison Papers Retirement*, 2: 190–91.
[54] Madison to Edward Livingston, 17 April 1824, in Hunt 9: 188.

1788, Madison took measures to influence the ratification debates by distributing copies of *The Federalist* to members of the Virginia convention.[55] Finally, as Gary Rosen points out, Madison acknowledged that the records of the state conventions were difficult to find. The New England states, with the exception of Massachusetts, were completely inaccessible, and Pennsylvania's were partial at best. Further, Rosen points out that Madison typically did not refer to the actual debates of the state conventions. Rather, "his usual practice was to recall, in the most general terms, the discussion in the Virginia convention of which he was a member," which is to say that "exhaustive historical research was not what he had in mind."[56]

Even though Madison varied in his solution to the problem, the key is that Madison saw it is as a problem that needed to be fixed. This problem derived from one that he had examined way back in 1788, in his *Federalist* No. 37. As was discussed in Chapter 2, Madison went out of his way in that essay to address the "difficulties" of the Constitution. The biggest difficulty, finding a line between state and national authority, brought Madison to reflect on the indeterminacy of language – the problem of words – with respect to human inventions in the science of politics. As Rosen notes, Madison returned to the problem of the malleability of words and added another: the meaning of words changes over time.[57] In the 1824 letter to Edward Livingston, Madison said the problem was the "constructive phrases." In his view, all debates must begin with "defining the terms in the argument," which is "the only effectual precaution against fruitless and endless discussion." This was "peculiarly essential" in constitutional debate, where old words too often get saddled with new meanings.

> Known words express known ideas; and new ideas, such as are presented by our novel and unique political system, must be expressed either by new words, or by old words with new definitions. Without attention to this circumstance, volumes may be written which can only be answered by a call for definitions; and which answer themselves as soon as the call is complied with.[58]

Two months later, Madison continued this point in his exchange with Henry Lee. Madison said the solution to constitutional controversies should not be found in the "changeable meaning of words." Rather, those definitions had to be fixed by "sense" in which they were originally "accepted and ratified by the nation." In his view, any unbiased study into the "origin and adoption" of the Constitution would reveal that the "language of our Constitution is already undergoing interpretations unknown to its founders." Accordingly, the meaning of the Constitution was to be found in the sense in which it was

[55] George Nicholas to James Madison, 5 April 1788, and James Madison to George Nicholas, 8 April 1788, in *PJM*, 11:10 and 14.
[56] Rosen, *American Compact*, 163–64.
[57] Ibid., 165.
[58] Madison to Edward Livingston, 17 April 1824, Hunt 9: 189.

"accepted and ratified by the nation" and in "that sense *alone* it is the *legitimate* Constitution."[59]

This statement would seem to offer more evidence for Rakove's version of Madisonian original understanding, but the phrase "accepted and ratified" potentially broadens it. Madison might have meant to include the tacit consent of the broader populace by the word "accepted," or perhaps he meant to include the proposal part of constitution-making by shifting some of the emphasis away from the ratification debates themselves.[60] At a minimum, the statement reveals that Madison believed there were at least two facts about the meaning of the Constitution. First, there was such a thing as the meaning of the Constitution that was fixed in the words of a specific time. Second, because this meaning was fixed in a specific time, it could be discovered in history. Given that Madison said that the fixed historical meaning of the Constitution mattered, it is important that Madison devoted his last years to presenting what would come to be our best record of the Federal Convention. Madison chose to leave posterity a record of the Convention of 1787, and he seemed to think this was more worthy of his labors than leaving a record of the Virginia ratifying convention of 1788.

What Madison's Notes Subtract from the Yates Version

For all of the work on the Constitutional Convention, there is surprisingly little scholarship on the differences between the Madison's *Notes* and the alternative accounts, the primary one being that by Robert Yates. Yates left the Convention on 10 July, so Madison's account is obviously much longer than Yates's version, and it is worth asking what Madison included that Yates did not.[61] But it is just as important, if not more so, to notice what Yates included and Madison left out. In most cases, it is impossible to determine whose memory was more accurate, and, for obvious reasons, this author would place more weight on Madison's records rather than those of Yates. But the differences can nevertheless be revealing, especially if they indicate where either Yates thought Madison might be embarrassed or where Madison might have been tempted to use his editorial judgment to soften his own speeches.

One obvious difference is that Yates records Madison as being more clearly antidemocratic in his views with respect to the need for the Senate. In his record of the debates on 12 June concerning the length of term for senators, Yates quotes Madison as endorsing a seven-year term, noting that Madison

[59] Madison to Henry Lee, 25 June 1824, Hunt 9: 190–92. Emphasis is my own.
[60] See also his 1830 letter to Andrew Stevenson, where Madison traces the meaning of the general welfare clause from practice under the Articles, through the Convention, and into the state ratifying conventions. Madison to Stevenson, 27 November 1830, Hunt 9: 411–24.
[61] Robert Yates and John Lansing, *Secret Proceedings and Debates of the Constitutional Convention* (Honolulu, HI: University Press of the Pacific, 2002 [reprint of the 1986 edition].

"Considers this branch a check on the democracy. It cannot, therefore, be made too strong."[62] On 26 June, as the tension between small-state and large-state delegates concerning representation in the Senate is mounting, Yates records Madison as defending the Senate as a protector of the rights of the "opulent," of "the man who is possessed of wealth, who lolls on his sofa or rolls in his carriage." Further, Madison is recorded to say,

> If these observations be just, our government ought to secure the permanent inter-
> ests of the country against innovation. Landholders ought to have a share in the
> government, to support these invaluable interests, and to balance and check the
> other. They ought to be so constituted as to protect the minority of the opulent
> against the majority. The Senate, therefore, ought to be this body; and to answer
> these purposes, they ought to have permanency and stability. Various have been
> the propositions; but my opinion is, the longer they continue in office, the better
> these views will be answered.[63]

If Yates's version emphasizes Madison's vision of the Senate as contributing permanence and [64,65,66] against unjust laws.stability by being a protector of the wealthy against the majority, Madison's version of those speeches provides a different picture. In his version of his comments on 12 June, Madison says that he "was not afraid of giving too much stability by the term of Seven years" because "his fear was that the popular branch would still be too great and overmatch for it." Nowhere does he say that the Senate could not be too strong. Likewise, in his speech on 26 June, Madison records himself in a very different way. Rather than casting the Senate as a necessary protector of wealth, Madison instead has himself defending the Senate "as a body in the govt sufficiently respectable for its wisdom & virtue." To be sure, Madison does say that this body would be necessary in "emergencies," some of which might be "agrarian attempts" arising out of the differences of property in any republic, but the point is that the Senate's contribution would add to the "pre-ponderance of justice by throwing its weight into that scale." While Madison does cast the Senate as a protector of the "minority" against the "major inter-est," and while he does provide examples of the difference between the two in terms of financial interests including the "rich & poor," he does not see the Senate explicitly as a protector of the "opulent." Finally, in his own notes, Madison records himself to say on 26 July that the "unjust laws of the states had proceeded more from this class of men [those with "landed possessions"], than any others." According to Yates, Madison saw the Senate as a protector of the rich, but, according to Madison, Madison defended the Senate as a necessary protector of stability

[62] Ibid, 124.
[63] Ibid.
[64] Madison, *Notes*, 110–11.
[65] Ibid., 194.
[66] Ibid., 375.

There is also a subtle omission with respect to the debate on federalism during the most heated part of the debate between small states and large states. According to Yates, Madison on 21 June said that it was impossible to determine the precise boundary between the state and national governments: "To draw the line between the two, is a difficult task. I believe it cannot be done."[67] Madison does not record this statement in his *Notes*; rather, he attributes a similar statement to Hamilton on 19 June. Madison, but not Yates, records Hamilton to say that "no boundary could be drawn between the National & State Legislatures."[68] Even though Madison did not attribute such a statement to himself, there is a good chance he agreed. As we have seen, in *Federalist* No. 37, Madison wrote that the problem of line-drawing is one of the five difficulties facing the delegates at the Convention, and he went out of his way to show that the difficulties were derived from the indeterminacy of words and the necessary imperfection of human inventions such as political science. Madison left the reader in No. 37 to come to the conclusion on his or her own that finding the line between the two is impossible, but he does not come out and say it in so many words. Moreover, the point that Madison eventually draws in *Federalist* No. 39, or at least says he draws, is that the new Constitution created a government that was neither wholly federal nor wholly national.[69] Hamilton, however, drew a different conclusion, at least according to Madison. Because no line could be drawn, the National Legislature "must therefore have indefinite authority."[70]

Throughout his life, Madison pointed to this formulation from *Federalist* No. 39 as representing his view of the subject and as evidence that he had not been inconsistent in his views about national authority over the course of his career.[71] It is in this sense, then, that Yates's version becomes more important. With respect to finding a line between state and national authority, Yates also records Madison saying, "I believe it cannot be done and therefore I am inclined for a general government. If we cannot form a general government, and the States become totally independent of each other, it would afford a melancholy prospect."[72] So, according to Yates, the impossibility of drawing lines led Madison to endorse a wholly national government. Madison's version, however, makes a different point, predicting that even if the general government were given "indefinite power," that power would be safe because "the conveniency" of the general government would almost always "concur with that of the people in the maintenance of subordinate Governments."[73] If Yates's

[67] Yates and Lansing, *Secret Proceedings*, 159.
[68] Madison, *Notes*, 152.
[69] Madison, *Federalist* No. 39, Scigliano, 242–46.
[70] Madison, *Notes*, 152.
[71] Madison to Jefferson, 27 June 1823, *Madison Writings*, 801–02.
[72] Yates and Lansing, *Secret Proceedings*, 159.
[73] Madison, *Notes*, 165.

account is correct, then Madison's entire argument in *Federalist* No. 39 would have been based on a deception.

Yates recorded another moment where Madison was especially sharp in his presentation of the differences between the national and state authority. That moment was on 29 June, when Doctor Johnson said that the "endless controversy" could be traced to the "differing grounds" of the arguments by the two sides. In Johnson's estimation, the large-state advocates considered the states "as districts of people composing one political Society," while the small-state advocates considered the states "as so many political societies."[74] According to Yates, Madison flatly rejected the premise, saying that "the States never possessed the essential rights of sovereignty," and instead that these rights of sovereignty "were always vested in Congress."[75] In his own account of the Convention, however, Madison records a softer version. There, Madison "thought too much stress was laid on the rank of the states as political societies," and he "pointed out the limitations on the sovereignty of the states" under the Articles of Confederation.[76] Again, according to the Yates's account, Madison is more unambiguously a nationalist, denying even the premise that states were sovereign at some historical time.

This subtle difference in the presentation of the 29 June speech extended to Madison's treatment of constitution imperfection. According to Yates, Madison worried that the compromise between the small and large states would become permanent. "I would always exclude inconsistent principles in framing a system of government. The difficulty of getting its defects amended are great and sometimes insurmountable. The Virginia State government was the first which was made, and though its defects are evident to every person, and we cannot get it amended."[77] But Madison recorded himself to make a different point. In his version, he predicted that the "unjust" principle of state equality "must infuse mortality into a Constitution which we wished to last forever."[78] The difference between the two accounts, then, amounts to whether Madison emphasized the undesirable durability of an unjust constitution (Yates) or whether he emphasized the undesirable temporariness resulting from an unjust constitution (Madison). Given that Madison had elsewhere pointed to constitutions that had not been amended, it would not be too far-fetched to conclude

[74] Ibid., 211. Johnson sided with the small-state theory: "The fact is that the States do exist as political Societies."

[75] Yates and Lansing, *Secret Proceedings*, 199–200. The full quotation is as follows: "Some contend, that the States are sovereign, when, in fact, they are only political societies. There is a gradation of power in all societies, from the lowest corporation to the highest sovereign. The States never possessed the essential rights of sovereignty. These were always vested in Congress. Their voting as States, in Congress, is no evidence of sovereignty."

[76] Madison, *Notes*, 213.

[77] Yates and Lansing, *Secret Proceedings*, 205.

[78] Madison, *Notes*, 214.

that Yates was the more accurate of the two in his placing the emphasis on Madison's desire for future constitutional change.

What Madison's Notes Add to the Yates Version

The most obvious difference between the two accounts is that Yates left the Convention on 10 July, so Madison's is longer and contains more extensive accounts of the speeches and covers more days.[79] Madison thus contributed the bulk of what we know about the Convention's debates. This is an obvious point, but it is worth noting what we would not have if Madison never offered his version. One striking example is Madison's 6 June speech, which was a preview of his famous *Federalist* No. 10. Yates summarized the speech in a single sentence. "The more extensive we made the basis [of the federal govt], the greater probability of duration, happiness, and good order."[80] Madison, on the other hand, recorded a version of his solution for the problem of faction that was more than 750 words long.[81] Even on those days in which Yates was present, Madison contributed the bulk of what we know about the Convention's debates.

This is especially true with respect to the problem of constitutional imperfection and Madison's failure to convince his fellow delegates of the need for the congressional negative. For 8 June, Madison's *Notes* record Madison as stating that the congressional negative was "absolutely necessary to a perfect system," but the accounts from Yates, King, and Hamilton make no mention of this language.[82] Later, when the convention was winding down, Madison again recorded his displeasure on 12 September, saying that an appeal to the Supreme Court would insufficiently protect rights in the states. "A negative on the State laws alone could meet all the shapes which these could assume. But this had been overruled."[83] There is no record of this statement elsewhere.[84]

It is also evident in the way Madison's records reveal other key delegates holding a dark view of the republican government. In his record of 28 June, Madison recorded the full text of Benjamin Franklin's 28 June speech recommending that the delegates begin each session with "prayers imploring the assistance of heaven." Notably, Franklin's speech, the text of which appears to have later been delivered by Franklin to Madison, begins by saying that the deliberations up to that point offered "melancholy proof of the imperfection of Human Understanding." Further, because examples from ancient and modern

[79] Clinton Rossiter, *1787: The Grand Convention* (New York: Norton, 1966), 188.

[80] Yates and Lansing, *Secret Proceedings*, 111.

[81] Madison, *Notes*, 75–77.

[82] Ibid., 88; Max Farrand, ed. *Records of the Federal Convention of 1787.* 3 vols. (New Haven, CT: Yale University Press, 1911), 1: 164–73.

[83] Madison, *Notes*, 631.

[84] Farrand, *Records*, 2: 583.

history were "suitable to our circumstances," they were "groping as it were in the dark to find political truth."[85]

Similarly, Madison's *Notes* also show that that Wilson and Morris shared Madison's doubts about the possibility of representation in the context of founding. Madison expressed these doubts in the context of concerns that the debates had exceeded their mandate and were thus acting without authority. For 12 June, both Yates and Madison record Madison to say that it was impossible to know the opinions of the people on the question before the Convention. Madison's version is worth quoting at length:

> Mr. Madison, observed that if the opinions of the people were to be our guide, it w[oul]d be difficult to say what course we ought to take. No Member of the Convention could say what the opinions of his Constituents were at this time; much less could he say that they would think if possessed of the information & lights possessed by the members here; & still less what would be their way of thinking 6 or 12 months hence.[86]

This statement is striking for the degree to which it asserts that representation is impossible, because no representative could actually know how his constituents would vote if they were in the same place as the representative. Madison made this point to make another, namely that the delegates "ought to consider what was right & necessary in itself for the attainment of a proper government," and that the people at large would probably follow the recommendations made by the "most enlightened & respectable citizens."[87] Madison records James Wilson, the delegate most willing to appeal to democratic arguments, and Morris as making that point.[88] These parts of Morris's comments go unrecorded by Yates and King, and, curiously, Yates records Wilson as saying something much different, namely that the people "expect relief," and as a result he believed the Convention had the authority to make a more national plan.[89]

All of this only underscores the impression that what really comes through in Madison's account is the degree to which the negotiation between the small states and the large states infected the way the Convention tried to deal with the already impossible problems of line-drawing in the context of federalism

---

[85] Madison, *Notes*, 209. Farrand notes that Madison originally had an "abstract" of 200 words but replaced that abstract with the speech that appears in Franklin's own papers. Farrand, *Records*, 1: 450.

[86] Madison, *Notes*, 107.

[87] Ibid.

[88] Ibid., 125 and 240. On 16 June, on the subject of the power of the Convention, Wilson said, "With regard to the sentiments of the people," it is "difficult to know precisely what they are." This is because people often confuse the sentiments of "the particular circle in which one moved" with the "general voice" of the whole. Likewise, on 5 July, Madison records Morris saying, "Much has been said of the sentiments of the people. They were unknown. They could not be known."

[89] Farrand, *Records*, 261.

and separation of powers. Indeed, this is what emerges in the records after the Compromise, during those days for which Madison's *Notes* are the only record. For example, on 16 July, Madison records Morris worrying that it was now impossible, *given the compromise between the small and large states*, to "bring the House [the Convention] to a consideration in the abstract of powers necessary to be vested in the general Government." Now, instead, "a reference" to that vote, either "mental or expressed," "would mix itself with the merits of every question concerning the powers."[90] Morris's prediction was accurate, for over the next six weeks, the debate turned to the power of appointment, the power of the purse, and presidential selection.

In each of these debates, it is difficult to determine whether the speaker is primarily interested in defending his prior position on large versus small states or with determining in the abstract the best constitutional policy. Edmund Randolph, for example, makes this very point on 18 July in the context of determining who would have the power to appoint judges. He says that he was for giving it to the Senate before "an equality of votes" had been granted to that body, and then says, "Yet he had rather leave the appoint[en]t there." His use of "yet" was clear in its intention to show that he wanted to find a way to shift that power to the large states but that his principles stood in the way.[91] More pointedly, Madison records himself on 13 August to say the origination of money bills in the House was the "compensation" offered to the large states in exchange for equality in the Senate.[92] Likewise, with regard to the war power, Madison records Mason as saying that it could not be given to the Senate because is was "not so constructed as to be entitled to it."[93]

This problem is especially true with respect to presidential selection, where it is very difficult to disentangle the interests of the small states from the arguments made against popular selection of the president. A considerable portion of the opposition to selection by the people is given by delegates from the small states, while the defenders of popular selection – Wilson especially – were among the most vocal defenders of the large states.[94] In this context, on 24 August, Nathaniel Gorham of Massachusetts criticized his fellow delegates and said that "it was wrong to be considering at every turn whom the Senate would represent" when trying to create the system for presidential selection.[95] With respect to Madison himself, it is illuminating that he unequivocally supported popular selection, claiming "the people at large was in his opinion the fittest in itself," on 19 July, three days *after* the compromise between the large and small states.[96]

---

[90] Madison, *Notes*, 302.

[91] Ibid., 316.

[92] Ibid., 447.

[93] Ibid., 476.

[94] Ibid., 578.

[95] Ibid., 523.

[96] Ibid., 327. Banning concludes from the letter to Wallace that Madison was open to popular selection before Jefferson. Banning, *Sacred Fire*, 134.

More generally, it would be very hard to say if the opposition against or support for popular selection can be extricated from the prior question of the contest between the large and small states. But the point here is that this very problem about the meaning of the Constitution becomes the serious interpretative problem that it is only because Madison's *Notes*, refocused by his explanation of a "fresh struggle" in *Federalist* No. 37, so clearly calls it to our attention.

The Status of 1787

These events show that Madison took unusual pride in the work of the Convention, making it in some crucial way his life work. But they also show that Madison's understanding of the forming and ratification of the Constitution was, like the framing itself, complicated by difficulties. Recall Madison's letter to Jefferson about Justice Johnson's history of parties. In addition to providing material for Justice Johnson's section on Washington's Farewell Address, Madison took the opportunity to curtail the dangerous application of Jefferson's proposal for constitutional conventions as a solution for constitutional conflict. Pointing to passages where Johnson was "indebted" to Jefferson, Madison wrote that referring "every point of disagreement to the people in Conventions" would be "too tardy, too troublesome & too expensive." On top of that, it would "lessen the salutary veneration for the instrument." So again, almost four decades after *Federalist* No. 49, Madison returned to his argument from veneration to chasten the argument for appeals to the people, this time in the context of federalism. But he also added another reason. Under the "prevailing view" of the Constitution that the people had "adopted and put forward," the federal judiciary was to be the "constitutional resort" for determining the line demarcating state and national authority. What is important to notice is that Madison supported the argument from veneration with a claim about the particular constitution that was put forward and ratified. It was true that the decisions of the Supreme Court had not, in fact, "corresponded with what was anticipated." In his view, the remedy was a constitutional amendment, fixing the judiciary, not a continual process of appeals to the people. More than that, he also said that the problem with Johnson's argument was that it "expected far too much, in requesting a precise demarcation of the boundary between the Federal & the State authorities." The real lesson is that the appeal to the people could not settle the matter because there was no such line.[97]

As we have seen, Madison sometimes looked to the Convention debates to find constitutional meaning, and he sometimes rejected these debates as ultimately authoritative. He also worried that the natural evolution of political language would fundamentally alter the meaning of the Constitution. But he

[97] Madison to Jefferson, 27 June 1823, *Madison Writings*, 800–01.

was also aware of putting too much stock in contemporary sources, for in the very letter to Livingston where Madison reflected on the malleability of language over time, Madison also recommended that Livingston be cautious when using contemporary sources to interpret the Constitution, because "the authors" then were "sometimes influenced by the zeal of advocates."[98] This point obviously undermines the authority of both the anti-Federalist and the Federalist writers made at the time of ratification. Tellingly, Madison made a similar observation in the context of a publication of the *Federalist*. To Jacob Gideon he objected to the inclusion of the Helvidius-Pacificus papers, in part because he thought the disagreement between himself and Hamilton would be distracting, but he also acknowledged that his own Helvidius papers, even if basically representative of his constitutional doctrine, were overly partisan, hastily written in the passion of the moment, and contained inaccuracies.[99] These points by Madison are unsettling in the sense that they clearly undermine his own argument that the ratification debates hold the highest ground in determining constitutional meaning.

But it is also likely that Madison also had in mind the Convention itself. Madison made this clear in an 1821 letter to Virginian politician John G. Jackson, which is perhaps the most underappreciated of Madison's treatments of his decision to source the Convention.[100] Madison wrote in response to Jackson's inquiry into Madison's plans for the "Mass of papers accumulated through a long course of public life," including his "voluminous proceedings of the Convention." Jackson's inquiry was probably related to the release of Yates's publication of his history of the convention. Madison explained that he continued to lean toward making the release of his own *Notes* a "posthumous one." He added that even though he had not yet seen Yates's publication, the "prejudices" of Yates undoubtedly led him to "egregious errors, in relation to others as well as myself."[101] But after criticizing Yates, Madison went on to discuss the Convention itself and to place it within the context afforded by his now larger perspective.

Surprisingly, Madison told Jackson that the deliberation in the Convention of 1787 was flawed in at least two respects. First, the delegates were overly influenced by current events, especially by the "recent and alarming insurrection

---

[98] Madison to Edward Livingston, 17 April 1824, Hunt 9: 189.

[99] "I cannot at this day but be sensible that in the pamphlet under the name of Helvidius a tone is indulged which must seek an apology, in impressions of the moment, and altho' in other respects it may be liable to criticisms for which the occasions are increased by the particular haste in which the several papers were written, to say nothing of inaccuracies in transcribing them for the press, yet I see no ground to be dissatisfied with the constitutional doctrine espoused, or the general scope of the reasoning used in support of it." James Madison to Jacob Gideon Jr., 20 February 1818, *Madison Papers Retirement*, 1: 223–24.

[100] Madison to John Jackson, 28 December 1821, *Madison Papers Retirement* 2: 441–44. There are important differences with the text presented in the older Hunt edition.

[101] Ibid., 441–42.

headed by Shays in Massachusetts." It was "natural for many in the Convention to lean to a higher toned system than was perhaps in strictness warranted." The problem was a confusion over what was a "temporary" cause of the disorder and what was "permanently inherent" in the popular form itself, combined with the fact that the honest objective to give the government more vigor was partially "stimulated" by the "backwardness" of the Convention's opponents, causing, Madison seems to suggest, the Convention's advocates to overreact.[102] Second, extreme negotiating tactics caused people to vote for things that they otherwise would not have. "Where so much depended on compromise, the patrons of different opinions, often set out on negotiating grounds more remote from each other, than the real opinions of either were, from the point at which they finally met."[103] From Madison's perspective in 1821, then, the deliberation in 1787 was in some sense flawed in its proximity to rapidly changing events and negotiations.

Had Madison stopped there, the letter to Jackson would still rank as one of the most striking commentaries on the Convention offered by Madison. But he went on, subjecting himself to the same kind of scrutiny. Like some of the other delegates, he entered the Convention with the objective of securing as "much energy as would ensure the requisite stability and efficacy." This was a rather common expression by Madison, but what is surprising is how much he qualified it in the next sentence. "It is possible that in some instances that consideration may have been allowed a weight greater than subsequent reflection within the Convention, or the actual operation of the Government would sanction." That is, Madison acknowledged that he would have opted for less stability had he then had the knowledge of the actual operation of the government that he had acquired by 1821. But more than that, Madison also said that he would have qualified his preference for stability had he had more time for "reflection" during the Convention. The problem was that "it sometimes happened" that "opinions as to a particular modification" or a "particular power" had a "conditional reference," and these opinions needed to "vary" accordingly. Importantly, Madison wrote that his own contribution to the Convention was less than perfect, not only because of his necessary inability to see the future but also because he did not have the time to think through the consequences of the deliberations as they were happening.

After making this revealing confession, Madison returned to familiar themes. He said that it was the "duty of all" to support the Constitution as it was understood "by the nation at the time of its ratification." He was saddened by the "constructive innovations" that changed the meaning of the Constitution in its first decade. He went on to say that the most dangerous threat to republican government comes from a majority in the legislative branch; that the most important constitutional controversies would arise over the size and number

[102] Ibid., 441.
[103] Ibid., 442.

of states, questions hitherto untreated by "the most oracular Authors of the Science of Govt;" and that the meaning of the Constitution lies in how it was understood "at the time of ratification." This was clearly meant to be a plug for his own argument concerning the importance of the extended republic, but that only underscored the importance of Madison's frank description of what he believed to be the failures of not only the Convention of 1787 but also his participation in it. For readers familiar with Madison's discussions of energy and stability in *Federalist* No. 37 and in the removal power debate of 1789, Madison's analysis of the Convention in the letter to Jackson should be nothing less than shocking.

This was more than an isolated remark. As we saw in the previous chapter, Madison continued to believe that the Constitution was flawed in its procedure for selecting the president in the House in a contingency election. In his view, state equality was simply unjust and needed to be changed, but it was unlikely that small states would ever agree to such an amendment. And Madison knew it was unlikely because of his own experience in the Convention itself. Calculations between the parties infected the negotiations even after the Connecticut Compromise. The Twelfth Amendment and the Election of 1824 reinforced these concerns for Madison. What is interesting is that in the context of 1824, Madison commented that the delegates had an especially "difficult" time in creating the Electoral College, and, albeit to a lesser extent, the debates were "not exempt from a degree of the hurrying influence produced by fatigue and impatience in all such bodies," as the delegates grew tired at the end of the Convention and eager to return home.[104] On this point, it is worth noting that Madison wrote Spencer Roane (a judge on Virginia's high court) in 1821 that we should give especially little precedential weight to "midnight precedents" passed at the end of a legislative session.[105] And, as was mentioned in Chapter 1, Madison in retirement praised Franklin and Morris in ways that disparaged the deliberative abilities of the other delegates to the Convention.

Like the other texts discussed in this chapter, the letter to Jackson reveals that there is more work to do in understanding Madison's presentation of the Convention. It is true that Rakove's award-winning analysis calls attention to important questions in political theory. Those questions include: Does tacit consent make sense if we can never know the meaning of the original compact, that is, if the law is not really settled and standing? And how are citizens governed by an original constitution if the original meaning remains elusive? The answers to these questions are important and get to the heart of Madisonian constitutionalism, but they leave unanswered a question about what Madison hoped to accomplish with his project to leave the definitive account of the

---

[104] Madison to George Hay, 23 August 1823, Hunt, 9: 147–55.
[105] Madison to Spencer Roane, 6 May 1821, *Madison Papers Retirement* 2: 317–21.

Federal Convention. That is, they do not identify Madison's *object* in composing his *Notes*.

The analysis in this chapter thus makes two arguments with respect
to Madison's object. First, Madison's decision to publish his records of the
Federal Convention was nothing less than a decision to prioritize the Federal
Convention over alternative sources of constitutional meaning. Even though
Madison from time to time said that the understanding of those who ratified the
Constitution was more important than that of those who composed the document, he frequently said the opposite and his decision to devote his energy to
the *Notes* speaks for itself. Second, Madison's *Notes* clearly emphasize the fact
that the greatest problem in the Constitution is the way the contest between the
small and large states mingled itself with the almost insurmountable problem
of marking the boundaries between state and national governments. Given that
Madison wrote in his "Sketch" that his reason for composing the *Notes* was to
offer future founders a resource that he lacked, namely a reliable history of the
founding of a confederacy, it stands to reason that Madison saw his *Notes* as
a manual for future founders of confederacies.[106] Moreover, the lesson of that
manual would be that founders must not underestimate the extent to which the
smaller members will insist, unfairly, on their equality with the larger members.
The lesson would also be that federalism is necessarily an imperfect blend of
contingency and compromise.

---

[106] For example, in 1828, Madison corrected Martin Van Buren, who had argued that the most
   important question at the Convention was the "degree of power" granted to the national
   government. Madison told him in clear terms that the real question was the "rule by which
   the States would be represented," with the "smaller States insisting on the rule of equality."
   Madison to Van Buren, 13 May 1828, Hunt 9: 314.

8

"Take care of me when dead"

Above all else, Madison's political thought and practice forces us to confront the problem of constitutional imperfection. Because no constitution can address every political problem, and because those who live under constitutions will find ways to make them compatible with their deepest ambitions, constitutions are necessarily imperfect. As a result, the philosophically inclined will want to understand whether their constitution recommends a doctrine of how to treat constitutional imperfection. With respect to this problem in the context of the U.S. Constitution, scholarship on the political thought and development of the early republic has uncovered three great traditions associated with the three most dominant political thinkers of the period: Hamilton, Jefferson, and Madison.

This evidence presented in this book, however, complicates our understanding of these traditions by showing where Madison departs from Madisonian constitutionalism. In place of Publius Madison, who argued for veneration of the Constitution and seemed to rely on elite representatives to "refine and enlarge" the public view, this book has presented a fuller Madison by considering in him in several of the contexts of his long career. This wider perspective reveals that Madison did not always see veneration of the Constitution as an unqualified good. Rather, at times, Madison worried that veneration would stand in the way of necessary reform. This wider perspective also further confirms that Madison's opinions about the Senate remained complicated by the deal with the small states, and it reveals that this deal – both its terms and its consequences – gave Madison additional reasons to doubt the possibility of true deliberation by legislative elites, both during times of founding and during times of normal politics. On a related point, this book also shows that Madison turned to the democratic logic of the argument for "responsibility" even before he was forced by his break with Hamilton to organize the opposition to Washington's administration. Further, in using responsibility to connect the president to a national majority, Madison was likely limiting the damage he believed resulted from the equality of states in the Senate, but he also laid the intellectual groundwork for Jefferson's Revolution of 1800.

Most of all, then, this book clarifies our understanding of Madison by focusing on Madison's lifelong alliance with Jefferson. Jefferson asked Madison to take care of him when dead, and Madison did, especially by reminding those who claimed his mantle that Jefferson always insisted that the majority should prevail.[1] Their alliance spanned half a century, and on 6 July 1826, when Madison heard of Jefferson's death on 4 July, Madison reflected that he had known Jefferson "for a period of fifty years, during which there has not been an interruption or diminution of mutual confidence and cordial friendship, for a single moment in a single instance." Mutual confidence for fifty years is a big claim to make of anyone, no less for someone like Jefferson. But Madison did not stop there. He said he knew Jefferson as a friend, but also knew him as the "wise & good" would remember him, as a "luminary of Science, as a votary of liberty, as a model of patriotism, and as a benefactor of human kind."[2] In a letter written a few months later, Madison wrote: "It may be said of him as has been said of others that he was a 'walking library,' and what can be said of but such few prodigies, that the Genius of Philosophy ever walked hand in hand with him."[3] It is almost certainly not an accident that these two statements – that Jefferson was both a philosopher *and* a votary of liberty – employ the very language that Madison had used in the context of Jefferson many years earlier in the *Federalist*.[4]

As this book has argued, Madison wrestled with the problem of Jefferson throughout his life. On the whole, Madison was more Jeffersonian than not, and more Jeffersonian than most scholars have acknowledged. This does not mean that he accepted all of his philosophic friend's arguments. Madison held out more trust in institutional arrangements, and he did not put as much emphasis on educating and leading a majority will. Most of all, even though he did think that appeals to the people were sometimes appropriate and necessary, Madison resisted them – as he resisted the other alternatives – as a catch-all solution to every problem that arises in constitutional politics.[5] But just as he did not wholly embrace Jefferson's executive and periodic appeals to the people as the final solution, he resisted Hamilton's argument from sovereignty. We might add that he did not throw himself on the solution later offered by

[1] Madison, "Notes on Nullification, 1835, Hunt 9: 589.
[2] Madison to Trist, 6 July, 1826, *Madison Writings*, 812.
[3] Madison to Samuel Harrison Smith, 6 November 6, 1826, Hunt, 9: 261. It is worth noting that Smith was working on memoirs, and Madison recommended Jefferson's 1825 letter to Henry Lee, the letter on the object of the Declaration, which Madison played a part in writing.
[4] See the use of "votary" in the discussion of republican government in No. 39 and the discussion of philosophers in the treatment of Jefferson in No. 49. Madison employed similar language in his treatment of Jefferson throughout the 1830s.
[5] Madison to Jefferson, 27 June 1823, *Madison Writings*, 798–802.

Lincoln, namely that the Constitution's flaws can be resolved by appealing to the argument of the Declaration. Likewise, he conceded that his most famous contribution, the extended republic, was qualified because it does not always solve the problem of faction.

This point reveals that Madison was more sober about the possibilities of political science than we have realized. Indeed, rather than being a proud advocate of the possibilities of political science, and its modern inventions of prudence, Madison was deeply concerned by its limits. This is evident in his treatment of veneration and deliberation. While scholars have long associated both with Madisonian constitutionalism, this book has offered evidence that Madison's views on each were mixed. At times, Madison thought the one was useful where the other would fail. So in place of deliberation by way of a second convention, Madison offered the argument from veneration. But veneration itself is no virtue, for veneration sometimes protects constitutional error or, perhaps just as bad, provides a cover for those who wish to construe the Constitution to their own liking and change it without the people's consent. So while veneration can sometimes nurture the necessary zeal to protect constitutional boundaries, the danger is that it can also lull people away from the vigilance necessary for that zeal. So too with deliberation, which, properly defined, cannot be done by people consumed by a holy zeal.

Further, separation of powers and federalism stand apart from other constitutional problems because of their complexity. Since it is frequently impossible to determine whether something is executive or legislative by nature, it is necessarily very difficult to manage political controversy about those powers and indeed sometimes impossible to engage in these controversies in way that can coherently be called constitutional. This is because the mixture of principled and interested calculation becomes more and more complex as the details of politics are negotiated, both during times of founding – constitutional conventions – and during times of ordinary politics. This is especially true in debates about the line dividing the respective authorities of state of nation, where the word "federal" demonstrates perhaps better than any other the limits of language. Separation of powers and federalism are necessary features of constitutional government in the United States, but, paradoxically, both are themselves resistant to constitutional rule.

As Madison's decision to create an opposition party shows, he believed that some ways to deal with this problem are better than others. In particular, Madison, like Jefferson, emphasized consent as the central requirement of republican politics, but he also believed that the intention of the founders – both proposers and ratifiers – was a better standard than were evolving meanings based on "broad and pliant" rules of construction or in meanings that change over time.[6] This point grows out of another. Namely, the lesson of Madison and constitutional imperfection is that even the better ways remain imperfect,

---

[6] Madison to Spencer Roane, 28 August 1819, *Madison Papers Retirement*, 1: 502.

because even founders, even the James Madisons of the world, cannot see clearly enough at the moment they are founding. Like the factious individual whose self-love obscures the dictates of reason, the philosophic legislator cannot extricate himself from the political details of deliberation and the received wisdom of the moment. On top of that, the task of deliberation remains a problem during normal politics for such a legislator because he is necessarily torn between the interest of his constituents and what is best according to the legislator's "conscience."[7] It is revealing that Madison never attempted to adjudicate the contest between these two visions of representation.

Equally revealing is that Madison never doubted his lifetime alliance with Jefferson. From this we can begin to discern the commonality of Madison's various solutions over time to constitutional imperfection. Put in the terms of Madison's masterful formulation in *Federalist* No. 37, this means that in the great contest between stability in government and republican responsibility, Madison leaned toward republican responsibility and away from stability. In this, as Madison knew, he hitched the permanence of the imperfect Constitution – his Constitution – to a necessarily Jeffersonian future.

[7] Madison to Henry Lee, 14 June 1825, Hunt 9: 216.

Index

Lightning Source UK Ltd.
Milton Keynes UK
UKOW05n1913191116
288068UK00005B/108/P